The Scottish Highlands

To Anne

The Scottish Highlands

John A. Lister

John Bartholomew & Son Limited
Edinburgh and London

Other Titles in this Series:

Already available:

Cumbria JOHN PARKER
Devon & Cornwall DENYS KAY-ROBINSON
South Wales RUTH THOMAS

In preparation:

South-East England OLIVER MASON
North Yorkshire LINDEN AND CHRISTOPHER STAFFORD
Somerset & Avon ROBERT DUNNING
Wiltshire & Dorset DENYS KAY-ROBINSON

First published in Great Britain 1978 by
JOHN BARTHOLOMEW & SON LIMITED
12 Duncan Street, Edinburgh EH9 1TA
And 216 High Street, Bromley BR1 1PW

ISBN 0 7028 1034 7

All maps © John Bartholomew & Son Limited

Book and jacket design: Susan Waywell

Printed in Great Britain by
Hazell Watson & Viney Limited,
Aylesbury, Buckinghamshire
Colour sections printed in Great Britain by
John Bartholomew & Son Limited, Edinburgh

Contents

* The map section at the end of the book is numbered separately, in bold type.

Regional Map

Showing the Area Covered by this Guide

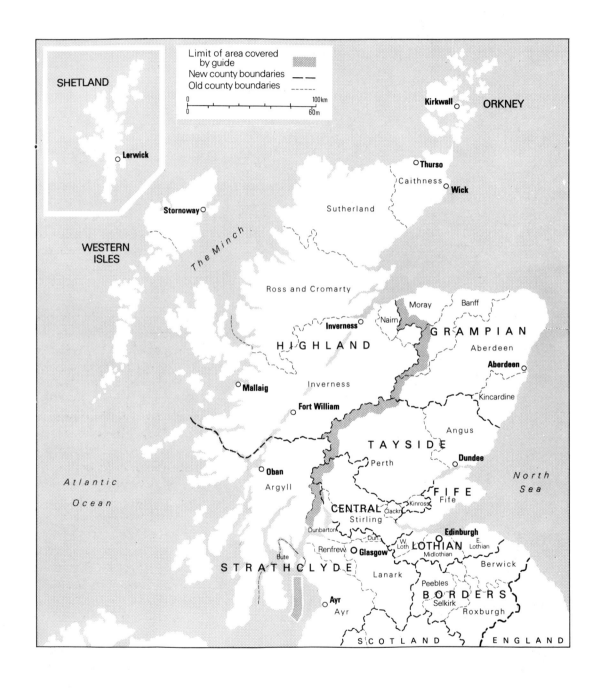

Preface

Although over 2 million people visit the Highlands of Scotland every year, either on holiday or on business, a remarkable number of misconceptions about this extensive area of Britain still survive. 'The Highlands' often conjures up a picture of rugged mountains, deep glens, and long lochs: an empty land, with a scattering of attractive islands off-shore. Superimposed on this impression are the kilt, the bagpipes, the clans, and, possibly, grouse-shooting, deer-stalking, and salmon fishing.

For the purposes of this volume the Highlands are the Seven Crofting Counties (as detailed in the Introduction), only about half of which conform to the popular notion of Highland scenery. The trappings of the 'tartan image' are agreeable irrelevancies, and the shooting and fishing on sporting estates a very minor part, now, of the Highland economy. The Highlands of pre-war years have largely vanished; the changes over the past three decades have been remarkable, and the pace is accelerating with the impact in particular of North Sea oil, the extension of forestry, and the work of the Highlands and Islands Development Board.

In trying to give (so far as space allows) an overall picture of the Highlands, my principal inspiration has been the experience of over thirty years' travelling in Scotland; for nearly twenty of those years – as Editor at the Scottish Tourist Board – I was in the happy position of being paid to find out about the country. The books that assisted me throughout that period were many and varied. For 'Ancient Monuments' an obvious source was the excellent series of guides produced by what is now the Department of the Environment; the publications of the National Trust for Scotland and the Forestry Commission were equally rewarding, in their respective spheres. My 'bibles' for reference for many years included earlier editions of the *Blue Guide* to Scotland (up to the 1959 edition), edited by L. Russell Muirhead, and the Automobile Association's *Illustrated Road Book of Scotland* (up to the 1969 edition); each, unfortunately, has now been replaced by a less detailed and less useful edition. *The Ordnance Gazetteer of Scotland*, edited by Francis H. Groome, *revised* in 1896, remains an invaluable reference book. Going even further back, there are the old *Statistical Accounts* of Scotland, which owed their first appearance to that great native of Caithness Sir John Sinclair, and appeared between 1791 and 1798, to be followed by the *Second Statistical Account*, on similar lines, which was published between 1834 and 1845. The *Third Statistical Account*, volumes of which, on different Scottish counties, have been produced at intervals over the past twenty-odd years, has not the substance of its predecessors. Other books found useful for reference have been included in the 'Further Reading'.

I must acknowledge the very many, often anonymous, writers in newspapers, more often local than national, who have, over the years, provided me with the material for volumes of press cuttings on all manner of subjects connected with the Highlands. Similar acknowledgement is also due to writers of local guide-books and to tourist officers in many parts of the Highlands.

Above all, though, I should like to thank my wife, who has not only endured the racket of many months' typing but has read and valuably criticized my text.

John A. Lister
Edinburgh
May 1977

Publishers' Note

The publishers of this guide are always pleased to acknowledge any corrections brought to their notice by readers. Correspondence should be addressed to the Guide-book Editor, John Bartholomew & Son Limited, 216 High Street, Bromley BR1 1PW.

Introduction

What are the Highlands?

Cutting north-east across Scotland from the Clyde Estuary to Stonehaven, south of Aberdeen, is a long irregular rift known to geologists as the Highland Boundary Fault. It would be convenient – but wrong – to suggest that everything north of that line is Highland, and everything south of it Lowland. North from the Moray Firth, the eastern part of the Highlands is essentially 'Lowland', both in the character of its countryside and of its people. Yet Caithness, the eastern parts of Sutherland and Ross and Cromarty, and Nairn are administratively in the Highland region. North of the Highland line are the mountains of Perthshire and the high hills around Deeside and Donside. But administratively the former are in the Tayside region, the latter in Grampian. The islands of Mull, Coll, Tiree, Islay, Jura, and Colonsay are part of the Inner Hebrides, intensely Highland in their Celtic background. But administratively they are in Strathclyde, the same region that holds Glasgow, Lanark, and Ayr.

Even before the new regionalization of Scotland, with the reorganization of local government in May 1975, defining the Highlands was difficult enough. To most people, though, and for the purposes of this book, the Highlands are what were known as the Seven Crofting Counties: Argyll, Inverness-shire, Ross and Cromarty, Sutherland, Caithness, Orkney, and Shetland. This was the area for the bettering of which the Highlands and Islands Development Board was set up in 1965 – though its jurisdiction has subsequently been extended to include the Isle of Arran in the former county of Bute, and Nairn and Grantown-on-Spey.

The Central Highlands can usefully be regarded as the area including the Spey Valley and the Great Glen. West of these is the seaboard of the Western Highlands. Then there are the North-West Highlands, archetypal Highland scenery of high mountains, wide moors, lochs, and a wonderfully varied coast. The wide eastern strip from northern Caithness to the Black Isle is not mountainous: but it is too far north to be called anything but Highland. The Western Isles are the Hebrides – an evocative name with an uncertain etymology: it probably derives from Ptolemy's *Hebudae*, although another explanation is that it comes from the Norse *Havbreday* ('Isle on the Edge of the Sea'). The northern island groups, Orkney and Shetland, are utterly different from the Western Isles, but just as inseparable from the Highland aura.

These areas, then, constitute a workable definition of the Highlands. They make up roughly one third of the area of Scotland, though overall they are the least populated part of Britain: in June 1974, out of a total Scottish population of 5,226,400, only about 6 per cent, 308,633, lived in the Seven Crofting Counties – and 36,595 of them were in Inverness.

The wide open spaces and often magnificent scenery that make up so much of the appeal of the Highlands to the visitor are also, of course, the very features to explain why so few people live there. Bare mountains and water-fretted moorland do not make for a flourishing agriculture: attempts have been made, on some of the islands, to transform peat into land that will grow more than rank vegetation, but the sheer expense of doing so has meant that there are only a few isolated green patches on the land. In much of the west and north-west Highlands it is crofting that maintains a sizeable part of the population – but 'maintains' is an exaggeration, for this mixture, usually of fishing and smallholder-type farming, is, in itself, not a viable proposition: the main source of income for a crofting family comes from other sources, not least of which is (often) tourism.

More than once in the history of the Highlands some prospect of making a living other than by scraping it from an ungrateful land has arisen. At times over the past two or three hundred years, for instance, the seas have promised a harvest that could lead to profitable gathering. In the eighteenth century, particularly, a number of Highland coastal villages and small towns were founded on the herring, which used to come along many parts of the coastline in vast quantities. But the herring, at various times since, has just disappeared, and many are the harbours that have fallen into decay. Sometimes the herring came back and fishing revived, but often only to fail again. Today, overfishing – not for herring alone, but for many other fish as well – is an international problem.

There is, though, still reward to be had from the sea and the sea lochs. Lobsters, for example, are caught from many a village and croft along the Highland shores, and for more than local consumption: from a number of places there is a profitable export trade as far afield as continental Europe; but as often as not the lobster-fishing is one of the adjuncts to crofting. Fish-farming is being developed in certain areas; but the numbers employed in this occupation are few.

Fish, black cattle, and seaweed are some of the commodities that have brought hope to the Highlands but in due course have failed. These, along with crofting and later developments – from forestry to the latest incursion, North Sea oil – are dealt with later in this introduction.

Anyone writing a survey such as this not much over a decade ago could have re-told the rise and fall of so many Highland hopes, but could hardly have anticipated the immense changes that have been wrought, not only in Easter Ross but in areas in the western Highlands and islands, and in some northern islands too, in the past few years. Industrial development – though in restricted areas – has made such a pace, and had its inevitable effect on the Highland scene, that it would take more than the Brahan Seer (*see* Conon Bridge in the Gazetteer section) to predict developments over the next decade or two. So far, at any rate, places where onshore developments connected with North Sea oil have changed the scene are very limited in number. It is possible to travel through most of the Highlands without a hint that an industrial explosion has taken place: the impact of forestry on the landscape and of tourism on the general scene is much more noticeable. There is little question that here is a land almost unique in scenic appeal, yet for natural resources still poor.

The poverty of the land is not the only reason for the lack of people in the Highlands. As potent, over much of its history, was the almost complete lack of communication. Until some 250 years ago there were virtually no roads in most of the Highlands. Inverness was a place frequently visited; but travellers to it went not by today's route – from Perth by the A9 through the Spey Valley – but, instead, journeyed further east, by Aberdeen. Inverness is a port, and for much of its long history was quite a prosperous one; but, other than by sea, choices of approach to the city were limited. One possible approach was by the Great Glen, the lochs of which take up two thirds of its length and whose southern end, where Fort William now stands, was accessible by water, up the

Firth of Lorn and Loch Linnhe. For long, the embarkation point for the western Highlands and the islands was Ayr.

After the 1715 rising the Government was determined to bring the Highlanders under control. In 1724 General George Wade, who had commanded the Government troops during the rising, was sent back to the Highlands; and his efforts resulted in the building of about forty bridges and some 400km. of roads. Much of this work was designed to give access to the Highlands, one route going from Perthshire on approximately the same line as today's A9 to Dalwhinnie, whence one road went over the Corrieyairack Pass to Fort Augustus and another by the Spey Valley to Inverness.

General Wade's surveyor or accountant was Edmund (or Edward) Burt, about whom little is known except that he wrote *Letters from a Gentleman in the North of Scotland* (which to him was Perthshire and Inverness-shire), which gives a fascinating picture of conditions at that time. Before the roads were built, he wrote, the ways through the Highlands 'consisted chiefly of stony moors, bogs, rugged rapid fords, declivities of hills, entangling woods and giddy precipices'. The Highlanders, not unnaturally, objected strongly to the new roads, which took away some of their isolation, but there was another, more favourable, reaction that gave rise to the tag:

> Had you seen these roads before they were made,
> You would lift up your hands and bless General Wade.

Burt also reflects the usual eighteenth-century attitude to wild country. Not until nearly a century after he wrote were mountains regarded as other than places to be avoided if possible. The Highlands, to Burt, were 'gloomy spaces', the mountains 'a dirty purple most disagreeable when the heath is in bloom' and of 'stupendous bulk, frightful irregularity and horrid gloom'.

Fifty years later another early traveller in the Highlands, the Welsh Thomas Tennant, looked westwards from a hilltop in Skye, a view entrancing to today's visitor, and described it as 'desolation itself; a savage series of rude mountains, discoloured black and red'. It was the Romantics of the nineteenth century, not least among them Queen Victoria, who made the Highland scenery eminently acceptable – though to her 'the Highlands' encompassed essentially her beloved Deeside in Aberdeenshire, the Spey Valley, Inverness, and a few other areas.

It took a long time for roads to be built into the remoter parts of the Highlands. In 1773 Dr Johnson and James Boswell made their famous journey (recorded in the former's *A Journey to the Western Islands of Scotland* and the latter's *The Journal of a Tour to the Hebrides*): Dr Johnson was unimpressed by the Highlands' 'wide extent of hopeless sterility'. After Wade's military roads little was done to improve communications in the Highlands until after the turn of the eighteenth century. Some thirty years later the position in the central and eastern Highlands had changed very significantly, largely due to a most remarkable Scot, Thomas Telford (1757–1834), who from being a stonemason in Dumfries-shire became, through his engineering skill, enthusiasm, and amazing energy, the greatest road and bridge builder in Britain. In 1801 he was commissioned by the Government to make a preliminary report on fishing ports and communications in the Highlands; this was followed in 1803 by an Act that established a Commission 'for making Roads and building Bridges in the Highlands of Scotland'. Telford had found that the old military roads were not fit to carry the traffic of his day; and by the time of his death he had virtually created a road system, building some 1,500km. of roads, improving – often extensively – most of the harbours of the east coast from Wick to Leith, as well as being responsible for the Caledonian Canal.

Telford's work did not extend to the remote west and north-west. North of the Great Glen, Strathpeffer developed as a spa from about 1820 onwards; but the west coast knew little of visitors. Although the island of Staffa, off the west coast of Mull, attracted some illustrious people to see Fingal's Cave – Sir Walter Scott (in 1810 and 1814), Keats (in 1818), Mendelssohn (in 1829), and Queen Victoria among them – in general other parts of the west Highlands were little visited; it was not until the coming of the steamboat in the 1850s and the railways a little later that even places like Oban began to attract any number of visitors.

By the 1820s there were but two proper roads to the north coast of Scotland, both from Bonar Bridge: these are represented by today's A9, the coast road by Wick to Thurso, and that by Lairg and Altnaharra, the A836, to Tongue. There was no 'maintained' road up the north-west coast.

For that matter, communications were not exactly fast in the far north-west even thirty years ago. To see what the roads of this remotest part of Britain were like after World War II, one has only to drive along the A835 north from Ullapool: long stretches of the old road may be seen from the new. The old road down Glencoe is another example: the new road in that magnificent glen was not opened until 1935; the old one now makes an excellent walkers' track.

At the other end of the Highlands, there were no roads in the 1820s in Knapdale and Kintyre; tracks, yes, but the main access to this peninsula was the 'natural' one – by sea.

It took a long time for the railway to penetrate into the Highlands. The line from Aberdeen north-west to the Moray coast was started in 1852, but it did not reach Inverness until 1858; five years later the more direct route from Perth to Inverness, over Drumochter, along the Spey Valley, and by Slochd Summit, was completed. But north from Inverness, Wick and Thurso were not reached by rail until 1874, and it was the 1890s before the Inverness–Kyle of Lochalsh and the Fort William–Mallaig lines were finished. West of Thurso and north of the Inverness–Kyle line there have never been any railways.

Very little happened to the railways in the Highlands during the Beeching era: the railways were not there to close. An exception was the closure of the branch line from Aviemore to Grantown-on-Spey and Forres; ironically, the stretch from Aviemore to the Boat of Garten, and possibly beyond, is being developed for steam locomotion by energetic enthusiasts. Even more ironically, in the 1960s British Rail uplifted – on the stretch over Drumochter – the second track of the main rail link with Inverness from Perth: in 1976 it was announced that vast sums of money were to be spent in restoring the second track. The line to Kyle of Lochalsh has been under threat of closure for years, and for a time there was the possibility too of the Inverness–Wick/Thurso line being closed, British Rail blandly suggesting that buses could be an alternative, ignoring the wild winter conditions that can afflict the north-east corner of Scotland. The vast on-shore developments connected with North Sea oil have ensured that the southern part of this line is safe, and not only for the life of the construction plant around the Cromarty Firth: the building of a major oil refinery at Nigg Bay, approved early in 1976, should ensure some permanence for the line; in 1974 British Rail actually re-opened a station on it.

WHAT ARE THE HIGHLANDS?

The physical make-up of the Highlands inevitably makes for poor communications and tells against industrial development in many areas. It is possible to fly from Glasgow to Stornoway in an hour (though there is no scheduled bus link between Stornoway Airport and the town!); but it takes twelve hours to do the journey by train, bus, and steamer. Similarly, by air from Glasgow to Campbeltown takes thirty minutes; by road, the only alternative, the distance is 220km.

There are no motorways in the Highlands, and very few roads that are dual carriageway for any significant distance. For the traveller in the Highlands using a car – and public transport being what it is, there is little alternative if any distance is to be covered – there are two extremes. One is the very many km. of single-track road still unwidened (usually supplied with passing-places). At the other, most disagreeable, extreme is the notorious A9 through the Spey Valley and Inverness as far as the Cromarty Firth. For years unpleasantly busy at peak holiday periods, the pressure of commercial traffic now makes demands that this road cannot adequately cope with. While there has been widening and straightening in parts, and some new stretches, such as the bypass round Dalwhinnie, have been built, the economic climate of the mid 1970s has hampered the proper development of what is known as 'The Great North Road'. To a lesser extent, the opening of the pulp mill at Fort William resulted in the roads leading to the town bearing traffic that they were never designed to take, although the congestion in Fort William itself was relieved early in 1976 by the opening of a bypass round the town.

Poor land resources have resulted in continuing depopulation of the Highlands for many generations: the leading export from the Highlands, over the centuries, has been the Highlanders themselves. This has led to a delightful situation for the visitor, who finds in the Highlands what in much of western Europe is the rarest of commodities – plenty of room. Maybe in some of the more publicized areas, in July and August, he will encounter rather more people than he had been led to expect; but, even so, it is not difficult to find seclusion. From mid May to early August, in the northern Highlands, there are but few hours of darkness, for even after the sun has set the twilight lingers long. The 'simmer dim' in Shetland, where it is never really dark for weeks on end before and after Midsummer Day, is memorable; but even 250km. further south, midnight golf contests are occasionally held at holiday resorts on the eastern seaboard – a gimmick, maybe, but quite feasible, given the weather.

The Highland climate, particularly in the north-west, can sometimes seem remarkably fickle. Days of rain can be succeeded by days of heavenly weather, equally unforgettable; and the very fact of the preceding rain brings brilliant colour, unknown in more southerly areas. A sodden morning can be followed by a sparkling afternoon – and vice versa. And except to those for whom sunshine is a holiday essential, there is great drama travelling through the hills against dark skies, seeing waterfalls pouring off the tops, and burns becoming sudden, tumultuous torrents of dark peaty water.

Highland weather is not only a matter of time (it is said to be more 'reliable' in spring, which itself cannot really be said to start much before late April in these parts), it is also a matter of place. Rainfall varies – and varies incredibly – from place to place in the Highlands. It is unfortunate that statistically the places with the highest annual rainfall lie between 56° N (just south of Arrochar) and 57°30′ N (the Torridons and Beinn Eighe), taking in much of the finest west-Highland scenery. The heaviest rainfall, over 250cm. a year, is on the mountains that stand high behind the coast: nearer the sea, the precipitation may not be much more than half that amount. The mountains at the northern end of Loch Fyne receive over 200cm. of rain a year; at the southern end of it, less than 150cm.

The island of Tiree has more hours of sunshine than anywhere in Britain except the south coast of England: the rain clouds pass over it, depositing less than 100cm. of rain a year, to release their wetting load further east: Ben More on Mull, not 60km. away, has double Tiree's rainfall. The Outer Hebrides receive less than 150cm. of rain a year; Orkney and Shetland have but half that amount.

About the only generalization that can be made about the climate is that the east is drier than the west and is usually colder.

The wise traveller in the Highlands takes rainwear and sweater. Although in the summer it is not uncommon to find temperatures going over the 25 °C. mark day after day, with only the slightest wisps of cloud to provide contrast to the blue sky, the only certain thing about the Highland climate is its unpredictability.

There is a more certain nuisance for the high-season holidaymaker in the Highlands than unpredictable weather. It features in few books on Highland travel, but, as it is at its most virulent at the very time when there are the most holidaymakers about, it is the subject of many an individual traveller's tale. It is *Culicoides impunctatus* and its relations, known generically as the midge, the smallest and at the same time the biggest menace to the Highland visitor, and to the Highlander too, for none, it seems, can develop immunity to its attack. Almost everywhere in the Highlands below 600m. (and most people stay or travel below that level) are midges, countless millions of them clouding the countryside and coast. They can affect the movements of man just as they can those of animals, driving the camper into a hotel (if he can find one) as well as the deer from the lower slopes to the high tops. For years research has gone on into means of controlling or even eradicating the midge, but as yet no form of control has been devised that would not also damage agriculture, forestry, and other essential resources.

The empty land, poor communications, weather, and insects of the Highlands may seem less than enticing. Yet they do not deter the traveller and holidaymaker: the first two are part of the compelling attraction that make the last two worth risking. And of course there is much more to the Highlands than these. In the Seven Crofting Counties are places as different from each other as the seaside resort of Rothesay and Sandwood Bay; buildings as disparate as Skara Brae and the Aviemore Centre; and people as varied as the crofter of the Outer Isles and the oil construction man of Nigg Bay.

The Start of the Highlands

In north-west Sutherland isolated peaks rise strangely from a waste of moorland riven with lochs. These peaks – Suilven (738m.) and Stac Polly (618m.) are examples – are of Torridonian Sandstone, pre-Cambrian rocks laid down over 600 million years ago. In geological terms they are not of great antiquity. But the rock on which they rest, Lewisian Gneiss, is much older, dating back some 2,700 million years: it is one of the world's earliest rocks.

These are only two of the rocks that make up the complicated geological picture of the Highlands. Much of this picture is still not properly understood: what is certain is that, geologically, Scotland, like Julius Caesar's Gaul, is divided into three parts: the Southern Uplands, the Midland Valley or Central Lowlands, and the Highlands. These parts are not only different geologically, they differ one from the other scenically and socially.

The Highland Boundary Fault, the geological demarcation line between the Highlands and the Central Lowlands, runs north-east from the Firth of Clyde to Stonehaven. The fault-line extends across the seas, producing the same geological demarcation in extreme north-west Ireland and in Scandinavia: for much of the world's existence what is today Britain was a north-westerly extension of the continental land mass, extending much further into the Atlantic than it does now.

Far more definite than the Highland Boundary Fault, which to the non-geologist is noticeable only in that north of it begins typical Highland scenery, is the great rift across the Highlands, running approximately in the same direction. This is the Great Glen, which splits the Highlands in two, from Loch Linnhe to the Moray coast near Inverness. About 350 million years ago there was a huge slip of mountain masses; the rocks north and south of the Great Glen are similar for much of the length of the fault, but the northern mass moved nearly a 100km. south-west alongside the southern one.

There are other geological features obvious to the non-geologist. The Moine Thrust is one: it runs for over 150km. north-north-east from the Sound of Sleat to Loch Eriboll. Here, as the Highlands 'tilted', older rocks were thrust westwards over younger ones: the demarcation can be seen particularly in Assynt, and near Inchnadamph, beside the road. More obvious still, in Skye, Mull, and Ardnamurchan are very visible reminders of the great volcanic activity in the Tertiary period, perhaps 50 million years ago, when sheets of basalt lava, 1,000m. or more thick, poured over much of the north-west Highlands (and extended as far as the Faroes and Iceland). The lava is not 1,000m. high today; but on Mull the terraces formed by various eruptions are a dominating feature of the landscape. The columnar cliffs of Staffa, with Fingal's and other caves, are of this basalt, which, in many areas, was later 'intruded' by huge masses of other rocks, ranging from pale-grey granite to dark gabbro.

These complicated rock formations contribute towards the drama and variety of Highland scenery, though what is seen today is but a remnant of rocks that once stood immensely higher.

For 37 million years after the volcanic eruptions largely ceased, the rocks were worn and shaped by rain, often continuous rain. Then, as the climate cooled, came the first of the four Ice Ages. Intermittently, for nearly a million years, the Highlands were covered by ice, and great glaciers from the Highlands spread south. The harder rocks of course resisted the erosion, but were 'smoothed over' by the glaciers. High-standing rocks were split by frosts to form serrated ridges, such as the Cuillins of Skye; the softer rocks gave way to form valleys; and the debris spread far and wide as the ice sheets melted, the glaciers retreated, and water swept down to the sea.

The Ice Ages came and went. Perhaps, between the later ones, Paleolithic man hunted the mammoth in the Highlands: but there is no trace.

The sea itself changed. First as the ice formed, its level fell; then, as the ice, which at its peak period covered the whole of north-west Europe, grew thicker, its immense weight depressed the land. When the ice melted and the huge burden of its weight was removed, the land gradually rose again, resulting in the 'raised beaches' to be seen along the coasts of the west Highlands and islands.

As the climate improved, vegetation gradually spread north from Europe. First there were mosses, then stunted willow and birch, then, in a kinder climate than to-day's, bigger trees became established – pine, alder, oak, elm, and lime among them. These forests covered much of the Highlands and stretched as far north as Shetland. In about 7000 BC a wetter, windier climate returned: trees in many areas became moss-covered and fell; in due course, from around 5000 BC, blankets of peat, covering much of the Highlands, were formed.

With the spread of vegetation came the animals. The wolf was among the first, and survived in the Highlands for thousands of years: the last, it is said, was killed in the area around Moy, south-east of Inverness, in 1743. Lynx, bear, elk, and reindeer, which used to roam the Highlands, have similarly disappeared (though reindeer were re-introduced to the Cairngorm slopes in the 1950s); but one of these early immigrants, the red deer, is still widespread in the Highlands.

History

Following – and hunting – the animals that returned to the Highlands after the last Ice Age came man. Nobody knows quite when of course – radio-carbon evidence remains open to varying interpretation – but it would appear that small groups of these people were in evidence in Scotland around 4000 BC, though there are suggestions that it might have been 1,000 years earlier when man first trod the shores of the Tay Estuary. It is generally believed that the first inhabitants of Britain spread gradually, over many, many centuries, from the South into Ireland, by which route they may have first come to Scotland.

These were the Mesolithic (Middle Stone Age) people, who lived by fishing and food collection: farming was unknown to them. They were few in number and were nomads, perforce staying near the shores of sea or loch, where the land was reasonably clear and where the waters provided some of their food supply. Their presence in the Highlands is known by the shell middens – the big heaps of shells they threw aside after eating the contents – that have been found in Argyll: one of the most important collections of these remains was found in a cave where Oban's main street now runs; another was on the island of Oronsay. At these sites, in addition to shell middens, flint arrowheads and knives were found: similar flint tools have also been found in Kintyre. The caves in which these people stayed may still be seen on the raised beaches of the west; and from this period, too, may date the remains of reindeer, cave bear, and lynx found in a cave near Inchnadamph. But there are few other traces: these people built no dwellings, and no graves have been discovered.

The picture changes with the emergence in the Highlands, probably about 5,000 years ago, of Neolithic (New Stone Age) man. These people were farmers, cultivating barley, wheat, and rye, the original grasses for which are not native to Scotland. They had cattle and sheep, and they settled (for periods at least, until they moved to new pastures); they knew the use of fire and could make pottery. They created graves for their dead; and their gradual advance through Europe from the Mediterranean can be traced by the tombs they built. In the Highlands they spread, slowly, over the centuries, by two routes, by the west coast and by the east, each route culminating in Orkney, where some of the most outstanding reminders of their culture are found, particularly at Skara Brae. This prehistoric village of ten 'houses' was built at some time between 2000 BC and 1400 BC: its survival today is due to its flag-stone construction, there being, even then, we may presume, no timber in Orkney. These flat stones were also used to create the 'dressers' and 'beds' to be seen today. At some time, probably about 3,000 years ago, this village, whose 'houses' are linked by low stone passages, was overwhelmed by some sudden natural disaster, almost certainly a storm of wind-blown sand, which buried it until 1850, when it was exposed by another storm.

The Standing Stones of Stenness and the Ring of Brogar, a great stone circle, probably date from the same period as Skara Brae, though even more imposing than these is another reminder of the Neolithic age, the Standing Stones of Callanish, built between 2000 BC and 1500 BC.

But older than these are the many places, some still traceable, where these people buried their dead. Onstan Cairn, near Stromness in Orkney, dates back to the third millennium BC, as do the Grey Cairns of Camster in Caithness and the South Cairn at Nether Largie in the Kilmartin area of Argyll, a region rich in early remains. These are a few of the more important; but remains of burial chambers and cairns are to be found in many places in the Highlands (with the exception of areas well away from the coast, usually too mountainous or densely forested for habitation). The cairns – some may be up to 70m. long – held passages leading to one or more chambers in which the dead were laid. Some are known as 'horned cairns' from their having a shallow crescent of stone walling at each end: they are not found outside the north of Scotland.

The Neolithic period lasted some 2,000 years before it merged, gradually, into the Bronze Age. During this period there was another 'invasion', by a different culture, the Beaker Folk, so called from their custom of burying earthenware vessels along with the dead.

It is from the later Neolithic age, rather than the Bronze Age, that some of the most impressive remains date. In Orkney it was Neolithic man, tending cattle and sheep (although not, apparently, growing grain), as well as getting food from the sea, who built not only Skara Brae but also, probably rather earlier, created the finest megalithic tomb in Britain, at Maeshowe, between Stromness and Kirkwall, an incredible achievement for men who had but stone tools.

The purpose of Maeshowe and the chambered cairns is obvious enough; they were for the burial of the dead. Much more mysterious is the purpose of the standing stones and stone circles. Why were they erected? Once Callanish (like Stonehenge) used to be referred to, by the more romantically inclined, as a 'Druid Temple'; but the Druids' period lay mainly in the first century BC and the first century AD (this Celtic priesthood, with its nature rites and veneration for the oak and the mistletoe – neither of which flourish on the island of Lewis! – was exterminated by the Romans; the Standing Stones of Callanish were erected well over a thousand years earlier). While these standing stones may have had a religious significance, there are also theories that suggest some kind of astronomical function, perhaps to guide the early farmers in sowing and harvesting.

Equally mysterious, though by no means so prominent, are the 'cup and ring' markings inscribed on so many stones. These are not unique to the Highlands: they are found in many places in Europe; in all, Scotland has about 300 such, with a large number around the Kilmartin area of Argyll. The markings, a round hollow surrounded by anything up to eight concentric rings, certainly date from Neolithic times (some markings have only the 'cup', without the rings). They may have had a religious significance (some people believe that the 'cup' held blood after sacrifices); it has also been noticed that many of them in Scotland are where gold or copper or other valuable minerals could be found: might they be 'lucky marks' made by early prospectors?

Skara Brae apart, there are no impressive remains of the dwellings of the Neolithic people (Jarlshof, in Shetland, dates back to late Bronze Age times). But often, on hilltops, or on peninsulas, can be found enclosures of earth or stone, which once held huts, probably of turf or wattle; some of these may date back beyond the Bronze Age.

Bronze gave way to iron for metal-working in Scotland in about 200 BC – though again the impact of the new culture varied extensively over the Highlands. It is from this time that the earliest duns – small stone-built forts – were built in the Highlands.

These evolved, after 100 BC, into those remarkable stone towers, unique to Scotland, the brochs. These were tall, circular buildings with immensely thick walls. Between the inner walls, which were perpendicular, and the outer, shaped like a narrow bell, there were galleries and, frequently, cells; inside there was a circular courtyard. There were no windows; and the narrow entrance could be barred from the inside. As the 'castles' of a family or group, they were triumphs of skilful building, and their drystone walls still stand, 1,800 to 2,000 years after they were built. The most impressive example is Mousa Broch, in Shetland, the walls of which still stand some 12m. high all round: they may originally have been 3m. higher. Dun Carloway in Lewis, the Glenelg brochs, and Dun Dornadilla in Sutherland are among other important examples of these buildings, which are only to be found in Scotland, with the overwhelming preponderance in the north and west Highlands.

The tribes who were living in the northern part of Scotland towards the end of the pre-Christian era are usually referred to as the Picts. Though little is known about their origin and background, it is assumed that they were not a race that at some time invaded the country (least of all that they were one of the Ten Lost Tribes of Israel, a theory put forward with all seriousness more than once!). They are more likely to have been an amalgam of the people who moved gradually through Britain – hunters first, then farmers. There would be the traders, for there was trade, in metals particularly, using, in the west of Scotland, sea routes to and from Ireland and around the Firth of Clyde. There would be conquerors: the Bronze Age itself possibly came to Scotland with invaders using bronze weapons. These different elements perhaps constituted the Picts. If none know exactly when and whence they came, equally puzzling is their sudden disappearance from Scottish history in the ninth century. Even the name of the Picts is a problem. They called themselves the Cruithni. The name Picti, first used by the Romans in 297, means 'Painted People': it is generally accepted that they decorated themselves by tattooing or daubing.

But the Romans had invaded Scotland over 200 years before this name was recorded. It was in 83 or 84 that the legions, advancing north under Agricola, found a wild, wretched country holding fierce warriors; they were unable to subdue the Picts for any length of time, and, over succeeding centuries, the northern frontier was rarely free from the menace of these warriors. Tacitus wrote of them as being red-haired men who fought with swords.

There are few if any dwellings that can be assigned to the Picts. The souterrains or earth houses that are occasionally referred to as Pictish dwellings are more likely to have been underground storage places, while the crannogs or lake dwellings – huts on 'stilts' built in a loch, of which remains have also been found in the Highlands and which are also referred to as 'Pictish' – cover such a long period, from late Neolithic times through to the Middle Ages, that they cannot be assigned to any particular people.

The Picts left no written records; but they were responsible for a distinct class of archaeological remains: the Pictish stones, incised or carved with symbols that are almost identical in design wherever they are found. There are two types of these stones, the first (which might date back to the tribes of the Iron Age) bearing Pictish symbols only, the second having Christian and other symbols added. While the finest and most numerous of these stones are to be found in the east of Scotland, there are occasional examples in the Highlands, including one north of the pier at Raasay, off the east coast of Skye, and, on Skye itself, at the entrance to Dunvegan Castle. A pre-Christian stone is to be seen at the church at Dingwall, and a post-Christian one, repaired, at Rosemarkie in the Black Isle. The latest of these stones seems to date from around 700.

For all modern research, the Picts remain a mystery: it is not even certain whether or not they were a Celtic race. There may have been two separate branches, the northern and the southern Picts, and over the centuries they evolved a system of 'representative government': men elected from the settlements themselves elected chiefs, who, in turn, chose overlords, who, in their turn, elected a king. From this there arose a number of Pictish 'kingdoms', which in 297, possibly to counteract the onset of the Roman attacks, merged into one kingdom: for over 500 years this kingdom dominated much of northern Scotland. It was a Pictish king, Brude, who in 565 received St Columba at his fortress beside the River Ness, probably where Inverness now stands. This is vouched for by St Adamnan, the biographer of St Columba: whether or not the king was converted to Christianity is unclear; but he did consent to St Columba's monks preaching the new religion to the Picts – which they did with remarkable success.

This, though, was a later development. When in c. 80 the Roman legions under Agricola set out to subdue northern Britain there was no 'Scotland', no Pictish kingdom as such. Hadrian's Wall, stretching between the Solway and the Tyne, was not started until forty years later; another twenty or so years were to elapse before the Roman geographer Ptolemy drew a map of the country, showing that the Caledonii inhabited the area including the Great Glen and Speyside. The Antonine Wall, running between the firths of Forth and Clyde, was yet further off: it was completed in 142. Agricola was not interested in splitting Scotland: he intended to conquer it up to the northern coast. But he, and subsequent Romans, never conquered – probably never even invaded – the Highlands, although they tried for over 300 years to contain the Picts. The most northerly point of the Roman invasion of Britain was Mons Graupius, where in 83 or 84 Agricola's troops defeated a native army, said to number 30,000 men, and killed its leader. Agricola might have gone on to conquer the Highlands, but he was recalled to Rome in 84 and Imperial commitments elsewhere deprived the forces in Britain of the necessary resources: unconquered Pictland remained a thorn in the Roman flesh for centuries.

It was not only by the Picts of the north that the Romans were assailed; by the fourth century raids into Roman Britain were being made from the west by the Scots from Antrim in Ireland, Gaelic-speaking people, who by about 500 started to settle in the land to which they were to give their name.

The start of this settlement seems to have been under the leadership of three brothers who established their small 'kingdoms' in Kintyre, Cowal, and the islands of Islay and Jura. Their homeland in Ireland was known as Dalriada, and it was this name that was given also to the Scots kingdom when it was established. Its 'capital' was Dunadd, a fort on an isolated hillock in the Moine Mhor, the flat expanse of country east of Crinan Loch and north-west of Lochgilphead, where rock carvings, including a footprint and a rock basin used at the inaugural ceremonies of the Scots kings, can be seen today.

The Scots were Christians, of a sort; and the Gaelic they spoke was the basis of that still used in the western Highlands and islands. Their kingdom was precarious at first, though they received some support when in 563 Columba (whose Gaelic name was Colum Cille) crossed from Ireland to establish his monastery at Iona. He was an Irish princeling who had studied at monasteries in his own country; why he left Ireland is not known: he may have been banished, or his journey may have been a self-imposed exile, following bloodshed during a quarrel. It is generally believed that he had to settle, with his small band of monks, where Ireland could not be seen. From Iona, off the south-west corner of Mull, his monks travelled widely, preaching Christianity and establishing churches. Although not the first to bring Christianity to Scotland (St Ninian established his church at Whithorn in Galloway in 397), St Columba's Celtic Church was widespread, and continued after his death in 597; eventually it succumbed to the authority and better organization of the Church of Rome and to the influence of Margaret, wife of Malcolm Canmore (Malcolm III), who brought a strong anglicizing influence to Scotland in the eleventh century.

The arrival of St Columba at Iona in 563 is one of the few reasonably certain dates in the centuries following the departure of the Roman legions from Scotland. This was the 'Dark Age' in the Highlands, as it was in post-Roman Britain generally. The Scots' foothold in Dalriada was precarious for over 300 years, but they managed to maintain it. Then, much further north, came the forerunners of the people who were to control a considerable part of the Highlands thereafter: the Norsemen. They came first, to Shetland, Orkney, and Caithness, not as invaders but as settlers; they were peasants, not warriors, looking for more rewarding land than they found in Norway. They probably established themselves with little opposition, for there were few people in those areas. Soon, however, the warriors followed, in their longships, raiding the northern islands and mainland, and soon spreading their attacks south. It was in 794 that they made their first attack on Iona, sacking the monastery; they returned to destroy the abbey there in 801, and five years later they attacked again, killing 68 monks: it was this event that led to St Columba's shrine being moved to Ireland, since when all trace of it has been lost.

Early in the period of their attacks and subsequent settling, the Norsemen had a momentous effect on the course of Highland history. At the beginning of the ninth century they inflicted a disastrous defeat on the Picts, the remnants of whose kingdom were taken over by Kenneth MacAlpin, king of the Scots of Dalriada.

Dunadd was no longer the centre of the kingdom. Kenneth MacAlpin's capital had been at Dunstaffnage, near Oban; but on gaining the Pictish throne he moved from there to Scone in Perthshire (at one time the capital of the southern Picts), taking with him the 'Stone of Destiny', on which he was crowned in 843, on the mote hill at Scone, as king of the two peoples. On this stone, reputed to confer a right of kingship, Scottish, and subsequently British, monarchs have been crowned ever since. Traditionally, this was the stone on which Jacob rested his head when he dreamed of angels, and was allegedly brought from Bethel to Ireland and thence to Dalriada. It remained at Scone until 1297, when Edward I had it removed to Westminster Abbey, where it still lies.

The domain over which Kenneth MacAlpin and his successors held sway – fairly tenuously, probably – was not the Scotland of today. His rule did not extend south of the Forth nor north of the Moray Firth, and in the north-west Highlands two factors prevented his having any control. One was the physical barriers: the mountains and forests and the lack of any communication except by sea; the other was the Norseman. Following the Viking raiders had come Norwegian settlers in greater numbers than the handful that had preceded the raiders: they colonized the northern islands and mainland, the Hebrides, and much of the western seaboard. A Norwegian overlordship was established in the west, and this grew into a kingdom over which the Scots kings had no control. Nor, for that matter, in due course, did the Norwegian rulers: the Norsemen established a powerful earldom in Orkney, which was more or less autonomous.

Orkney and Shetland remained under Norse rule until the fifteenth century; but their hold elsewhere was shorter lived. Malcolm II, who reigned from 1005 to 1034, regained the Hebrides and the mainland for his kingdom, which at his accession was known as Alba – it was in 1018, after the conquests that added Lothian to his territory, that the country was first known as Scotland. Malcolm II was succeeded by Duncan I, who also inherited Strathclyde, and thus ruled over a comparatively united south Scotland, whose borders were not dissimilar to those of today.

These events were outside the Highlands but not irrelevant to their story; for with the development of Scotland came the tensions between the Highlands and the south.

Duncan was married to a Northumbrian, and his conquest of Lothian was the first stage in a process of 'anglicization' of Scotland. Working against this influence was the Celtic one, personified by Macbeth, who in 1040 murdered Duncan and (despite Shakespeare's version) reigned for seventeen years, until overthrown and succeeded by Malcolm III. This was Malcolm Canmore ('Bighead') who married the English princess Margaret, exiled by William the Conqueror: hers was a powerful personality and she did much to further southern ideas.

One result of the Norman Conquest was that many Anglo-Norman leaders were granted estates in Scotland; and while these English influences did not directly affect the north and west Highlands, they did lead to the Highlands withdrawing even more into themselves, emphasizing the difference between Gaelic Scotland and the Lowlands – a difference that is still to some extent apparent today.

Malcolm Canmore died in 1093, and in the following four years Scotland had five kings: perhaps, in such a context, it is not surprising that in 1098 Magnus Barefoot, King of Norway, recaptured the Hebrides. In the same year the Treaty of Tarbert between Barefoot and the Scots king Edgar ceded to Norway all the islands round which a ship could sail: traditionally, Magnus claimed Kintyre by having his ship dragged overland from West to East Loch Tarbert while he sat at the helm. The Norse domination of much of the west of Scotland ended after the death of Magnus in 1103 with the rise to power of Somerled, 'King' of Argyll. He was a tempestuous character; but he was also the only man who defeated the Vikings at sea, in 1156, driving them out of Argyll. It was he who became the first 'King of the Isles', a title later changed to Lord of the Isles in nominal deference to the kings of Scotland. His grandson, Donald of Islay, was the founder of Clan Donald.

In 1243 Alexander III of Scotland tried to regain the western seaboard by purchase, but failed; and a military expedition in 1249 had no greater success. Not only were the kings of Scotland anxious to gain this territory: in 1263 King Haakon of Norway assembled a great fleet to try to regain the west of Scotland; but he was defeated at the Battle of Largs, in the October of that year. His fleet returned to Kirkwall in Orkney, where he died. Only Orkney and Shetland continued to be ruled from Scandinavia, and this continued until 1468/69, when they were pledged by King Christian of Denmark and Norway to meet the dowry of his daughter Margaret on her marriage to James III of Scotland.

In theory, after 1263 all Scotland apart from the Northern Isles was one nation. But behind their wild mountain barriers, the Highlanders were subject to little control. The Lords of the Isles regarded themselves as sovereign princes in their own territory; and in the Central Highlands, still well covered with forest – and above the tree line could be found only bare rock or soil too thin to cultivate – there were few people and little traffic, apart from that along the recognized routes, such as the Great Glen, along which men could travel using boats. Yet though they were a land apart from much of Scotland, the Highlands could not, after the thirteenth century, be divorced entirely from the mainstream of Scottish history. In the first stages of the Wars of Independence, with the rebellion of William Wallace, they were little concerned; but when Robert the Bruce sadly miscalculated his support after the murder of the 'Red Comyn' at Dumfries in 1306, it was to the Highlands he fled. At Dunaverty Castle, at the extreme south of Kintyre, Bruce was given refuge by Angus, King of the Isles, who, when the enemy's ships closed in, helped him to escape to Ireland.

After wintering in Ireland, Bruce took ship to the Isle of Arran in the spring of 1307, probably landing at Lochranza and staying at Brodick Castle, to start his seven-year conquest, which culminated in the Battle of Bannockburn (1314) and the routing of Edward II's army.

The Highlands saw little of this action; but one minor affray had momentous consequences. In 1308 Bruce had his revenge on the MacDougalls (who had tried to intercept his earlier flight to the Highlands), defeating them in a battle at the Pass of Brander (between Loch Awe and Loch Etive); the MacDougall's forfeited lands were given to Neil Campbell, a consistent supporter of Bruce. This was the start of the rise to power of Clan Campbell, which, by the end of the Middle Ages, controlled most of Argyll except Kintyre. With an uncanny knack of almost always backing the winning side, they became the most powerful clan in the Highlands. They established their main seat at Inveraray in the early fifteenth century, and became successively Earls then, in 1701, Dukes of Argyll.

Towards the end of his career, in 1326, Bruce tried to subdue the power of the Highlanders of the west and gain more control over Kintyre: at Tarbert he repaired and extended the castle, and it was while he was here in occupation of the castle that he emulated the feat of Magnus Barefoot, over two centuries earlier, by having his ship hauled, on log rollers, across the narrow neck of land between East and West Lochs Tarbert. (Avoidance of the long sail round the Mull of Kintyre was finally solved by the cutting of the Crinan Canal in 1801.)

After the death of Robert the Bruce in 1329 much of his achievement was lost by weak successors. In 1371 Robert, the High Steward of Scotland, son of Bruce's daughter Marjory, ascended the Scottish throne, founding the House of Stewart.

During the reigns of Robert II and III and of James I, II, and III – a period of over 100 years, from 1371 to 1488 – the Highland chiefs usually supported the King, provided it suited them. But by the time James IV came to the throne, the Highlands were in rebellion. Alexander of Lochalsh, a kinsman of the Lord of the Isles, tried to obtain the earldom of Ross: the clans took sides, and from 1493 James was often in the western Highlands, trying, through a mixture of edicts and force, to bring peace. Apart from the capture of the Lord of the Isles at Stornoway in 1506, the main result of this warfare was the appointment of two sheriffs to look after northern Scotland: the Gordons of Huntly, Aberdeenshire, in the north, and the Campbells of Argyll in the south-west.

James V was only a year old when his father was killed in the military disaster of Flodden Field in 1513; for some 150 years after that the Highland clans grew in power, and intrigued and feuded as, further south, the great families intrigued and feuded on the national scene.

The Reformation had little immediate effect on the Highlands; there were few Presbyterian ministers there, the clan chiefs being uninterested in establishing churches. Similarly, the Union of the Crowns in 1603, when, on the death of Queen Elizabeth, James VI of Scotland became also James I of England, had little effect on the Highlands: they had been remote from the King when he was in Edinburgh; they were even more remote when he was in London.

In the civil wars of the seventeenth century, when the Covenanters – those who had signed the 'Solemn League and Covenant' to continue Presbyterianism in Scotland – were opposed to Charles I's Episcopacy, there was the usual division of support in the north of Scotland. As the Campbells supported the Covenanters, their enemies, including Cameron of Locheil and the Macphersons and Mackintoshes of Speyside, supported the King (though the Grants, also on Speyside, were Covenanters). The confusion of sides in this conflict is not simplified by the fact that the great Marquis of Montrose, although a Presbyterian, fought for the King. His arch enemy was the Earl of Argyll, chief of Clan Campbell, whose forces he defeated in the heart of the Campbell country as well as routing the Covenanters at Auldearn, near Nairn, in 1645. But when Montrose advanced from these Highland victories into south Scotland, he was disastrously defeated. Escaping to Holland, he returned in 1650 to raise an army for the exiled Charles II, marched with his forces from Thurso down the east coast, and was defeated at Carbisdale, near Bonar Bridge. He fled west and sought refuge with Macleod of Assynt at Ardvreck Castle, the gaunt ruins of which still stand near the head of Loch Assynt; but he was handed over to his enemies, taken to Edinburgh, and executed.

Oliver Cromwell was more determined – and better equipped – than his royal predecessors to subdue Scotland. Much of the Highlands was subjugated, as was the rest of the country: at Inverness a great citadel was built to hold his garrison; and, at the other end of the Great Glen, Fort William was first established by General Monk (who called it Inverlochy) to control the western Highlands.

With the Restoration of 1660, the English troops moved out. But Charles II tried to enforce Episcopacy again: there was another Covenant and more brutal conflict, until, after James II had fled the throne, peace finally prevailed. It was not a universal peace, of course: in the special conditions of the Highlands it could not be; and what peace there was had little chance of lasting. Many Highland chiefs had supported the Stewart kings, but William III extended an amnesty to them, an amnesty that led, indirectly, to the infamous Massacre of Glencoe (*see* pp. 91–2).

Yet despite the amnesty, there were still in the Highlands many with Jacobite sympathies. As the years lengthened, perhaps the return of the Stewarts, when 'the King shall enjoy his own again', was more a romantic dream than a practicable proposition, though Highland loyalty to 'the King over the water' maintained for a long time. The best-known of the Jacobite risings, the 'Forty-Five', took place fifty-seven years after James II had lost his throne. There had been two risings in Scotland before then. In 1715 the Earl of Mar raised the standard of the Old Pretender (the son of James II) at Braemar, at the head of Deeside in Aberdeenshire. Initially, this rising had some success – Inverness was occupied by Mar's troops for a time – but it was defeated in about ten weeks. The rising of 1719 was a trivial affair. Two frigates and a few hundred Spaniards under the command of two leading Jacobites, the Marquis of Tullibardine and the Earl of Seaforth, sailed to Lewis and then set up a base at Eilean Donan Castle on Loch Duich. They were to be the spearhead of a great Jacobite rising; but they got little support from the chiefs, a British frigate attacked and largely destroyed the Castle (which was not rebuilt for nearly 200 years), and the Jacobites – if such forces could be so called – were routed in Glen Shiel. The rising of 1745 was a much bigger affair, but, for all its high hopes, was doomed to failure from the start; in the upshot it was a crushing and final disaster for the Highland way of life.

There can be no doubting the courage and personality of the 23-year-old Young Pretender, Prince Charles Edward Stuart, who sailed from France to first set foot on Scottish soil on the island of Eriskay on 23 July 1745. Yet when he crossed to Moidart, the chiefs at first refused their support until Cameron of Locheil, despite his conviction that this was a hopeless cause, allowed his loyalty to the Stewarts to sway him and threw in his lot with the Prince. After the standard was raised at Glenfinnan, many more joined the Jacobite army for the march south. Twenty months later, after reaching Derby and then, on the advice of his Highland officers, retreating to Scotland, the Prince's army was massacred, and the Jacobite cause lost forever, at Culloden on 16 April 1746. The Prince escaped, and for five months was a fugitive in the Highlands, with a price of £30,000 on his head – an immense sum, yet he was not betrayed.

The atrocities committed after Culloden by the victorious army of the Duke of Cumberland (which earned him the sobriquet 'Butcher') were really only a side issue. The Government, determined to stamp out resistance once and for all, enforced an Act of 1725 aimed at disarming the Highlanders, banned Highland dress and the pipes, in some cases formally abolished the Highland chiefs' right of heritable jurisdiction (which was in fact a dead letter), and by disparaging the Gaelic speech and the whole Gaelic way of life sought to reduce the Highlanders, whichever side they had taken, to the status of second-class citizens. For thirty years the Highlands were under military control. Many of the Highland chiefs' lands were forfeit, along with their powers, and their place was taken by landowners.

The sheep and the Clearances were yet to come; but 1746 was, for the Highlands (as was said of Scotland at the Union of the Parliaments thirty-nine years earlier), 'the end of an auld sang'.

The abolition of the right of many chiefs to heritable jurisdiction over their people extinguished just one part of the clan system, a rather unique form of society that had existed over many centuries. In some cases, these rights of the chiefs to exercise jurisdiction were used with the tacit consent of the king, in some cases by long-established custom, in some cases without any legal backing. It was an acceptance of the fact that if the Highlanders isolated among their hills could not be governed by the king, government by the chief was preferable to no government at all.

The clan was a family, not a tribe, though probably clans stemmed from the break-up of the Pictish tribes: *clann* is the Gaelic name for children. Today, over 200 years after the defeat of the Highland way of life, the clans survive mainly as a tradition, romantically embroidered no doubt but still a tradition that commands intense loyalty.

It would be a nice line in historical continuity to think that the clans grew up from the system of government developed by the Picts: but it would not be true. The clans stemmed from the feudal system introduced by the Normans, and can be dated back to the time of Malcolm Canmore (Malcolm III, 1057–93). His queen, Margaret, a determined woman set on extending southern ways to Scotland, persuaded him to grant estates on a feudal basis to Norman and English lords who established themselves and their retainers in different territories. (Some of them were ejected by Malcolm's successor, Donald Bane – but he only reigned for a year.) Some of the nobles held on to their lands; some clan territories were gained by conquest; some granted as estates forfeited by previous occupiers who had rebelled or fallen into disfavour; some by marriage. The system was essentially feudal; but as it developed in the Highlands, with people in isolated communities tending to intermarry and be much of the same kin, the clan chief was regarded as being of the family of the 'chief of chiefs', the king, embodying the family, its traditions, and its lands. The system was oddly democratic: the clansman could, and did, regard himself as being equally as good a man as the chief, yet offered him an unswerving loyalty: the clansman was not a feudal serf; above all, he was a fighter, ready and glad to battle whenever called on to do so – which was not infrequently, for the clans were constantly feuding with each other. Between feuds there might well be extensive cattle reiving.

Within a clan individual families might well rise to power and form 'little clans', almost as powerful, in some cases, as the clan itself, yet owing loyalty to the clan chief. These were known as septs, and there are many more septs, naturally, than clans: the extreme case, probably, is the septs of the Campbells. There are over eighty septs or families 'entitled' to wear the Campbell tartan. The Campbell septs range, alphabetically, from the Ballantynes to the Ures, and embrace such diverse characters as Robert Burns and Kenneth MacKellar.

The Campbells' hereditary enemies, the MacDonalds, have as their progenitor Somerled, one of the most famous names in earlier Highland history, who, although possibly of Norse descent, wrested control of Argyll from the Norsemen. He was killed at Renfrew in 1164 and was succeeded by his son Reginald, whose son was the founder of Clan Donald, from which came many branches of the MacDonalds (there are MacDonalds of the Isles, of Sleat, and of Clanranald, all separate clans, as are the MacDonells, in this complicated 'family tree', which also has many septs).

Although the clans as such do not date back much before the twelfth century, clan chiefs were adept at building up mythical pedigrees: the Campbells claimed to trace their lineage back to King Arthur. Equally suspect are the maps that show Scotland as being neatly divided into clan territories. Over the centuries – the clans were an important feature of Highland life for some 400 years – clan territories varied considerably. A clan chief could well have land in widely separated areas of the country; he could lose his land, or extend it; and while in many areas of the Highlands there is often a preponderance of people with the same surname, this is due more to the people tending to stay, until comparatively recent times at least, in the same area than to any clan basis.

Over the years, the clan developed into a fixed structure and became much more rigid and undemocratic. The chief, who owned the clan lands, would lease them out, in large part, to 'tacksmen' who, in turn, rented out small areas to tenants, who might well have sub-tenants. Rents would normally have been paid in kind, and the tenant was usually under an obligation also to work on the tacksman's land when called on to do so.

In practice, although the chief was the head of the clan, the operation of the clan lands was left to the tacksmen; some were good masters and conscious of their responsibility for the welfare of the people; others, perhaps the majority, were not. It was a system that only worked because there was little or no alternative.

There was nothing 'romantic' about the Highland way of life. At its best, it was precarious, with tenants trying to scrape a subsistence living, using primitive instruments, from an ungrateful land. When crops or labour failed, starvation was the inevitable outcome. For much of the clan period there was no alternative to this existence, in a society that had little money and where there was an intense, though inarticulate, loyalty to the land.

Communities near the coast, with the harvest of the sea at hand, and more chances of communication, were in a better state. From some of the islands, particularly Skye, and from parts of the western mainland, too, there was an 'export trade' in black cattle (not half the size of today's cattle); but although this is recorded from the sixteenth century onwards, the main droving period was in the eighteenth and nineteenth centuries, after the clan system had collapsed. Essentially, though, Highland communities had to be self-supporting, and the insecurity of existence was accepted by a people who had little knowledge of the outside world, and few needs.

Though Culloden marked the end of the old order, with the clans as a power in the land finished, it could not have survived very much longer in any case. The isolation that gave the system its strength was ending before Culloden. After the 1719 rising General George Wade was given the task of building roads to control the Highlands, and by the 'Forty-Five' over 400km. of roads leading into the Highlands had opened up communications. In this period, too, the Government realised that the best way to utilize the Highlander's warlike tendency, his hardihood, and his fighting skill was to recruit him into the King's service, and some of the most famous Scottish regiments were formed in this period – the oldest, the Black Watch, dates from 1725. Later in the eighteenth century the Highlands were a major recruiting ground for the armies that built up the British Empire; to the young and fit recruitment offered an escape from the glens.

Even before the 'Forty-Five', Highlanders had gone overseas to seek a better way of living. After Culloden, with their way of life condemned, many more clansmen and their families emigrated. But it was not only this that led to mass emigration from the Highlands. There was a population explosion (from the mid eighteenth to the mid nineteenth century the population rose from 255,000 to 396,000, despite emigration) and no land to till; there could be no further extension of cultivable land: the vast Caledonian Forest, which had covered much of the Highlands for so many hundreds of years, was virtually all cleared by the eighteenth century. Rents were increased: Dr Johnson on his journey to the Western Islands of Scotland recorded the case of a farm where the rent had increased from £5 to £20 in twenty-five years.

With the failure of the Jacobite risings, some of the Highland chiefs forfeited their lands as well as their powers. The tacksmen, already largely an anachronism, were also dispossessed or made redundant, and their holdings were let to groups of existing tenants or sub-tenants or to incomers. With better communications – the roads continued to be steadily extended during the eighteenth century – farmers from the south, with more modern ideas, were moving into the Highlands, bringing sheep, and paying more in rent than the previous tenants could afford. Enclosure was necessary to develop the land, and this again reduced the scope for the more primitive methods of the past: 'common grazings' for cattle were as often as not the first lands to be taken in.

This process did not happen overnight; it continued over many decades, and the picture was not entirely black. In some areas, towards the end of the eighteenth century, the British Fisheries Society established fishing centres in many places. Not all were successful, in part due to the vagaries of the herring shoals; but many coastal ports – Ullapool is a case in point – owe their existence today to this enterprise.

Another new, and for a time very flourishing, industry developed along the seaboards of Wester Ross, Skye, and the Outer Hebrides. The 'tangle o' the Isles', the seaweed that grows along the rocky shores, when calcined between layers of burning peat results in kelp, a valuable source of alkali, much needed in the eighteenth century for bleaching linen, then a major industry in Scotland. It became even more valuable when alternative sources of alkali from Spain were cut off by the Revolutionary and Napoleonic wars. After the Napoleonic wars, when it was cheaper to import the alternative barilla from Spain, the Highland industry virtually collapsed.

But these changes, and others, took place against a very different background to that existing in earlier years. More important than the chiefs losing their powers was the resulting change in relationship between landlord and tenant. Despite the fact that clan lands had been let out to and by tacksmen, there had been a mutual interest in the land; after the break-up of the system the peasant became a 'tenant-at-will' of a landlord who, as a rule, had more interest in the rent than in the person who paid it. From this arose the class of people that come again and again into any survey of the Highland scene – the crofters, the tenants of separate holdings into which farms or lands were divided. The name appears early in the kelp industry in Skye, where farms divided into these holdings were known as crofts, probably from the Gaelic *croit*, which referred in parts of the central Highlands to the 'infield', the better land around a township, as compared with the 'outfield', poorer land more distant. Kelp was a seasonal and spasmodic occupation, so the men working on it had in the croft a part-time smallholding; and the croft, today, is still, usually, that: a smallholding that is a home and a sideline for the crofter, who has another occupation such as fishing or estate work.

Transient developments like fishing and seaweed did little to relieve the main problem of the Highlands: too many people on too sparse land. Black cattle and scant crops could not sustain the communities, which, by the mid eighteenth century, had in many cases been reduced to a potato diet, introduced in the early part of that century. As in other 'peasant areas', the potato was at first regarded with the deepest suspicion, and at first rejected as a crop. But for many it became the staple, sometimes the only, food; and when the crops failed the result was starvation. Various projects in the Highlands, such as 'Destitution Road' between Braemore and Dundonnell, are witness to the efforts made to relieve this position by giving work to starving men and their families.

In such circumstances landlords could not rely on rents, and they realized that sheep were more profitable than men. And so came the infamous Clearances. While the rights and wrongs of clearing out people to make way for sheep are still debated, there can be no doubting that whatever the economic justification the effects were in some cases as brutal as anything in Highland history. In many parts of the Highlands whole communities were forcibly evicted to make grazings for sheep, which needed but few men to look after them – and the Highlanders were not skilled shepherds.

Many of the dispossessed emigrated; some, indeed, were forcibly put on ships bound for the Americas. Others found their way to the rapidly growing cities and towns of the south, and to the Industrial Revolution. Wherever they went away from their glens, not only were they penniless but they could not, usually, speak any language but the Gaelic.

Some of the clearances, it is claimed, were done with the best of intentions on the part of the landowners. In Sutherland, perhaps the most notorious area, they were part of a policy of land improvement by the Countess of Sutherland and her husband, the Marquess of Stafford (later Duke of Sutherland). As one of the leading landowners in the country, the Marquess spent some £60,000 on improvements; he and the Countess believed that people evicted from inland areas such as Strathnaver would settle on the coast, where their diet could be supplemented by fishing. However well meaning these actions, though, he and those of his agents who directed some of the more vicious evictions are reviled to this day.

Not all landowners had even good intentions, except for themselves, in clearing out people. Others at first rejected this way of making their estates viable, until economic pressure forced the issue. Some created settlements in the Americas for their people to go to; some did not embark on the clearances policy at all. Generally, clearances were fairly widespread, in the northern Highlands and the western islands, from the end of the eighteenth century to a peak between 1820 and 1840. Many a 'rickle o' stanes' that was once a house can be seen in the glens and behind the coasts today, though not a few date from a later period – emigration from the Highlands has never ceased. (Although it is now suggested that by the late 1970s the Highlands may show a net gain in population, for the first time in over a century, it is not to the crofts and the deserted dwellings that people will return.)

Incidentally, it is worth recalling that the first evictions of men to make way for sheep in Scotland were not in the Highlands but in the Borders and Galloway, at the end of the seventeenth century: it was sheep farmers from these regions who later looked to the Highlands for more grazing for their flocks.

Ironically, in many places in the Highlands, the sheep in due course cropped the grass so close (which cattle had never done) that the pastures became useless. The sheep went and the bracken took over; and where the sheep remained, they became increasingly unprofitable because of mutton and wool imports from New Zealand and Australia.

For the landowner, and to a lesser extent his tenants, the situation was saved by the growing popularity of deer stalking and grouse shooting. Vast areas of land became 'sporting estates' for Victorian and Edwardian magnates whose interest in the High-lands usually started on 'The Glorious Twelfth' (of August, when grouse shooting begins) and ended when the due number of grouse, deer, and other quarry had been disposed of.

For those crofters who were left, life in the nineteenth century was often grim indeed. With no security of tenure, no incentive, and no capital to develop their land they were too often at the mercy of rapacious landowners, and liable to be evicted at will. One series of evictions, in Skye in 1882, had unexpected results: instead of accepting their fate, the people rioted and a battleship was sent to Portree to restore order to an island that even then was beginning to attract the attention of the early tourists. In itself not notable, this incident at least drew attention, far away in Westminster, to the straits in which the crofters lived, and resulted in the passing in 1886 of the Crofters' Holding Act, which gave security of tenure, and the establishment, in the following year, of the Crofters' Commission. Replaced by another body, the Commission was re-established in 1954, and there was a Crofting Act in 1961. But attempts to improve crofters' conditions have proved to be limited in value, in part due to the very set-up of the organization appointed to look after them – a croft has been described as 'a piece of land surrounded by regulations' – and in part to the conservatism of the crofters themselves, unwilling to consider, or at least actually do, anything about suggested re-organization. By 1972 there was a suggestion that the rigid basis of crofting tenure could be replaced by a system of owner-occupation: three years later this was still being argued.

To put present-day crofting in perspective it should be realized that not one in five of the 308,000 people in the area covered by this survey actually live on crofts. In the past half century, and in the post-World War II period particularly, a much wider view has been taken of the 'Highland Problem'. Developments range from the establishment of the Forestry Commission, in 1919, to the unexpected arrival on the Highland scene of North Sea oil operations, which, depending on what way you look at it, may be either a blessing or a disaster.

Industry and Development

Over 1,000 years ago much of the Central Highlands was covered by the vast Caledonian Forest. It consisted mainly of pine trees: Rothiemurchus in the Spey Valley is an anglicization of the Gaelic *rath a'mhor ghiuthais*, 'Plain of the Great Pines'. But from the arrival of the first settlers, the forests were steadily eroded as ground was cleared for cultivation. Later, when timber was in demand for shipbuilding, trees were felled in great quantity and floated down the rivers: pine logs from Rothiemurchus, for example, went down the Spey to a shipyard at Garmouth, near Fochabers in Moray.

Not all the forests were pine. There were extensive oakwoods in Argyll: Taynuilt on Loch Etive and Furnace on Loch Fyne were two places where iron-smelting was established in the late eighteenth/early nineteenth century, both of course using charcoal from the oak woods (and further depleting the stock of trees).

Laws to protect the forests had little effect; but a few farsighted landowners did take steps to maintain the forests: even 400 years ago Sir Duncan Campbell of Glenorchy was re-planting trees with seed taken from pine cones. He was perhaps the first tree-conservationist in the Highlands, and his example was followed by other landowners in subsequent years.

There were Crown forests in the early years of the twentieth century: Inverliever Forest, on the western shores of Loch Awe, was one of the first in Scotland: here planting started in 1907. Until after World War I, though, forestry was largely the concern of private estates, which still have a considerable interest in it. But the extensive felling of trees during the War made the conservation of trees a national concern, and in 1919 the Forestry Commission was established. It is now the most important landowner in Scotland, controlling some 750,000ha. of land, and in the Highlands there are some eighty forests owned by the Commission.

The forests are not all big, and they are not all covered with trees. In parts of the Argyll Forest Park, covering much of the area west of Loch Long towards Loch Fyne, for instance, many of the mountain tops are above the tree line, and here, as elsewhere, emerging from paths through the trees can lead to sudden, wonderful views. It was partly because of this that the Argyll Forest Park was formed, out of six Commission forests in the area, in 1935. It was the first National Forest Park in Britain: there are now seven, of which two are in the Highlands, the other being Glen More, under the Cairngorms, opened in 1947. For all its beauty and its wealth of wildlife, Glen More is the smallest of the Forest Parks, with 2,600ha. compared with Argyll's 25,000ha.

The original idea behind these Forest Parks was to offer free access to large forest areas so that the public could enjoy wide stretches of unspoiled countryside. In the earlier years of its existence, while the first trees were growing, the Commission did not normally welcome visitors to its forests. In the past decade in particular, though, many more forests than those covered by the Parks have been opened up, all with one merciful proviso: 'no cars'.

The main object of the Forestry Commission and the private landowners involved in forestry is of course to grow and sell timber. The most noticeable aspect of its use in the

Highlands is the pulp and paper mill at Corpach, near Fort William, which, at its completion in 1966, was the biggest new industrial development in the Highlands. In its process of making specialized papers (it cannot compete with overseas suppliers to the bulk paper market because of the high cost of bringing timber from the forests to the mill) this establishment, operated by Wiggins Teape Ltd, uses as about one third of its input hardwoods from Canada, ready chipped for pulping. The other two thirds is in the form of softwoods from Scottish forests, which supply some 500,000 tonnes annually to this mill.

This is only one customer for the impressive production of timber from Scottish forests, which it is estimated will exceed 3 million tonnes annually by 1980.

Sadly, from the scenic point of view, the Forestry Commission's profitability flag has to be nailed to the softwoods. Not only can conifers thrive on the poor soil that makes up so much of the Commission's property, their commercial yield is much quicker than that of the hardwoods, however much more picturesque the latter are. So some areas of Highland hillside are increasingly covered with monotonous dark-green blankets of trees, blurring the once bare, if unprofitable, beauty.

However regrettable this may be scenically, though, the fact remains that this is the only use to which much of the land can be put; and in the Highlands, the Forestry Commission employs about 2,000 people.

While forestry impinges on many areas of Scotland, the main activities of the North of Scotland Hydro-Electric Board are in the Highlands, where it has over forty power stations. It employs about 4,000 people; but many, including the headquarters (in Edinburgh, as are those of the Forestry Commission), are outside the Highlands.

Were it not for the excellent water supplies in the Highlands, not only would there be some 4,000 people in different (or no) jobs, but nearly half a million consumers would have to look elsewhere for their heat and light. Half a million consumers, of course, sums up more than the Highland population: the Board 'exports' much of its output of nearly 7,000 million units of electricity a year.

The North of Scotland Hydro-Electric Board was established in 1943. But Highland water was used for generating electricity over fifty years before then: in 1890 a small water turbine installed near the Abbey at Fort Augustus gave the first public supply of electricity to Scotland; it operated for sixty-one years. Across Loch Ness from Fort Augustus, in 1890, the British Aluminium Company brought into commission the first large commercial hydro-electric undertaking in Britain, for aluminium smelting. It operated for seventy years; then the factory closed, the Hydro Board installed a turbo-generator to use the water, and in 1968 started to build a 'reversible pumped storage station' on the site, with a capacity of 300 megawatts; this went into operation in April 1975.

It was the second such station, the first being that at Ben Cruachan above Loch Awe, where a 'visitor centre' explains the system, and from which minibuses take visitors to see the vast power station built inside the mountain. Briefly, these stations transfer water from a low-level reservoir to a high-level one when consumer demand for electricity is low, then use the water to generate electricity at times of peak demand. At Cruachan the low-level reservoir is Loch Awe; to create the upper one, the Board built a dam some 400m. above sea-level, high up on Ben Cruachan. At Foyers the low-level reservoir is Loch Ness, the high-level one Loch Mhor, up in the hills to the east: the two are linked by an underground tunnel 2,750m. long, and the station is remotely controlled by micro-wave radio link from Fort Augustus. The Foyers station was the last of the Hydro Board's major projects to go into operation in the 1970s, and when it opened there were no further water-powered stations planned. The Board's first major scheme was at Loch Sloy, east of Loch Fyne, the power station of which is beside Loch Lomond: this started to generate electricity in 1950.

A quarter of a century separates Sloy and Foyers. Obviously, the power stations cannot be disguised; but the Board has been genuinely concerned to spoil the scenery as little as possible. Certainly the level of many lochs has been raised – often to the benefit of the scenery. Many new roads have been built – often giving a new opportunity to the tourist to see great Highland views. Many of the power stations are built of local stone, to fit into their surroundings, and with very few exceptions they have been remarkably successful in doing so.

Inevitably, there are protests when new power lines have to be installed: in 1975 there was controversy over the route of overhead cables to Skye – should they go via Glen Shiel or over the hills to Glenelg? Nobody likes pylons, but the alternative of put-ting the cables underground for these distances was too expensive to consider. So, in this instance, was the suggestion that electricity could be locally generated in Skye instead of bringing it across from the power station at Loch Quoich: even that was going to cost an extra £2·54 million. In the event, the Kinloch Hourn–Glenelg route was chosen. The National Trust for Scotland, which owns Kintail (*see* Shiel Bridge in the Gazetteer sec-tion) was delighted, the Glenelg Action Group disgusted. Basically, though, this, as ever, was a conflict between people who visit Scotland or have their own little patch of it, and the people who live there, some 98 per cent of whom can now get electricity from the operations of the Hydro Board.

Hydro-electricity is one use for a resource that the Highlands have in plentiful sup-ply: water. It has other uses.

Barley was grown by the first farmers in Scotland – neolithic man. Peat was laid down over much of the Highlands 7,000 years ago. Clear water has been running off the Highland hills ever since the glaciers melted. These three natural resources, in combina-tion, help to make up the most famous of all exports from Scotland – 'Scotch'.

While the adjective pertaining to Scotland is either 'Scots' or 'Scottish', there is only one legitimate use of the adjective 'Scotch', and that is in its application to whisky. The whisky purists will maintain that there is only one form of whisky – pure malt – which is certainly the traditional form of the drink, although far and away the largest consump-tion of whisky is not of the 'straight malts' but of 'blended', a mixture.

There are three forms of whisky: malt, grain, and blended. The first is made entirely from an extract of malted barley, dried in a kiln over a peat fire, fermented with yeast and then twice distilled. Grain whisky is made from maize, and is seldom drunk as such but is used mixed with malts to make blended whisky.

How many different malt whiskies are used in blending, and in what proportions, is a secret jealously guarded by each and every one of the firms producing whisky; and the traditional skill that goes into blending is another reason for the pre-eminence of Scotch whisky. Traditionally, also, Scotch is Highland. But in fact, of the 100-odd distilleries producing malt whisky today, only about one third are in the Highland area. Many of the greatest malt whiskies come from Banffshire, in what is now Grampian region, where the characteristic onion-topped or pagoda-like towers of the distilleries are a feature of the landscape.

From Orkney to Campbeltown there are Highland distilleries, including a dozen between the well-known one at Tomatin, south of Inverness, and Balblair on the Dornoch Firth. Others include the charmingly incongruous intrusion on a bleak moorland outside Dalwhinnie and the famous Talisker distillery on Skye. But the greatest congregation of distilleries in the Highland area is on Islay: eight of them, including those that produce some of the really great malts like Lagavulin and Laphroaig. There used to be many more distilleries than there are today: Campbeltown once had thirty-four: now there are two.

Forestry, hydro-electricity, and whisky – some of the Highlands' principal industries – reflect how far outside the traditional pattern of industrial development this area stands. The absence of such development in the Highlands has been due to a variety of causes, all fairly obvious from the general make-up of the area. These include not only the lack of raw materials – there might well be more that could be exploited – but also the sparseness of communications, the distance from the markets, and also, perhaps, even the traditional image of the Highlands as an area where industry just does not happen.

There are isolated instances in the Highlands where minerals have been discovered and exploited. The mine at Brora, where coal was worked from the end of the sixteenth century, the mines at Strontian (*see* Sunart in the Gazetteer section), whence strontium originated, and the diatomite that used to be mined in Skye are examples, very small in scale. Bigger are the silica-sand industry at Lochaline (*see* Morvern in the Gazetteer section), which is still going strong, and slate quarrying at places like Ballachulish and Seil Island, neither of which now function. There are other instances, but nothing that could make more than a tiny dent in the 'Highland Problem' of continuing emigration and high rates of unemployment, even in the 'reconstruction years' after World War II.

Governments, and plenty of other people, recognized the problem, but it was only tinkered with until, in 1965, the Highlands and Islands Development Board (largely fostered by an Englishman who was a Labour Minister of State for Scotland at the time, with a Lowland Scot, Sir Robert Grieve, as its first chairman) was set up, with the task of creating jobs and stemming depopulation (and even, if possible, reversing it). Its scope obviously included tourism, the promotion of which for nearly twenty years previously had been the function of the Scottish Tourist Board set up by Tom Johnston, then Secretary of State for Scotland, in 1946.

Tourism was nothing new to the Highlands. Even before wild mountain scenery became 'romantic' instead of 'horrible', Scotland in general and the Highlands in particular had exercised a fascination to many, including Dr Samuel Johnson and James Boswell. As the Romantic Age dawned, other literary figures, including the Wordsworths, Coleridge, and Southey, came. Sir Walter Scott was an untiring publicist for romantic scenery, and the seal of respectability on Highland touring was set by Queen Victoria, whose *Leaves from the Journal of Our Life in the Highlands* (1868) and *More Leaves from the Journal of a Life in the Highlands* (1884), though by no means confined to the Highland area of this survey, are worth reading.

Before World War II tourism was not an important factor in the Highland economy. The coastal resorts and the country centres had their clientele, the former for seaside holidays, the latter as often as not for angling; but touring in the modern sense was largely confined to the young and adventurous, who stayed, as like as not, in youth hostels (the Scottish Youth Hostels Association was founded in 1931) or in bed-and-breakfast accommodation.

For some twenty years the sole job of the Scottish Tourist Board was to attract more people to visit Scotland, and this it did with remarkable success – though probably the facts of increased leisure, holidays with pay, and increasing numbers of car owners contributed considerably to the build-up of tourism in that period.

With more holidaymakers coming to the Highlands, not only more accommodation and many more outdoor activities came into being: side issues included a mushrooming of 'craft shops', often operated by craft workers who saw in the Highlands an opportunity to work and sell their products where they wanted to be. There was also a blossoming of 'souvenir shops' of less genuine value, and 'tourist information offices' were set up, often working on a shoestring budget. Throughout this time the only contribution made by the Government to the development of tourism in Scotland was a £15,000-a-year grant for a few years for developments in the Highlands, although towards the end of the 1960s tourism was generally estimated to be worth about £100 million a year to the Scottish economy.

From 1965, however, promotion and development of tourism in the Highlands was largely the province of the Highlands and Islands Development Board, whose task was by no means confined to tourism (and which, in fact, has always been faced with the problem of differentiating between the often conflicting claims of tourism and industry).

The value of tourism as an industry of value to the local community has been increasingly questioned in recent years. This was pinpointed particularly in a paper produced by the Fraser of Allander Institute in 1976. In this it was maintained that 'The benefits from tourist expenditure are more apparent than real – it involves a lot of noise and activity, but at the end of the day locals have little to show for it'. In the accommodation field, 'the main item of tourist expenditure', the researchers found 'leakages' in the form of 'profits to non-local owners, wages to non-local labour and, most of all, goods and services imported'; it was suggested that each pound of tourist expenditure would generate only 34p of local income.

Be that as it may, few people dispute that tourism will remain an important factor in the rural Highland economy for years to come.

The Highlands and Islands Development Board now concentrates much more on industrial development. During the first decade of its existence it dispensed £26·4 million in grants and loans to 3,437 projects, ranging from fish farming and seaweed processing to the manufacture of spectacle frames on Barra (which, unfortunately, was not a success). The Board has added over 100 new and second-hand trawlers and other fishing vessels to Scotland's fleet, done much to establish craft-working shops (some of which have entered successfully into the export field), helped to re-open a distillery on Mull and to establish an oyster hatchery at Loch Creran. One of the Board's most significant successes was to persuade British Aluminium to open a major smelter at Invergordon. This provided upwards of 600 jobs and cost £37 million – which provoked the unkind comment that if that money had been used for a network of small industries 22,000 jobs could have been created. The £37 million was not, of course, Highland Board money.

There were also plans, quite elaborately worked out, to create a 'linear city', along with a vast industrial complex, round the Moray and Cromarty firths from Nairn to Tain, with Invergordon as its hub. It would, it was projected, have a population of 300,000 people (larger than either Aberdeen or Dundee) and its industry would be largely based on petro-chemicals.

But the problem of making additional employment available in this area of the eastern Highlands ended through no action of the Highlands and Islands Development Board: the catalyst was the discovery of large oil fields in the North Sea.

The Industrial Revolution in Scotland affected the Highlands hardly at all, except in drawing Highlanders, many of whom were being dispossessed by the Clearances, into the squalor of the cities. The true industrial revolution in the Highlands can be said to have started in February 1972, when work started on constructing what was then the largest graving dock in the world, for the fabrication of steel production platforms, at Nigg Bay. Within three years nearly 4,000 jobs had been created, and by mid 1976 Professor Kenneth Alexander, the Highland Board chairman, could say that between 12,000 and 13,000 people in the Highlands were involved in the oil industry.

Exploratory drilling for North Sea gas and oil had started some years before then. Licences to explore for oil were first granted in the UK in 1964. In the early days, when resources were not proved, to encourage as many firms as possible to search for oil, an 'Exploration Licence' cost £20; a 'Production Licence', giving the holder the right to search for and 'get' oil or gas in a 'block' of sea, cost £200. In 1971, when resources were starting to be proved, Shell/Esso paid £21 million for one 'block'; and within a year, the Brent oilfield in this area was found to have estimated reserves of a 1,000 million barrels of oil. This field lies over 150km. west of Shetland, which is now becoming a major service centre for the industry.

The first oil to come to Scotland started to flow in November 1975 from the Forties Field, nearly 400km. south from the Brent; it was then estimated that within two years the yield would be 400,000 barrels a day from this field alone; peak production from the Brent Field would be around 300,000 barrels a day. If predictions are correct, by 1985 the oilfields off Scotland will yield between 2·7 million and 3·6 million barrels a day. The estimates of oil production vary almost as much as do prophecies as to how long the flow will last. But whether the end of the reserves is reached within twenty or forty years (and new 'strikes' continue) the need for construction yards will largely have disappeared long before then.

Although, inevitably, there must be references to North Sea oil through much of this book, the impact on the Highlands is, of course, fairly localized. The Cromarty Firth area is the most affected, and early in 1976 the Secretary of State for Scotland agreed to the establishment of a £150 million oil refinery at Nigg Bay, obviously in the hope that this would encourage similar developments in the area – the 'linear city' may well be growing up. Probably the traveller in the Highlands will avoid the Cromarty Firth in future.

Flora and Fauna

Just as there are birds and animals that are to be found only in the Highlands (*see* below), or very rarely anywhere else in Britain, so there are a few species of plant in that category. The most notable, perhaps, and unique to the Highlands, is *Primula scotica*, the Scottish primrose, found only near the northern coastlines of Caithness and Sutherland and in Orkney. This small but most attractive plant with purple-red flowers, quite unlike the common primrose, is not easy to find: although it grows in short grass, even that is sufficient almost to hide it.

It is for the small plants that the Highlands are of most interest to the botanist. These are the alpines of the high mountains, particularly the Beinn Eighe Nature Reserve, where two rare species of saxifrage, the drooping *S. cernua* and the tufted *S. caespitosa*, relics of those that were in the area at the end of the last Ice Age, may be found. The National Nature Reserves in the Highlands – the Cairngorms and Inchnadamph as well as Beinn Eighe – are rich stores indeed for the lover of alpines, as are the mountains of Glencoe and Kintail. The purple, alpine, and starry saxifrages, the alpine forget-me-not (*Myosotis alpestris*), and the rock speedwell (*Veronica fruticans*), though by no means common, may be found in these areas, along with many other plants that are not so rare, the 'cushions' of pink campion, for example. (In fairness it should be added that one of the richest areas for alpine flora in Britain – Ben Lawers – is not in the Highlands at all; while geologically it is Highland, Ben Lawers is in Perthshire, not one of the Seven Crofting Counties.)

Below the bare mountain tops, springs create 'rock gardens' with a great variety of mosses, ferns, butterworts, willow herbs, and the like; and below these again may be expanses of white cotton grass.

At a lower level are the moors that make up much of the Highlands, and here are the vast areas of heather, a plant that is one of the stock Scottish symbols; in late August and September it emerges from ten months of dreariness to clothe the moors with vivid purple. This is the ling *Calluna vulgaris*: bees love it (hives are still taken up on the moors, in summer, for the bees to visit the bell heather *Erica cinera* – which blooms earlier than the heather itself – with heather honey resulting in due course). Some of the moors are forbidding: for example, a blanket bog such as the Moor of Rannoch, where huge areas of peat have built up over the past 9,000 years or so on a wet plateau; it is an acid area where, nevertheless, the asphodels, sundews, and mosses provide considerable botanic interest. Once this moor was densely covered with trees, the bleached stumps of which, many hundreds of years old, are still to be seen.

The woodlands of the Highlands, though not without interest, cannot compete in variety of flora with their English counterparts. The birch woods are widespread, and it is interesting to recall that these stem from the dwarf birch *Betula nana*, one of the typical growths on the tundra that followed the Ice Age. As the climate improved the birch trees grew. The birch woods grow largely out of tumbled rocky ground, so the ancillary botanic interest is limited – though not as limited as in the new pine forests, where, by and large, little grows around the trunks, which, packed closely together, create a permanent dry shade.

To the non-expert, the plant that makes the most stunning appeal is the rhodo-dendron, largely ignored by the botanist in the Highlands. Even if the rhododendron is not a Highland, nor even a Scottish, native, there are those who maintain that it should be Scotland's 'national flower' rather than the unlovely Scotch Thistle (*Onopordon acanthium*), which is not Scottish either: it is found throughout Europe. In early summer vast areas of rhododendrons (*R. ponticum*) in full bloom make travelling, particularly in Argyll and Bute, a delight only equalled, at the same time of year, by the wide expanses of brilliant-yellow gorse and broom. The fuchsias, again, may be garden species gone wild; but on Arran and in parts of Argyll their beauty in the hedgerows is memorable.

Botanist and non-botanist alike can enjoy the many flowers found in the meadows: clover, orchids, vetches, and daisies in the drier places, marsh marigolds, marsh orchids, and lousewort in the wetter ones. But it is more likely to be the gardener and garden-lover than the botanist who will visit some of the 'Gardens of the West' in the Highlands, most notable of which is Inverewe in Wester Ross (*see* Poolewe in the Gazetteer section). The collection there is not, of course, Highland, though it is set on a rocky promontory jutting into Loch Ewe, among typical Highland scenery. As well as the ubiquitous rhododendron, there are eucalyptus and a great variety of Chilean and South African plants, with Himalayan lilies and giant forget-me-nots from the South Pacific – exotics of many kinds. Inverewe is the most striking of these gardens in the western Highlands; but there are some fifteen others, many including sub-tropical trees and shrubs, and they should not be ignored.

The flora of the Highlands – a point already made – is not often unique, or nearly unique, to our region: the fauna, on the other hand, is frequently more localized, some-times not being seen anywhere else in Britain.

On many a loch in the north and west Highlands – and on Mull, Jura, and other islands of the Hebrides – it is not unusual, with patience and a quiet approach, to see the sleek beauty of the black-throated diver. It is a clumsy bird on land, and stays in the water except when nesting; but it is a superb and graceful swimmer, capable of swim-ming up to 400m. under water. It can be elusive; but it is there – and has been for some 10,000 years. The black-throated diver is one of those birds that was in the Highlands long before man came. Other birds in the same category include the red-throated diver, which prefers lochans to lochs, the ptarmigan and the dotterel of the high tops, particu-larly in the Cairngorm area, the red-necked phalarope, which breeds, albeit in small numbers, in Orkney and Shetland, and the golden plover, flocks of which may be seen over much of the Highlands. These birds were among the first to come to the Highlands after the last Ice Age retreated and left, for many centuries, a bleak, tundra-like land-scape that offered little sustenance to wildlife.

There are said to be around 400 different species of bird in Scotland. Most are to be seen in the Highlands; some – within Britain – are exclusive to this region, while many others that are rarities elsewhere may well be plentiful in the Highlands.

On the Isle of Islay alone, ninety-seven different birds were seen in two days of winter birdwatching: the different types of terrain – woodland, moor, hill, sea cliff, machair, sand-dune, agricultural land, river, marsh, freshwater loch, and shallow sea loch – are no doubt responsible for such variety.

A similar range of terrain may be found in other parts of the Highlands, particularly on the islands, and results in the same abundance of birdlife. Easter Ross and the Black

Isle, for example, list about 120 species; and this is far excelled by Orkney, where no less than 280 have been recorded, and by Fair Isle, north from Orkney, with its famous Bird Observatory, where some 300 species have been put on record, many of them rarities on passage. Just as important as Islay's ninety-seven species in two days' watching is the season in which it was achieved – in winter. As in the rest of Britain, the dullest time for wildlife in the Highlands is exactly that period when most people take their holidays.

The time to see the widest variety of birds in the Highlands is late winter and spring, before the winter visitors have departed but after the summer breeders have arrived: when, in fact, the pinkfoot goose and the cuckoo can be heard on the same day. The Highlands have the advantage over many other areas of a long and varied coastline and, of course, a profusion of islands: myriads of sea birds are always to be seen.

The Highland bird most often looked for by the non-ornithological traveller is the golden eagle. So far as Britain is concerned, this magnificent bird breeds only in the Highlands and in the mountains of the Grampian region, though in recent years it has been suggested that one or two pairs may be breeding in south-west Scotland, and there are reports, not always accepted as reliable, of sightings in Cumbria. Golden-eagle numbers were quite drastically reduced by the introduction of sheep dips based on chemicals such as dieldrin: the golden eagle, a carrion-eater, could include dead sheep in its diet, with disastrous results. Now that the use of dieldrin has been forbidden, the reproduction rate of the eagle, along with that of other predators even worse affected, has improved and the population (believed to be about 150 pairs on the mainland) is on the increase. But golden eagles are still not as numerous as stories from inexperienced observers might indicate – many a buzzard has been 'recognized' as a golden eagle. The golden-eagle's habitat is the barren mountain, where it nests on ledges, or on tall pine trees, on a huge nest of sticks. Neither knowledgeable locals nor dedicated ornithologists are prepared to reveal where these eyries are: this majestic bird with a wing span that exceeds 2m. is too much at risk for its whereabouts to be divulged. But it may well be seen soaring high over the mountains as it hunts for ptarmigan, grouse, or hare. The best chances of seeing it are available in Wester Ross and Skye, though anywhere in the Highlands where there are high, bare mountains, such as the Cairngorms, may yield a sighting.

The other great predator that has caught the public imagination is, of course, the osprey. Although there are far fewer of these fishing hawks than there are golden eagles – a dozen pairs, or at most a score – there is much more chance of their being seen; or, to be more accurate, of one pair – that at Loch Garten – being seen (see Boat of Garten in the Gazetteer section). Where the other pairs are is an even more closely guarded secret than the location of golden-eagle nests; but to see the osprey fishing above a loch (it is exclusively a fish eater) and plunging, feet-first, to grab a fish from below the surface, then flying off, fish in claws, to its eyrie is a magnificent sight.

Another bird that has attracted attention in recent years is the snowy owl, huge and white; it soars more like a buzzard than an owl as it hunts silently for its prey, which can include birds up to the size of an oystercatcher. A pair came from their Scandinavian home to nest on Fetlar, Shetland, in 1967, and single vagrants may be seen, some years, in northern Caithness, Orkney, and Shetland. The frequency seems to be determined by the fluctuations in its main item of diet, the lemming, on its normal tundra territory.

Even if the snowy owl does not materialize – and its future as a breeding bird is always in doubt – Shetland is immensely rewarding to the bird watcher, as are all the northern coasts with high cliffs, on whose ledges sit and screech and squabble hundreds of sea birds: fulmars, kittiwakes, puffins, razorbills, guillemots, and gannets. This last, the gannet, is the most spectacular of fishers: white with black tips to its wings (which may span nearly 2m.), it soars above the sea, then, as it spots its prey, 'dive bombs' from a height of perhaps 30 or 40m., with wings folded, into the water. It can be seen fishing off almost any coast of the Highlands, and the biggest breeding ground for gannets in the world is on St Kilda, where some 40,000 pairs nest.

The 'dive-bombing' attacks of the gannet harm only the fish. But another notable 'dive-bomber' has no hesitation in attacking man and any other animals that intrude on its breeding colonies in Shetland, Orkney, Fair Isle, the Outer Hebrides, and the northern mainland. This is the great skua, the 'bonxie', a brown pirate, which lives by harrying other birds, forcing them to disgorge and, at times, killing them. Perhaps the best place from which to watch the bonxies is from a ship: on land, in the breeding season (the birds spend at least three quarters of the year at sea), a stout hat is advisable!

Another bird that has no hesitation in attacking man is the tern, of which at least four species – the arctic, common, little, and sandwich – can be seen at various places around the Highland coasts. These terns are not confined to the Highlands; but, in Britain, the arctic tern, distinguished in summer from the common tern by its blood-red bill, nests mainly around the Highland coast. All these handsome but belligerent 'sea swallows' are intensely aggressive.

These are but three of the predators and some of the sea birds that may – and in the case of sea birds most certainly will – be seen. Of the predators, the slim, long-tailed hen harrier (the cock bird is pale grey, the hen brown) is the one bird of prey that has successfully increased its range in the past forty years. Before World War II its breeding grounds were only in Orkney and the Outer Hebrides; now it can be seen over much of the Highland area (though rarely, if at all, in western Sutherland and the Hebrides), hunting low and lazily over the moors. The sparrowhawk can be seen dashing along the hedgerows in areas that have them, or imitating the gannet with a plunging dive; the kestrel may be seen hovering almost anywhere; and in Argyll, Skye, and other areas of the west the buzzard is even more common, not only in its moth-like flight above the woods but perching placidly on many a roadside telegraph pole, moving only when the walker gets within a few m. of it. Other birds are much more wary. The capercailzie, a huge native of the pine forests, with a turkey-like tail, a glossy blue-green breast contrasting with its grey and brown body, and a shaggy beard, became extinct in Britain at the end of the eighteenth century. Re-introduced some fifty years later into Perthshire, it soon spread to the Highlands, where the extension of forests in recent decades has given it even more encouragement to multiply. Easter Sutherland, Easter Ross, and the Central Highlands, particularly the Glenmore Forest Park, are places where the song of the capercailzie may be heard. It is perhaps the most unmusical (with the corncrake as runner-up) and certainly one of the most extraordinary 'songs' in nature: rattlings followed by a popping noise, then gurgling, grating, and whispering. At times of courting display, when this remarkable noise is heard, and when the cocks posture and battle, a human onlooker may well think it wise to beat a retreat: this bulky bird can weigh up to 8kg., and brooks no interference with its ritual. At other times, a clattering flight through the woods and a brief glimpse may be the only sighting of the capercailzie.

Another bird of the pine forests to indulge in remarkable displays is the black grouse. The cock bird, the blackcock, is unmistakable with its glossy blue-black plumage and its lyre-shaped tail; the hen (rather confusingly known as the greyhen) is less distinguished; each sex has a scarlet wattle above the eye. The birds congregate at their display grounds (known as leks), where cocks joust with cocks and, to a lesser extent, hens with hens.

The blackcock is bigger than the familiar red grouse of the moors, the slaughter of which is a ritual practised by 'sportsmen' each year, starting on 12 August, 'The Glorious Twelfth'. It is unusual to walk the moors of the Highlands without seeing the red grouse and hearing it call 'go-back, go-back' as it whirrs away over the heather.

Another notable bird of the pine forests, the crested tit, is tiny by comparison: it is $11\frac{1}{2}$cm. long compared with the 62cm. of the capercailzie and the 53cm. of the blackcock. The crested tit is, in Britain, exclusively a Highland bird. Even in the Highlands its range was restricted until recently to the Glenmore Forest Park; it is now spreading into the forests of Easter Ross, eastern Inverness-shire, and Nairnshire. The same size as a bluetit, the crested tit with its prominent speckled black-and-white crest is a charming creature.

The forests of the central Highlands and of north-east Scotland are the home of the Scottish crossbill, *Loxia curvirostra scotica*, which has a much heavier bill than *L. curvirostra*, the crossbill that every few years irrupts across the North Sea from Scandinavia to spread out anywhere in Britain where it can find conifers. The Scottish race is an all-year-round resident – the only resident crossbill in Britain except for a small colony in East Anglia. Both cock and hen – the former with bright brick-red plumage, the latter olive-yellow – are handsome birds; their distinguishing feature is the crossed mandible: the tips of their beaks cross so that the birds can more easily pick out seeds from fir cones. If there is a litter of dropped, open cones on the ground beneath a fir tree, it is a sure sign that the crossbills have been feeding.

Above the tree line in the Glenmore Forest Park is the home of two birds that are exclusively Highland as far as Britain is concerned. The ptarmigan nests only in the Highlands, mostly in the Cairngorm area, and in the extreme north of Europe, Asia, and Canada. It is a bird of the high, barren mountains, seldom coming below 750m. above sea-level. The dotterel's range is similar, though even more restricted; but these two birds have little else in common. The ptarmigan, the grouse of the high mountains, changes its coloration according to the season: in winter it is pure white except for a black tail and a small red wattle over the eye; in summer the head, neck, and body are dark (grey in the cock, brown in the hen), but the wings and belly are still white. The dotterel, little more than half the size of the ptarmigan, is an attractive bird in its summer plumage; in winter the plumage change is only for its smart markings, with a white band between brown upper parts and orange/chestnut merging to black underneath, to become paler and blurred. While the ptarmigan will normally take flight at any hint of danger, the dotterel is too tame and friendly for its own good: it was easily caught in the past, and now there are probably not more than fifty or sixty pairs in the country.

The car park for the chairlift up Cairngorm lies well under the lower limit of these two birds' habitats. Nevertheless, the impact of the skiing and the vastly increased number of summer tourists taking advantage of the chairlift have had their effects, which again affect these two species of bird differently. The ptarmigan has become slightly more approachable; to a limited extent it has learnt to live with the skier and the tourist. The dotterel, though, has retreated further into the mountain fastnesses.

Among the curlews, common on the mud flats and estuaries, and whose ringing call on the moors from early spring onwards is easily recognizable, there may well also be seen, at migration times, small flocks of whimbrel. These birds are not unlike the curlew, though smaller, with a slightly shorter bill, and a different song. In Britain – in western Europe, in fact – there are only two places where the whimbrel breeds: Shetland and Lewis.

As magical a call as the curlew is that of the wild geese, skeins of which can number hundreds or even thousands of birds, flying in in autumn and leaving for the north in the spring. By and large, these are winter visitors only, an exception being the greylag, whose native breeding grounds are the extreme north of the Highlands and the Outer Hebrides.

It is not necessarily the rarities, some of which are noted above, that make up the joy of observing bird life in the Highlands. All round the coasts of the mainland and the islands the eider is commonly seen bobbing on the sea, the drake with its white back and dark belly, the duck brown barred with black; and another beautiful sound on these coasts is the crooning of the drake. The dipper in a Highland burn; the flocks of fieldfare and redwing in late autumn and winter, ransacking the berries; the harsh infuriating call of the seldom-seen corncrake, not as common as it once was because of modern farming methods, but still heard in Orkney and the Outer Hebrides; the waders along the mud flats, bays, and estuaries; the piping performance of a small flock of oystercatchers, running up and down in circles with red bills pointed to the ground; the hooded crow, known as the 'hoodie' or the 'corbie', handsome in his grey and black plumage as he struts over moor or seashore (his breeding range goes barely south of the Highland line) . . . these are some, but still only a part, of the intriguing variety of bird life in the Highlands.

The wild life of the Highlands of course encompasses more than the birds. As typical as the golden eagle, and far more numerous, is the red deer. Anyone travelling the roads running through glens flanked by high, bare mountains, at any time between late autumn and spring, is fairly certain to see herds of red deer, each herd often numbering several hundred. The deer will be feeding almost up to the roadside, taking little account of passing traffic – providing it passes. In the summer months the deer retreat to the high tops; the feeding is there then, and they are above the worst attacks from midges and mosquitoes: in clear weather small numbers may be seen, from the glen bottom, on the skyline; if a sudden storm should develop – always a possibility in high mountain country in the Highlands – they may well retreat downhill.

There are probably too many red deer; the population perhaps approaches 180,000 (there are believed to be about 5,000 on Jura alone; Rum, where there are about 1,500, is used for research on red deer). The numbers have to be kept down by an annual cull, which disposes of about 30,000 stags and hinds. There are regular protests at this, of course; but the fact remains that unless a proportion of deer was killed off there would be insufficient feeding, and the weaker animals would perish miserably. Too many deer could be a danger to two of the Highland's major industries: forestry and agriculture; and venison is a useful export; so the cull serves several purposes.

The red-deer stag is the largest land animal in Britain. In appearance he is also the noblest, his head crowned with magnificent antlers. But in fact he is not master of all he surveys, nor Landseer's Monarch of the Glen. He lives in a matriarchal society, and the roaring of the stags in rut – the beginning of the breeding season – is awesome as they get among the hinds to collect as many as they can for a 'harem'. Even then, though, the hinds, who keep themselves to themselves, with their own hind leader, are quite capable of moving off, with the stag following abjectly behind. Once the rut is over, the hinds go their own way; the stag, exhausted by the rut, will in due course lose his place to a fitter animal.

Among other deer in the Highlands is a herd of reindeer. These are not descendants of the reindeer that used to roam the Highland forests: they were extinct by the twelfth century; today's Highland reindeer are to be seen only in the Cairngorms, to which they were re-introduced from Sweden in 1952. At first they did not flourish, and others were brought in to strengthen the herd, which for the past fifteen years has bred successfully.

There are other Highland animals that, while definitely there, are rarely seen. Most notable, perhaps, is the wildcat, bigger than the domestic cat and unmistakable with its heavy, black-ringed tail. It hunts, taking anything from voles to big grouse, not excluding insects and fish, from sundown through to dawn, in the forests lying higher up the mountains, and over the bare slopes above the tree line. It is a lone hunter in lonely places, and can give vent to blood-curdling screams when on the prowl. Avoiding man if it can, it reacts when cornered by spitting ferociously.

The pine marten, a bushy-tailed weasel about the size of a domestic cat, is even less often seen than the wildcat. By the early part of this century it was near to extinction, only a few remaining in the north-west Highlands; but with the extension of the pine forests, its range is spreading, and there is always a chance – if rather remote – of seeing its spectacular leaping from branch to branch in pursuit of birds in the Highland forests. Its main stronghold is in the Beinn Eighe Nature Reserve.

Stoats and weasels, otters and badgers are by no means rare, and there are polecats on Mull if nowhere else. Less expected, perhaps, is the mink, which may be seen – most likely swimming in a river – in many parts of the Highlands. Mink farming has been going on for upwards of fifty years, and the descendants of escapers from the farms would appear to make up quite a considerable population.

As with birds, this is but a selection of the mammals that may be seen. There are some forty species in all, ranging from the blue hare – which turns white in winter – to bats; from the smallest mammal in Britain, the pygmy shrew, to the largest, the grey seal. Almost anywhere around the coasts of the Highlands the seal may be seen. The grey, or Atlantic, seal is the larger of the two seal species, the other being the common, which is considerably smaller. The breeding habits of these two differ: during the summer the grey seals may occasionally be seen off the coast, but in early autumn they move to their breeding grounds in the remoter Orkney and Shetland islands, or to the biggest grey-seal breeding place in the world, the island of North Rona, 65km. north-west from Cape Wrath. Common seals breed at sea: as their name indicates, it is this species that is most generally seen.

Brown bears used to roam the Highlands when the Caledonian forests covered much of the country; but they became extinct probably 1,000 years ago. There were beavers, too; they lasted in the Highlands for a further 500 years, eventually to be exterminated by man, for their skins. The wild boar followed the beaver into extinction in the Highlands not long after; again, man was probably responsible for its disappearance, although in this case it was not so much for its skin as for the pleasures of the hunt. The wolf was everybody's enemy, but it survived into the eighteenth century.

Those people who like to see animals such as these in captivity – animals that once roamed wild in the Highlands – may do so at the Highland Wildlife Park at Kincraig (*see* p. 116). More satisfactory (though this park is a very good example of its kind) is the wealth of wildlife in the Highlands that flourishes in natural habitats, and, in general, is on the increase.

Short-stay Guide

This page is intended for the person whose time in the Highlands is limited to a few days. What, out of all that is described in this book, is most worth visiting? The question is an invidious one, but below are some unashamedly subjective thoughts on the matter. Naturally, the traveller will have to make a further selection to take account of the area he happens to be in. The lists are alphabetical and not in order of preference or of geographical sequence.

Many items are not the subject of a separate gazetteer entry: it is suggested that the index will provide the most convenient way of tracing descriptions.

Archaeological and Historical Remains
Callanish Standing Stones, Lewis
Clickhimin Broch, Shetland
Dunadd, Argyll
Dun Carloway Broch, Lewis
Jarlshof, Shetland
Kildalton Cross, Islay
Kilmory Knap Sculptured Stones, Knapdale
Maeshowe, Orkney
Skara Brae, Orkney

Castles
Cawdor Castle, Nairn
Duart Castle, Mull
Dunvegan, Skye
Eilean Donan, Loch Duich
Inveraray Castle
Kisimul Castle, Barra
Rothesay Castle
Castle Tioram, by Acharacle
Castle Urquhart, Loch Ness

Churches and Chapels
Iona
Italian Chapel, Orkney
Rodel church, Harris
St Magnus Cathedral, Kirkwall

Towns and Villages
Inveraray
Lerwick
Plockton
Oban
Stornoway
Stromness
Tobermory
Ullapool

Scenery
There is so much superb scenery in the Highlands, especially along the western seaboard looking to Hebridean islands, that almost any list is inadequate. But here are some suggestions:
An Teallach from Little Loch Broom area
Cape Wrath
Duncansby Stacks
The Five Sisters of Kintail, from Dornie
Gairloch, looking to Skye and the Torridons
Glencoe
Glen Nevis
Gribun, Mull
Kyles of Bute, from road above Loch Riddon
Loch Alsh, from Mam Rattachan
Loch Coruisk, Skye
Loch Leven
Lochs Nevis and Hourn from a boat trip
Loch Torridon from Shieldaig road
The Old Man of Hoy
The Paps of Jura, from Kilmory Knap

The Quiraing, Skye
St Kilda
The Small Isles from Smearisary
Suilven and Canisp from around Elphin
The Summer Isles from Achiltibuie

Special Features
Auchindrain Farming Museum, Loch
  Fyne

Cairngorm Chairlift
Commando Monument, Spean Bridge
Culloden
Cruachan Power Station, Loch Awe
Fingal's Cave, Staffa
Glenfinnan monument and Glen Shiel
Landmark, Carrbridge
Falls of Measach, Braemore
Smoo Cave, Durness

Gazetteer

Abbreviations

NTS for National Trust for Scotland

Entries in the Gazetteer

The first figure of the map reference supplied to each entry refers to a page number in the map section at the back of the book. The subsequent letter and figure give the grid reference.

Population figures are based on the *Annual Estimates of the Population of Scotland*, 1975 edit.

Acharacle Highland 6E2
Although in a wonderful setting at the foot of Loch
Shiel, with Ben Resipol (853m.), a notable Sunart
landmark, rising 10km. to the east, this scattered village
has little attraction in itself. But as well as being popular
with anglers, it is a good place from which to explore
the wild country of Moidart, Ardnamurchan, and Loch
Shiel (which runs its fjord-like length between high hills
from here to Glenfinnan on the Road to the Isles).

Near the village a minor road crosses Kentra Moss to
Ardtoe, where in 1965 the White Fish Authority started
an experimental fish farm. Initially, the 200,000 plaice
released into it were eaten by crabs and eels; but this
tribulation overcome, the fish farm flourishes.

CASTLE TIORAM, superbly set in the south channel of
Loch Moidart, is reached from Acharacle by the road,
just past Shiel Bridge, that goes through the woods to
Dorlin. This stout castle, with high curtain walls and
a turreted keep, was built in 1353 by Lady Anne
MacRuari, divorced wife of John MacDonald, Lord of
the Isles. Their son Ranald was the founder of Clanranald, and with this clan the Castle remained, never
captured, until 1715 when the chief came out for the Old
Pretender. Fearing that if he fell his castle would be
taken by the clan's hereditary enemies, the Campbells,

he had it destroyed by fire, though he himself could not
bear to stay and see its destruction. Set on an island
linked to the mainland except at high tide, the ruins look
across the wide bay to Eilean Shona.

Achiltibuie Highland 19A6
Some 12km. north of Ullapool a minor road goes west
under Cul Beag (769m.) and Stac Polly (612m.). It
runs beside three lochs – Lurgain, Baddagyle, and
Owskeich – and looks across the first to the great mass of
Ben More Coigach (743m.); past Loch Owskeich it
turns south to the coast, there looking across to the
Summer Isles.

Achiltibuie, south-east along this coast, is a scattered
crofting township with a hotel; the road continues by
even smaller places – Polglass and Achavraie – to peter
out at Culnacraig. None of those settlements is particularly picturesque; but the views of the Summer Isles are
magical. Boat trips may be taken from Achiltibuie to the
islands, a group of about twelve, the biggest of which,
Tanera Mor, once had some seventy inhabitants: the
last left in 1946. Now there is an 'Adventure Centre'
there, for sailing and canoeing holidays.

The nature interest is considerable and varied: seals
have bred on Tanera Beag, which has a herd of wild

OPPOSITE: *'The Lobster's Claw' on Stac Polly, E of Achiltibuie*

BELOW: *(left) Cul Beag and (right) Stac Polly seen from the
Lochinver–Achiltibuie road*

Dun Dornadilla, NW of Altnaharra

goats; and breeding birds on Priest Island further out to sea (not, strictly speaking, a 'Summer Isle') include greylag geese, which are also found on Glas Leac Beg, a wintering ground for barnacle geese.

North-west from Achiltibuie are more crofting townships: Polblain, the picturesque cluster of Alltan Dubh, and Reiff, now largely deserted, where the road ends but beyond which are fine, though not high, sandstone cliffs. Achnahaird Bay has good sands.

Achnasheen Highland 14B2
Were it not for its position on the A832, one of the main roads from the east to the west coast, this hamlet at the head of Strath Bran would remain unnoticed, being little more than a hotel, a railway halt, and a few cottages.

Here, however, the road divides, the A832 continuing west beside Loch a' Chroisg to the grand view down

Glen Dochertie to Loch Maree, the A890 running by Achnashellach Forest to Loch Carron, much of the way beside the railway line, and to Kyle of Lochalsh. The railway is the Kyle line, one of the two most scenic rail routes in Scotland (the other being that from Fort William to Mallaig); frequently threatened with extinction, it has successfully survived, more perhaps because of the oil-related developments at Loch Carron than for the social needs of the few people who live alongside it.

Altnaharra Highland 18F4
On one of the loneliest roads in Scotland, this small angling centre – only a hotel and a few houses – stands at the head of Loch Naver, 32km. north of Lairg. To the south, the steep schist peaks of Ben Klibreck rise to 960m.; north, the A836 to Tongue (qv) goes beside Loch Loyal and under Ben Loyal (763m.).

The minor road west from Altnaharra to Loch Hope passes, in 16km., DUN DORNADILLA, one of the most notable mainland brochs in Scotland, some of its walls still standing over 6m. high, though built some 2,000 years ago. Just north of this is the Allt-na-Cailleach ('the old woman's burn') coming down from Ben Hope, higher (927m.) than Ben Loyal, though not so shapely. Here, though, is a fine waterfall, which, for devotees of Gaelic poetry, has an extra significance: Rob Donn (1740–78), the bard, was born at the foot of it (*see* Durness). Those interested in alpine flora will find the ascent of Ben Hope – the track up the shoulder starts near here – a rewarding expedition.

East from Altnaharra a minor road goes beside Loch Naver and through Strath Naver, a major scene of the Clearances (*see* Bettyhill).

Applecross   Highland   16E4
Leaving the Lochcarron–Shieldaig road (A832) at Tornapress at the head of Loch Kishorn, you cross the bridge over the Kishorn River and turn briefly along the south side of the loch. Until 1975 there was a wonderful view down the loch to Skye; now, this beautiful open water has been hideously destroyed by the oil men.

It is a sorry story. The first proposal was that construction platforms be built at the rather dull crofting

The ascent to Applecross; Loch Kishorn is in the background

hamlet of Drumbuie, between Kyle of Lochalsh and Plockton. This was owned by the NTS, which is said to have spent some £50,000 fighting the development, draining its resources disastrously in the process. The Secretary of State for Scotland upheld the NTS; the oil men turned their attention to the infinitely more attractive Loch Kishorn, and were given permission to bu'ld there with little delay. Despite reassurances, which included an undertaking to respect the local residents' views on Sunday working, the contractors have caused havoc in the area – and, incidentally, at the end of 1975 insisted on the need for Sunday working.

It is a relief to turn into the hills of the Applecross Forest and the tortuous ascent of one of the highest road passes in the country, the Bealach na Bo ('Pass of the Cattle'), rising, after dramatic scenery, hairpin bends, and a maximum gradient of 1 in 4, to 636m. above sea-level in a distance of 6½km. The top is no peak, but a barren plateau of stones; across the Inner Sound can be seen Raasay and the Isle of Skye.

The descent to Applecross is long, gradual, and for some of the time – through bleak moors – uninteresting. Applecross comes as a complete surprise – a charming village among trees looking across its bay to Skye – not

Dulsie Bridge on the R. Findhorn, NE of Ardclach

the image of what, until 1976, was perhaps the most inaccessible village in Scotland.

Applecross was originally a sanctuary: St Maelrubha founded a monastery on the north side of the bay 1,300 years ago; and in this green oasis he was abbot for nearly fifty years. On his death, while on a mission in Sutherland, his body was brought back to Applecross: two stones traditionally mark his grave, and a sandstone cross (remains of which are to be seen in the church) is also said to be from his monastery, which was destroyed some fifty years after his death by Norse invaders.

The road south runs for about 6km. by charming little farms and lochans full of rushes and flags to Camusteal, a crofting township, then continues beside a bay to end at Toscaig, from where you can walk round the point back to Tornapress.

The story that Applecross got its name from five apple trees being planted in cross formation is a harmless fiction. Many centuries ago the name of the place was Apor-crossan, the estuary of the River Crossan: and the trees were chestnuts.

The village, as already mentioned, is no longer as cut off as it was. If weather closed the Bealach, access used to be possible only by boat. But in 1976 a new road past the church on the north side of the bay linked the village to Shieldaig. With the spoliation of Loch Kishorn that, were it not for the views from the Bealach, would be the way to go in future.

Ardclach Highland 15H3

A minor road off the A939 11km. south-east from Nairn goes by this tiny place, from where a lane leads to Ardclach Bell Tower, a detached belfry on a promontory above the River Findhorn. Built in 1655, it has two storeys and had a dual purpose: to call worshippers to the nearby church, and to act as a fortified watch tower.

Some 8km. further along this minor road the river is crossed by Dulsie Bridge on one of its most beautiful stretches, where it goes through a deep gorge. Footpaths above the river in this area are well worth following, and a stone near the top of a chasm records the incredible height reached by the great flood of 1829.

Ardfern Strathclyde 4A4

The main road north from Lochgilphead reaches its summit 166m. above sea-level, then drops steeply down to Kintraw at the head of Loch Craignish. Across the bridge over the river running down from Gleann Domhain a minor road turns off along the north-west side of this long, narrow loch: like the best of so many such roads in Argyll, it 'goes nowhere'; and you must walk the last stretches to the point.

A fair number of people now drive the first 3km. of this road, to the village of Ardfern, looking across a narrow strait to the wooded Eilean Mhic Chrion; in recent years the village has been developed as a small sailing centre, where a hotel and a restaurant provide for the sailors' shore needs.

In spring and summer, too, some traffic will go on to Craignish Castle, whose gardens, open to the public, include a rhododendron garden laid out by Osgood Mackenzie, creator of Inverewe (see Poolewe). The Castle, now part of a modern mansion (not open to the public), is a sixteenth-century keep built on the site of an earlier (twelfth-century?) fort.

At the foot of Loch Beag, a sea inlet at the head of which Craignish Castle stands, the road ends by a derelict pier, with little room available to park a car.

Walk the 2km. to Craignish Point; and if there is a strong westerly wind, all the better. For westwards from this point is the most famous whirlpool in Scotland, in the Strait of Corryvreckan, between the islands of Jura and Scarba. The tides flooding up the Sound of Jura press west through the narrow strait and, striking a huge underwater rock, go into a vast whirlpool in which many a small craft has been lost. Although over 6km. away, the tide race can be seen from the low hill above Craignish Point; and with a westerly wind, its roaring heard (in a gale, Corryvreckan's noise can be heard at Crinan and beyond). Sailors from Ardfern, fortunately, have more sheltered waters for their enjoyment.

Ardgay Highland 19F7

Just off the road where the A9 turns to cross the head of the Dornoch Firth to Bonar Bridge, the village of Ardgay has an odd reminder of former times in the 'Clach Eiteag', the White Stone of Kincardine. This quartz stone marked the place where markets could be held: the people of Ardgay secured this right by building the stone into a wall (now on a plinth beside the main road); the village's winter markets were famous for many years.

Ardgay stands at the foot of Strath Carron, with pleasant roads on either side of the river; they join at Baileandounie and continue as one to Croik, 16km. west of Ardgay. In Croik churchyard crofters evicted during the Clearances of 1845 at nearby Glencalvie took refuge; the messages they scratched on the church windows are still to be seen. Two km. up Strath Carron from Ardgay, Gledfield Mill, a small two-storey stone-built mill, c. 1850, is now open to the public. Oatmeal was ground there until about 1940.

South-east from Ardgay, in 6½km., the 'top road' A836 leaves the A9 and climbs up Struie Hill, 212m. above the Dornoch Firth. Here is the deservedly-famous panorama of Sutherland, stretching to the north-west as far as Ben More Assynt, 80km. distant. At the top of the road is the Aultnamain Inn, the only building in a wide expanse of high rolling moors.

Ardgour Highland 8B5

Ardgour village stands on the west side of the Corran narrows of Loch Linnhe, some 16km. south-west of

The Silver Sands, nr Arisaig

Fort William. A frequent car-ferry service plies across the loch at this point, where there is also a lighthouse.

The name Ardgour, though, is usually used for the whole of the area lying between Loch Linnhe, Loch Eil, and Loch Shiel – some 400 sq. km. of fine mountain scenery untraversed by any road. While the area is best seen from across Loch Linnhe, equally from Ardgour itself are wonderful views of Lochaber to Ben Nevis.

The village lies under the slopes of 730m. Sgurr na h'Eanchainne. To the south, between Glen Gour (no road) and Glen Tarbert (the A861 to Strontian), 895m. GARBH BHEIN is very popular with climbers.

Ardnamurchan Highland 6C3 (*pop.* – district – 1,506)
West from Salen, this long peninsula juts for 30km. to end at Ardnamurchan Point, the most westerly headland of the British mainland, with a lighthouse built by Alan Stevenson in 1848.

Just north of the point itself are the white sands of SANNA BAY, and from Sanna Point are fine views of Muck, Eigg, and Rum (*see* Small Isles) to the north, and Coll (qv) to the west. The north coast of the peninsula can also be gained by a minor road, leading to several tracks, that leaves the B8007, the only road to the Point. The minor road, narrow and tortuous in places, runs from Salen beside Loch Sunart for some 15km. before turning inland. It returns to the coast near Kilchoan, a few km. east of which is MINGARY CASTLE, splendidly set on a cliff and ideally placed to dominate Loch Sunart and the Sound of Mull.

Dating from the thirteenth or fourteenth century, this castle was the stronghold of the MacIains of Ardnamurchan, a sept of Clan Donald. James IV stayed there in 1495 during his long campaign to quell the island chiefs. During its history it has endured several sieges: in 1644 it was taken by Montrose's army and used as a prison for the Covenanters who opposed him. It is a typical west-Highland curtain-wall castle, and is still impressive.

KILCHOAN is a small village from which there is a passenger ferry to Tobermory on Mull.

Arisaig Highland 6E1
The magic of the phrase 'The Road to the Isles' has cast, for many travellers, a rare gloss over the A830 from Fort William to Mallaig – which is not the original Road to the Isles at all.

Added to this are the 'romantic' associations this district had with Prince Charles Edward Stuart and the rising of 1745. He landed at Borrodale, at the head of Loch nan Uamh, a beautiful sea loch, and from there went to Glenfinnan. The road west from Loch nan Uamh, crossing a peninsula too wooded for any views, comes back to the sea at Arisaig, an undistinguished little village desperately overcrowded in summer; only by leaving the car and going to the shores of Loch nan

Ceall to look across to the Small Isles can one breathe beauty again.

It is difficult, in holiday periods, to see the superb scenery of the area. North from Arisaig, trees are left behind as you cross the Back of Keppoch, a low hill, and come to the SILVER SANDS, stretching for over 6km. almost to Morar. From coves and bays of pure white sand there is a superb view across the machair to Skye, Rum, and Eigg. The sunsets deserve every praise that has been lavished upon them: but to see them, and the view, at any time during the summer holiday period, you look across a sea of tents, caravans, and attendant clutter.

The Silver Sands have suffered hopelessly from the popularity generated by their sheer beauty. But before the tents and caravans arrive the seals and the herons will still be there and the cry of the curlew may still be heard. Then, and only then, is the time to go to Arisaig: though, to some sensibilities, it may still seem too much like the picture postcards.

Arnisdale Highland 17F7
The road from Glenelg high above the Sound of Sleat and round to the mouth of Loch Hourn gives wonderful views of Skye, although, more and more, these views are obscured by conifers: as you descend the very rough road to Arnisdale, a forestry village on the shores of Loch Hourn, only glimpses – though superb ones – can be seen through the trees.

The road ends a little further south at the beautiful little clachan of Corran, with magnificent views down Loch Hourn to the Black Cuillin of Skye in the distance.

Beyond Corran, inner LOCH HOURN bites deep among great mountains; at its head is Kinloch Hourn and the road down to Loch Quoich. But there is no road along the north side of this superb loch, though a track goes along the south side from Kinloch Hourn to Inverie on Loch Nevis.

Arran Strathclyde 3F4 (*pop.* 3,552)
Anyone wanting to take the boat from Ardrossan in Ayrshire to Brodick on Arran at peak weekends in the high summer season has to obtain an Embarkation Ticket in advance. It is even necessary to have an application in on a certain day, some weeks in advance. Without following this procedure, although there are car ferries doing the 55-minute run each way six times on weekdays and five times on Sundays, chances of making the journey are remote, whether you have a car or not. That is a measure of the popularity of this remarkable and beautiful island in the Firth of Clyde. Yet, somehow, it has remained comparatively inviolate and uninjured, although you cannot walk along the 90km.-long road that circles the island with quite the same freedom as you could before the car ferries were introduced in the 1960s. Even a 'pop festival' inaugurated as an annual event (so the organizers hoped) some years

Brodick Castle, Arran

Arran: harvest scene nr Blackwaterfoot, looking E

ago excited, as it turned out, more pity than ire: those who attended had scant shelter from the rain.

Arran, some 32km. long and half as wide, is often, in tourist brochures, described as a microcosm of Scotland on the grounds that it has high mountains in the north, rolling but much flatter country in the south, two notable castles (each linked with Robert the Bruce), and most of the outdoor activities to be enjoyed throughout the country. But Arran cannot be dismissed with any slick summary. It has little industry apart from farming (including famous strains of potatoes) and tourist-related occupations. It has no towns: BRODICK, the main

centre for the island, from which coaches connect to other places round the coast (there are no inland centres), is but a village of around 1,000 people. It lies on the south side of Brodick Bay, its pier a short walk from the village centre, and is dominated by the highest, though not the most rugged, mountain on the island, shapely Goat Fell, 874m. above sea-level.

Above the north side of the Bay, Brodick Castle stands on a site that was a fortress in the days of the Vikings. This ancient seat of the Dukes of Hamilton (the Hamilton family owns most of the island) dates in part from the fourteenth century, with additions made in 1652 and 1844; since 1958 it has been a property of the NTS, which also owns over 2,800ha. of mountainous country to the north, including Goat Fell and Glen Rosa, the long, lovely glen between Goat Fell to the east and Beinn Nuis and Beinn Tarsuinn to the west.

Silver, porcelain, and paintings are among the contents of Brodick Castle, which is open from Easter to the end of the holiday season. The gardens, though, are open all year; there are two: a formal garden of 1710, and a woodland garden outstanding, in spring and early summer, for its rhododendrons, which are also an attractive feature of the road along the north of Brodick Bay. This road leads to the pleasant villages – strings of houses and cottages along the road, and looking to the sea – of Corrie and Sannox; it then turns inland.

There is another way to Sannox: up Glen Rosa (which has more than its fair share of campers in the peak summer period) is the steep path to the Saddle, high in the heart of the ridges and pinnacles of Arran's mountains, haunt of, among other predators, the golden eagle. From the Saddle, the path leads down Glen Sannox to the coast – an exhilarating walk of some 13km.

from Brodick to Sannox – and buses to take you back, if you wait long enough.

The road cuts inland and comes back to the coast at LOCHRANZA, where on a stone and shingle beach stand the impressive remains of a castle said to have been built as a hunting seat in the fourteenth century. In this position, standing out on a peninsula, it must also have found service as a fortress; Robert the Bruce is said to have gone there from Rathlin Island in Ireland at the renewal of his campaign for Scottish independence in 1307. The ruins seen today, however, are essentially those of a sixteenth-century building.

Lochranza is a small holiday centre, and in summer there is a car ferry to Claonaig (see Skipness) on Kintyre, of which there are pleasant views all the way down the west coast of Arran.

Past Lochranza the road hugs the coast nearly all the

Arran: the Standing Stones of Tormore, Machrie Moor, looking towards Goat Fell (right)

way, by the tiny villages of Catacol, on a delightful bay, and Pirnmill, where 'pirns' – wooden bobbins – were once made, to Machrie.

In the triangle of MACHRIE MOOR, through which the Machrie Water runs, are some impressive reminders of the fact that prehistoric man lived here: these include burial cairns – none in very good condition – and stone circles, of which the most remarkable are the Standing Stones of Tormore, remains of five Bronze Age circles, some stones still standing up to 4½m. high.

On the coast south of Machrie, the King's Caves are reputed to have sheltered Robert the Bruce, and there are claims that this was the scene of the 'Bruce and the Spider' story. If there is any truth in this story, the more likely setting would be Rathlin Island, where Bruce sheltered for some time during the winter of 1306/7.

BLACKWATERFOOT on Drumadoon Bay has pony trekking as well as sands, cliffs, and a golf course; and from here the 'String Road' cuts across the island to Brodick. There is only one other road across the island: it leaves the main road just before you get to Lagg Inn,

an inn set in charming wooded surroundings where subtropical plants and trees grow happily. This is the 'Ross Road', which goes to Lamlash. Just south of Lagg Inn, at Torrylinn, there are more, but not very impressive, Bronze Age remains and, more to the point today, a creamery where Arran cheeses are made. Nearby, round the south-east corner of the island, can be had the best views from Arran, at Dippin Head.

North of Whiting Bay, a popular though rather characterless resort, LAMLASH stands on a deep bay sheltered by Holy Island, a narrow island not 3km. long, yet with a central peak rising to 314m. above sealevel. 'Holy' because the seventh-century St Molaise had a cell there. Boat excursions go to the island in the summer from Lamlash: boats, indeed, have been a feature of Lamlash Bay for many centuries. Here the Norwegian King Haakon's fleet – what was left of the planned armada of 200 ships – assembled before the Battle of Largs in 1263. From here, also, Robert the Bruce sailed to the Ayrshire coast in 1307. But the conquest aimed at by today's sailors is over cod and conger, skate and rays: Lamlash is a major sea-angling centre, with dinghies and larger boats available.

For all its sense of activity, and for all its nearness to a considerable proportion of Scotland's population, Arran is essentially a Hebridean island, and a very beautiful one at that. There is a relaxed air about it; even on landing, there is that indefinable Hebridean feel that the clock has slowed down and does not much matter. It is too easy, perhaps, to forget the other side of the coin: the population of Arran has dropped by around 1,000 in twenty years. There are few opportunities for employment outside the holiday industry; youngsters who have to leave home during the week for the higher grades of education tend not to return to the island for long once their training is complete; and because of freight charges, prices are noticeably higher than on the mainland.

Arran, of course, is not unique in these respects.

Arrochar Strathclyde 5E4

Here, at the head of Loch Long, is the northern gateway to the Argyll Forest Park and, for those coming from the Central Belt of Scotland, the main approach to Loch Fyne, Loch Awe, and the wonderfully-fretted coast of south Argyll.

Not surprisingly, then, Arrochar is very much a tourist village, coping with people who stay there and, to a greater extent, cars passing through it. To supplement the limited accommodation in hotels and guest houses, here and at Ardgartan, not 3km. away, there are a youth hostel and three fairly large camping and caravan sites operated by the Forestry Commission, the Camping Club of Great Britain and Ireland, and the Caravan Club: these sites alone at peak periods can add between 1,500 and 2,000 (or even more) people to the area.

There is a lot to explore. Two km. east of Arrochar is TARBET on Loch Lomond: it was over this neck of land, in 1263, that King Haakon's galleys were manhandled from the head of Loch Long to Loch Lomond, in the Norse king's last campaign to gain this part of Scotland: he was finally defeated, at Largs in Ayrshire, some months later. Two km. to the west of Arrochar are the 'Arrochar Alps', of which Ben Ime (1,011m.) and Ben Vane (916m.) are the highest. But the most striking is rather smaller: BEN ARTHUR (881m.), better known as 'The Cobbler', rears its jagged peak above Arrochar; this mountain helps to make the village a popular climbing centre.

The ARGYLL FOREST PARK, some 24,000ha. of forests, mountains, and moors, lies to the west of Loch Long and extends, at its most westerly point, almost to Loch Fyne. Loch Goil, an arm of Loch Long, bites deeply into the Park up to Lochgoilhead; and another lovely stretch of water within its bounds is Loch Eck (see Benmore). The Park has a tremendous range of vegetation, and as rich a variety of fauna, which includes red and roe deer, wild cats, and, pre-eminent among the birds of Scotland, golden eagles. There are tracks and paths in profusion, many of which are within easy reach of Arrochar – there is, in particular, a maze of forest roads south from Glen Croe.

At Ardgartan, having ignored so far as is possible the Royal Navy Torpedo Testing Station on Loch Long, the traveller heading for the west passes between richly-forested mountains before going up GLEN CROE. From the main road, climbing easily under the slopes of the Cobbler, can be seen, in the valley bottom, the old road constructed after the 1745 Jacobite rising. It climbs steeply at the head of the valley, with a hairpin bend near the top, and was a notorious traffic hazard in the earlier years of this century. Near the top 'Rest and Be Thankful' was inscribed on a seat – and that gave the road its name. But the seat has gone and the old road is used only by walkers, riders, and, very occasionally, for car trials. At the summit, where the main road drops down to Glen Kinglas and Loch Fyne, a minor road goes south-west to Lochgoilhead. In summer, the top of the 'Rest' is a pleasant place to stop for a walk – there is space for cars to park – but in winter, north-westerly gales can funnel across it at ferocious speed to make this the windiest pass in west Scotland.

From the head of Loch Long, just north of Arrochar, a pleasant little road running up Glen Loin eventually becomes a path, which leads to the road up to the dam at the south end of LOCH SLOY under Ben Vorlich. The distance is some 7km. This dam, part of the first major project of the North of Scotland Hydro-Electric Board, was opened in 1950. 'Loch Sloy' was earlier the battle cry of Clan MacFarlane, whose gathering ground this was; and when the hydro-electric project was announced it raised another cry of protest from the comparatively few people who even knew where it was. This protest has been repeated at virtually every project of the Hydro Board, which has been outstandingly successful, in almost every instance, in ensuring that its power stations and other buildings 'fit in' to the landscape. In most cases, too, the reservoirs created have added to the appeal of the scenery, not detracted from it. In this particular case, the views from the Loch Sloy dam are superb.

Aultbea Highland 16F1

The sheltered waters of Loch Ewe were used by the Navy in both world wars, and its piers and quays can be seen from the road between Poolewe and Braemore, high above the loch. Aultbea (pron. Aultbay) is just off this road as it cuts across the Greenstone Point peninsula: it is the first of five crofting communities on the 5km.-long minor road along the shore, the last of which is Mellon Charles.

While the navy base is a rather unattractive intrusion on a lovely coast, it has brought extra employment to the area, and, as a result, Aultbea is a more prosperous-looking township than many others in the area. Its two hotels have good reputations.

Aviemore Highland 15H6
Until the mid 1960s this Spey Valley village was one of the most depressing in the Highlands. It looked what it was: a collection of houses, a few hotels and guest houses, and a ramshackle collection of shops, all of which had grown up around a railway station that seemed much too big for its setting.

It was the railway that was responsible for Aviemore. Until that was built, in the mid nineteenth century, Aviemore was little more than an inn on the old road built by General Wade. But when the rail link was established, houses and hotels were built around the station, and the place became popular for anglers (the Spey is one of the premier fishing rivers of Scotland) and for country holidays. Mountaineers and hill-walkers lured by the Cairngorms also found Aviemore a useful base, although it was a long walk to the slopes: even after the Forestry Commission road to Loch Morlich was built in the 1930s there was still only a track thereafter into the mountains.

At its peak period of activity the railway station employed 140 people, and this provided the main employment in the village. With the decline in rail traffic and the rise of touring holidays by car, Aviemore slumped; after World War II only twenty people were employed

Aviemore: the chairlift on Cairngorm

*Part of the Aviemore complex: bland 'international' architecture
in a Highland setting*

on the railway. The village still enjoyed a fair amount of
summer holiday trade, but at the end of the season it
virtually closed down.

The tide started to turn with the opening up of the
Cairngorm ski ground: some of the hotels then found it
worthwhile to remain open for part, at least, of the
winter. In the early 1960s the 'Ski Road' was built from
Loch Morlich into the Cairngorms, and the upper section of today's chairlift was opened.

The man who saw the opportunities for developing a
big all-year-round resort was Sir Hugh Fraser, later
Lord Fraser of Allander, a remarkable man who in
thirty years, from being the managing director of a
family drapery store in Glasgow, built up the House of
Fraser, an extensive chain of departmental stores
throughout Britain. His original plan for Aviemore was
the creation of a 'holiday village' with seven or even
more hotels. This proving impracticable, he formed,
with two leading Scottish brewery firms, Scottish and
Newcastle Breweries and Tennent Caledonian Breweries, a consortium that invested over £3 million in creating the Aviemore Centre, the most comprehensive
tourist project in Britain.

Lord Fraser died a few weeks before the Centre was
opened on 14 December 1966. Since its opening it has
continued to grow. Indeed, outside the Centre more
hotels, restaurants, and other facilities have grown up,
along with an estate of unpleasant-looking houses for
the hundreds of people who make a living catering for
visitors to Aviemore.

The Centre is a remarkable project, attracting some
600,000 visitors annually. It also strikes many – if not
most – of those who see it as utterly alien to the Highlands; and the towering Strathspey Hotel lacks totally
any sense of proportion. Aviemore's protagonists say
that you can have a good holiday without ever leaving
the Centre. Its detractors retort that it could just as well
have been somewhere else: so it could – except for the
skiing.

Ballachulish Highland 8C5
For decades motorists on the A82 between Crianlarich
and Fort William were faced with the alternatives of
waiting to take the car ferry between North and South
Ballachulish or driving some 26km. round Loch Leven.
A new bridge, opened early in 1976, avoids this delay

but gives no time to admire the superb mountain scenery up the loch, or down it across Loch Linnhe to the hills of Ardgour (qv).

Ballachulish village, on the south shores a little west of the old ferry, is unpleasantly dominated by extensive slate quarries first started in 1761 and now disused. West from North Ballachulish, past Onich, Loch Linnhe can be crossed by the Corran Ferry to Ardgour, saving a detour of 70km. via Fort William.

Barra Highland 22D3 (*pop.* 1,110)
Like all the Outer Hebrides, Barra, the southernmost main island of the group, has a rocky, almost forbidding east coast and fine bays and machair on its western shores.

But there are exceptions to this general Hebridean rule. North from the island, a long peninsula, in places not 300m. wide, juts to Scurrival Point; on the east side of this is the spectacular TRAIGH MHOR, the Great Strand, famous beyond the Hebrides on two counts. It is also known as the Cockle Strand: a traveller in 1549 said it produced the best cockles in Britain, and nobody seems to have disputed the verdict since. Here, too, every weekday during the summer months, and three days weekly in winter, the plane from Glasgow lands on one of the most remarkable 'airfields' in Britain; the airfield consists of just the firm, ripple-marked beach: there is little more than a hut to serve for the airport. For many years – and long before discrimination between the sexes became a matter of legislation – the airport was 'manned' by one lady. Until 1975 the air service was run by British European Airways (later British Airways); when this company pulled out of the service, the lady retired – and continued her job the next day in the service of Loganair, who had taken over the run.

The plane service operates, 'weather permitting', at all times. As the Traigh Mhor faces east across the Oitir Mhor, the wide bay sheltered by many islands, it is, except in the worst weather, fairly reliable. The plane takes sixty-five minutes to fly from Glasgow to Barra. There can be few scheduled journeys that take one in so brief a time from one world to another, from the biggest city in Scotland, which, in its attempts to rid itself of the worst legacies of nineteenth-century industrialization, has torn down vast numbers of buildings to create motorways and flyovers, to an island utterly remote from either architectural insult.

True, many crofters of Barra have been rehoused – but in neat white dwellings. One road goes round the coast of Barra: the interior of the island is hilly, rising to a summit at Heaval (384m.). Another, even smaller, road runs by Northbay, with lobster boats moored in its creeks, and lazybeds between its rock ridges, to the crofting township of Eoligarry, beyond which it stops. There are no other roads.

Barra's major centre is CASTLEBAY, a most attractive village scattered on the grassy hills around the bay on the south side of the island. It is dominated by a Roman Catholic church of 1891; this, like South Uist (qv), is a Catholic island, and on the path from the village to Heaval is a statue of the Blessed Virgin and Child, in Carrara marble, erected in 1954.

The quite easy walk to the summit of Heaval – not 5km. there and back – is worth making for the views along Hebridean islands. To the south you look to the end of the Outer Hebrides where, beyond Mingulay (whose 230m.-high cliffs are an important breeding place for kittiwakes and auks), are Barra Head, crowned with a tall lighthouse, and Berneray. There are no regular boat services to these islands, though hiring arrangements may be made.

For the visitor the great attraction of Castlebay – apart from the charm of the place and people (day-to-day speech, incidentally, is in the Gaelic, though English is also spoken) – lies in the bay itself, where, on an offshore rock, stands KISIMUL CASTLE, ancient seat of the MacNeils of Barra. The story that an early chief refused Noah's offer of a place in the ark on the grounds that 'The MacNeil has a boat of his own' need not be taken too literally; but certainly the clan has been there for a long, long time.

When the Castle was built is also uncertain. The chief who restored it, himself an architect, considered that the curtain wall was built in the eleventh century and that the massive square tower and ancillary buildings were complete by 1430. Other authorities suggest the thirteenth and even the early fifteenth century as possible dates. Whatever the truth, it is a splendid example of a Highland stronghold, and an example, too, of what can be achieved by dedicated restoration.

Often besieged, and at times lost to the clan, in 1937 the 45th chief, Robert Lister MacNeil, an American architect, bought the Castle and started to restore it in the following year. The restoration was completed in 1960, and was celebrated by a gathering of MacNeils from all over the world. It can be visited by boat from Castlebay on the afternoons of Wednesday and Saturday during the summer.

Visitor accommodation on Barra was roughly doubled with the opening in the mid 1970s of the Isle of Barra Hotel at Castlebay. In addition to other hotels and guest houses, there are bed-and-breakfast places and some self-catering accommodation. There are car ferries from Oban and Lochboisdale in South Uist to entice the visitors – who, however, are unlikely to come in sufficient quantity to spoil the immense charm of the most colourful island of the Outer Hebrides.

Beauly Highland 15E3
At the head of the Beauly Firth, 20km. west of Inverness on the A9, is this small market town, traditionally named from the French *beau lieu* – not an impossible theory, as the Lovat Frasers, in whose country this is, were originally a Norman family.

Its history is long: at the north end of the wide main street is the roofless shell of a church, the rather beautiful remains of a Valliscaulian priory founded in 1230, though much reconstructed in the fourteenth and sixteenth centuries.

There are few other reminders of is history, but today's Beauly is still a pleasant spacious place.

South of the village, before the road from Inverness crosses the River Beauly at Lovat Bridge, the A832 goes west beside the river and into the beautiful valley of Strath Glass (*see* Cannich).

Benbecula Highland 22E2

Benbecula is an island. Yet no boats go regularly to it; its only port is an airport.

The causeways that now link Benbecula to North Uist and South Uist (qqv) are comparatively recent. The southern link was established during World War II, the northern in 1961: before then, the only link was by fording the strait between Creagorry and Carnan Inn at low tide – a risky crossing in bad weather.

'Airport' is too grand a name for the air strip with services to Barra, Stornoway on Lewis, and Inverness. It is near BAILIVANISH (Balivanich) on the north-west coast of the island – the only place, one might almost think, where there is sufficient ground for a plane to operate. For Benbecula, a flat island whose highest point is Rueval, 125m. above sea-level, holds countless lochs and lochans; yet Rueval gives good views of the southern Outer Hebrides and of the area stretching

Beauly: the remains of the Valliscaulian priory

from St Kilda in the west to the Cuillins of Skye in the east. (There is another Rueval, only some 13km. away, at the north end of South Uist.)

With an east coast that is a maze of islands and inlets, and its west coast machair and beaches, Benbecula, measuring some 8km. north to south, 11km. east to west, supports a population of about 1,000 people, most of whom, perforce, are in and around Bailivanish. Benbecula, along with the Uists, is composed of Lewisian Gneiss, one of the oldest rocks in the world; but Benbecula's emergence as an island is comparatively recent: all the Outer Hebrides were one island until after the last Ice Age.

Prince Charles Edward Stuart took refuge among the lochs of the island in 1746 after his escape from Culloden (qv), and it was from Benbecula that Flora MacDonald, the 23-year-old daughter of a clan chief, took him in a rowing boat to Uig on Skye. A grimmer episode in the island's history was when it shared with South Uist some of the most vicious of the Clearances prior to 1860: many crofters and their families were rounded up and forcibly transported to America, to make way for sheep. Between 1841 and 1861 the population dropped from 2,107 to 1,468: but even the 1861 figure is more than today's population level on this windswept island, which yet, for those tuned that way, has an inexplicable fascination. Not many people can stay there, however: apart from a small hotel at Creagorry, there is very little accommodation for visitors.

Benmore Strathclyde 4D6
'There is no finer expanse of highland forest scenery in

Britain than that from Strone Point on the Firth of Clyde up the shores of Loch Eck to Glenbranter, with the peaks of Beinn Mhor and Beinn Bheula towering above the green woods in the glens and the blue waters of the lochs'. While there may be some pardonable exaggeration in this statement by the Earl of Radnor (in a 1967 edition of the *Argyll Forest Park Guide*), there is little doubt that this area, north of Dunoon, is one of the more satisfactory achievements of the Forestry Commission, of which the Earl was chairman from 1952 to 1963.

The area he praises is part of the southern section of the Argyll Forest Park, and at Benmore, just south of the head of Loch Eck, the Younger Botanic Garden makes an excellent introduction to it. The entrance to these 34ha. woodland gardens, planted between 1889

Looking NW from the snowclad slopes of Ben Nevis

and 1925 by Mr H. G. Younger and his father, is through a magnificent avenue of sequoias, giant redwoods, each towering over 30m. high. Here, also, or so it is claimed, is one of the largest collections of rhododendrons in the world: over 200 species, unforgettable when seen in full flower around the end of May or early June.

Mr Younger gifted these gardens to the nation in 1925; now administered by the Royal Botanic Garden in Edinburgh, they are open to the public.

Mr Younger's mansion house (not open to the public) was a forestry training school from 1929 to 1965, when it was bought by Edinburgh for use by its Education Department as an Outdoor Activities Centre.

Just south from Benmore, stone steps lead from the roadside to PUCK'S GLEN, which, despite its rather twee name, and the rustic bridges you find when you get there after a longish climb through well-varied trees, is worth the walk. There are rhododendrons as well as trees on the approach, and at the top many paths to follow and small waterfalls to see. This, again, was part of the Younger estate.

More natural is the dead-end road up Glen Massan, which comes down to Benmore from a narrow valley west of Beinn Mhor. A short way up from Benmore, the 'Golden Gates' (actually finely-wrought iron) are a private entrance to the mansion; then, above the road, in the Forestry Commission's Benmore Arboretum, are huge conifers planted over a century ago. Further still up the Glen, the Falls of Massan plunge into deep potholes and under a natural rock-arch scooped out by the water.

North from Benmore is lovely LOCH ECK, nearly 10km. long but never 1km. wide. The road runs beside it, past Whistlefield and, beyond the end of the loch, to Glenbranter. This estate once belonged to the Scots comedian Sir Harry Lauder, but his mansion has now been demolished and replaced by a Forestry Commission village of timber houses. Just north of the village, on a hillside west of the main road, is a monument erected by Sir Harry in memory of his son, killed in World War I. It makes a good viewpoint; but there are many such in this area – when you can get away from, or look through, the trees.

Ben Nevis Highland 8C4

Although the highest mountain in Britain – 1,361m. above the level of the sea, which is only 6½km. away – this huge granite mass tends to disappoint those who expect to see a soaring peak. Its top is a rounded wilderness of huge boulders, and the recognized route up, from Achintee Farm in Glen Nevis, is fairly easy, fairly uninteresting, and, at peak holiday periods, fairly busy.

'The Ben' was ascended by car for the first time in 1911, and more recent gimmicks include pushing a piano to the top (to raise money for charity). But even in summer it is not to be lightly regarded. The 8km. track to the summit, though well-defined, is rough, and the

Ben Nevis seen from Carn Mor Dearg

weather can change with remarkable rapidity: records of the observatory established on the summit in 1883 – it continued its work until 1904 – showed that there was an average of 261 gales over 50 m.p.h. every year; furthermore, because of its nearness to the sea, the mountain is frequently covered in cloud.

But from the A830 around Corpach and Loch Eil, the Ben takes on a very different appearance. From this angle, and from north of Fort William, can be seen the great north face of the mountain – the highest cliffs on mainland Britain, rising 460m. This North Face is an ascent not to be attempted by any save the most experienced mountaineers.

Glen Nevis, over which the Ben towers, is one of the most beautiful glens in Scotland, and may be followed much of the way by car. The road deteriorates into a track eventually, and by this the Steall Waterfall may be reached. Good walkers can continue along this track to Loch Treig, Corrour Station on the Glasgow–Fort William line (*see* Bridge of Orchy), and to Loch Ossian Youth Hostel. From upper Glen Nevis there are also paths to Kinlochleven (qv).

Berriedale Highland 21D5
At the bottom of the hills where the A9 drops down to the mouth of the Berriedale Water, here joined by the

Langwell Water, this rather charming little hamlet lies just off the road, with pleasant trees around it – in surprising contrast to the wild, bleak Caithness moors behind.

Berriedale Hill, north of the village, was a notorious hazard until comparatively recently, and its hairpin bend is still not to be disregarded. South from Berriedale the A9 climbs and twists past ravines to the great rock bulk of the ORD OF CAITHNESS (227m.).

Bettyhill Highland 20A2

Even today, over 150 years after the event, there are people in this small village on the north coast, where the River Naver comes to the sea, who speak bitterly of the Clearances. Strath Naver, which runs due south for some 25km. before turning west to Loch Naver, was one of the worst affected of the areas where crofters were forcibly evicted to make way for sheep.

It is said that Bettyhill was named after Elizabeth, Countess of Sutherland, whose husband (the Marquess of Stafford, who married the Countess and was created Duke of Sutherland in 1833) was the landowner responsible for the evictions. He believed that if the people living in wretched circumstances in the strath – whose poor ground was quite incapable of supporting them – were moved to the coast, they could supplement their living by fishing, and the strath, instead, be turned over to sheep. Violence had to be used to move the crofters, however, and the crofts were burnt before their eyes. Whatever the intention, the land at Bettyhill was equally poor, and the place was more a refugee camp: there was not even a harbour. Probably about 1,200 people were evicted; most found their way to other parts of the Highlands and many eventually emigrated. It was no consolation to them that the Duke spent a vast amount of money – building over 700km. of roads and over 100 bridges – to improve his extensive estates.

Today, Bettyhill is a rather untidy village amongst barren, rock-strewn moorland, with some delightful, though exposed, bays near at hand. It is popular with anglers: the Naver is a leading salmon river.

Beside the main road just east of the village is FARR church, now the Strathnaver Museum of Local History. This developed from a local school project on the Clearances, and makes for a most interesting visit. In addition to detailing the story of the evictions, there is a collection of local miscellania; one room has a number of fine grave slabs of the mid eighteenth century. In the churchyard is an elaborately-carved, though rather weathered, slab standing over 2m. high and dating from about the ninth century.

Black Isle Highland (Ross & Cromarty) 15F2

There are several ingenious explanations why this green peninsula between the Cromarty, Beauly, and Inverness firths is called the Black Isle. The least convincing is that it is seldom snow-covered; another, from the *First Statistical Account of Scotland* (1791–9), that it was once covered with black peat; a third, that the Gaelic Eilean Dubhthaich – St Duthac's Isle – became Eilean Dubh (the 'Black Isle').

Whatever the reason for its name, this is a quiet, fertile area of farmland and forest rising up to a central ridge, Millbuie, which, oddly, was granted by Mary Queen of Scots to Darnley on their marriage. As his ambition was to be King of Scotland, this gift can have been but little consolation. It is now extensively forested.

Access from the south is by the Kessock car ferry from Inverness. These straits are due to be bridged to make for quicker road approach to the North-Sea-oil construction centres on the Cromarty Firth; the crossing will be some 8km. north-east of Conon Bridge. But the project has been held up by economy measures, and is not likely to start before 1978.

While the Black Isle itself is not directly affected by the industrial explosion on the north shores of the Cromarty Firth, the once pleasant views from the shores of Cromarty Bay to Nigg Bay cannot now be recommended; nor, when the wind blows from Invergordon (possessor of an aluminium smelter), is the air as pure as it once was; the oil refinery at Nigg, plans for which were approved early in 1976, will not improve matters. Nevertheless, it is pleasant country to wander around in. (Cromarty and the resorts around Fortrose are noted separately.)

FERINTOSH, 5km. north-east of Conon Bridge, owes its fame as a whisky-distilling centre to the Forbes family: from 1690 this family, for their loyalty to the Crown, were exempted from excise duty; by a quirk of circumstance this whisky area also saw the first Communion of the Free Church of Scotland in 1843.

JEMIMAVILLE and POYNTZFIELD, near Cromarty Bay, are so named because the Munro who built them in 1822 married a Dutch girl, Jemima Poyntz. There are some good caves – though not easy of access – between Cromarty and Rosemarkie: one of these, Caird's Cave, was inhabited by prehistoric man (and as recently as 1930 by a Captain Devine and his wife).

MUNLOCHY BAY is noted for vast numbers of duck, waders, and wintering greese; but, again, access is not easy: the birdwatcher in winter and spring has more satisfaction on the shores of the Beauly Firth west of North Kessock.

Near the picturesque hamlet of Kilmuir, south from Munlochy Bay, is Loch Lundy, reputed to be the haunt of a water bull whose herd bellows under the ice in winter. As the loch does not freeze over, this flight of fancy is on a par with the many Brahan Seer legends and prophecies (*see* Strathpeffer and Conon Bridge), with which the Black Isle is somewhat overburdened.

Boat of Garten Highland 15H5

Lying 3km. east of the main A9 road, this village is much less harassed by traffic than other Spey Valley centres.

It has a railway station but, normally, no trains. It was a station on the branch line from Aviemore to Grantown-on-Spey, a line that was closed by Beeching. Now it is being restored by the Strathspey Railway Company, a private concern run by steam-engine enthusiasts: the line is complete from Aviemore to Boat of Garten, and it is expected that regular trips for tourists and holiday-makers will be a feature. The line may be extended again to Grantown-on-Spey; but the re-building of a bridge is involved.

Boat of Garten derives its name from the ferry that used to cross the Spey here – long since replaced by a bridge leading to the B970, the 'back road' between Aviemore and Grantown. Leading from this road is the minor road into the Abernethy Forest and Loch Garten: the signpost 'To the Ospreys' indicates its importance to the birdwatcher.

The osprey, once common in Scotland, was mercilessly persecuted by 'sportsmen', and the last was shot in 1910. The first pair to return came in 1959 and nested near Loch Garten, and ospreys have come back every spring since. Their treetop eyrie is now in a reserve controlled by the Royal Society for the Protection of Birds, whose members and other volunteers maintain a day-and-night watch over it during the breeding season. Despite elaborate precautions, the nest has been raided and the eggs stolen or smashed on more than one occasion; but usually the birds have bred successfully. A track from the road leads to a hide where the birds can be observed through fixed binoculars.

In November 1975 the RSPB bought some 600ha. of pinewoods, moorland, loch, and marsh surrounding the nesting site.

About a dozen pairs of osprey nest annually in Scotland now; but only at Loch Garten and Loch of the Lowes, near Dunkeld in Perthshire, are there arrangements for viewing them. The sites of the other nests are not revealed.

Less dramatic, but equally interesting to the bird-watcher, is the crested tit, only to be seen in this area. Crossbill, capercailzie, goosander, greylag goose, and whooper swan are among many other birds to be seen in the new RSPB reserve; and there are many delightful walks through the Abernethy Forest.

Bonar Bridge Highland 19F7
This village, popular with anglers, stands on the north side of the narrow strait that separates the Kyle of Sutherland from the Dornoch Firth. It also stands at the junction of tempting roads: to the north-west Highlands, or to the north coast, or, east, to Dornoch and the long coast to Caithness. Much less well known is the minor road north-east from Bonar Bridge, which climbs and plunges and climbs again to Loch Buidhe, then runs beside the Torboll River to Loch Fleet. At the southern approach to the bridge is Ardgay (qv) and the minor road up Strath Carron.

The Falls of Measach, Corrieshalloch Gorge, Braemore

The Firth used to be crossed by boat from Meikle Ferry, 14km. east; but after a disaster in which over 100 lives were lost, a bridge was built by Thomas Telford in 1812; this was replaced in 1892, after a flood, by the present structure.

Braemore Highland 19C8
From this small village, 77km. by road from Inverness, two roads each lead to some of the most superb scenery in Scotland.

Turn south-west on the A832 and you cross the empty moors of the DUNDONNELL FOREST, climbing up to 350m. above sea-level before dropping down to Dundonnell (qv). This is 'Destitution Road', built in 1851 to give work (rewarded, it is said, by food only) to those suffering from the potato famine. Beyond Dundonnell the A832 continues by Little Loch Broom to Poolewe and Gairloch (qqv).

Continue from Braemore on the A835 and you go through beautiful Strathmore, then by Loch Broom to Ullapool and the far north-west coast. Just after leaving Braemore there is a large car park by the road, from which leads a short path through the woods to the narrow, 62m.-deep CORRIESHALLOCH GORGE; the Gorge is spanned by a fragile suspension bridge, with spectacular views of the Falls of Measach below. The Gorge is in the care of the NTS.

Bridge of Orchy Strathclyde 5E1
The old road to Fort William ran north from Tyndrum to cross the River Orchy at Bridge of Orchy, skirted the western end of Loch Tulla, then climbed over the Black Mount to the Kingshouse Hotel near the top of Glen Coe. The new road, completed in 1935, follows a different track – up the west wide of the valley from Tyndrum to Bridge of Orchy, then east of Loch Tulla, to skirt the desolate Moor of Rannoch to Glen Coe.

The old road from Bridge of Orchy is suitable for motor-cars only to Forest Lodge. Then it is a 13km. walk along a good track that reaches its summit over the shoulder of Meall a' Bhuiridh, now equipped with chairlift and tows for skiers, before descending to the Kingshouse Hotel. Before this summit, though, the track crosses the River Ba at Ba Bridge. There is no track up this river, which emerges from the Corrie Ba lying under Clachlet (Clach Leathad). If you follow this river up – few do, for it can be wet and heavy going – you will come to the largest corrie in Scotland, lying under the 1,100m.-high mountain.

Or there is a track west from Forest Lodge to Loch Dochard – some 5km. long, though the track continues to Loch Etive – lying under a huge crescent of

'Destitution Road', between Dundonnell and Braemore: An Teallach mountain is in the background

mountains, which reach their peak at Stob Ghabar (1,077m.) and carry scores of tumbling streams. This, north and west of Bridge of Orchy, is the BLACK MOUNT FOREST, whose seven peaks over 900m. make up some of the most impressive mountain wildernesses in the country.

By Loch Tulla, north from Bridge of Orchy, the railway, which has taken a similar route to the road since leaving Crianlarich, strikes to the north-east, across the MOOR OF RANNOCH, over a 100sq. km. of peat hags. Pools of peaty water, bleached branches of long-fallen trees (this was once part of the Caledonian Forest), and cut almost in two by lochs Ba and Laidon, the Moor in bad weather can be desolate indeed. But walking across it in good weather gives not only immense views but, in their seasons, waving masses of bog cotton, wild swans, duck, and breeding black-throated and red-throated divers.

At the north-east end of Loch Laidon is remote Rannoch Station and, nearby, a nature reserve for bog plants and small trees. This station can be reached by road – over 60km. west from Pitlochry in the Tayside region. There is another station for Rannoch Moor: Corrour (marked 'Halt' on the map), which has no road to it at all; it is 2km. south-west of Loch Ossian, where there is a youth hostel – but nothing else.

The Black Mount and the Moor of Rannoch make up as wild and empty a scene as any in Britain. Most travellers look at them – or, rather, the fringes of them – from the comfort of their cars as they drive along the A82. There is a hotel at Bridge of Orchy – there are few other buildings – and as likely as not the hotel residents are there for the angling or stalking. Across the road from the hotel the steep slopes of Beinn Dorain sweep up to a fine peak.

Brora Highland 21C6
Although this small resort makes its appeal to the holidaymaker for its sands – golf and angling are also to be had – it has much more interest than many superficially similar places.

Brora has an unexpected industrial background: a privately-owned coalmine too small to have fallen into the grip of nationalization. Coal was found in 1529, and mining started in 1598, chiefly to provide fuel for the production of salt. Over the centuries the mine has been closed and re-opened and extended more than once; for some time it was operated by the few miners who worked there, as a cooperative enterprise. 'Finally closed' some years ago, coal was again mined during the fuel crisis of 1974.

A distillery, started in 1819, and a woollen mill – round which visitors are shown – are among other activities; but the once busy harbour is now little used.

The village stands at the mouth of the River Brora, noted for salmon, which flows through Loch Brora, 12km. west. Above the west bank of the loch, the Carrol Rock stands over 200m. high. Just south of this crag is the Carrol Broch, whose walls stand about 3½m. high; this is but one of many ancient dwellings in the area, the most important of which is the CINN TROLLA BROCH at Kintradwell, 5km. north of Brora. The Cinn Trolla Broch was excavated and cleared out over 100 years ago to reveal an entrance passage 5½m. long and 2m. high; a notable feature is the 2m.-deep well inside, with a flight of steps leading down to it.

Bute Strathclyde 3G1/G2 (*pop.* 7,956)
To many visitors Bute means, pre-eminently, one place – Rothesay. This resort, from the early nineteenth century, was the mecca of Clyde paddle-steamer passengers, out-rivalling even Dunoon (qv) as *the* place to go from Glasgow.

Fashions have changed; but Rothesay is still a very popular seaside holiday place, despite its not having a large beach: that deficiency is made up for by the good sands at ETTERICK (Ettrick) BAY, some 8km. away on the west side of the island, and easily attained by buses.

Until recently, with the introduction of roll-on, roll-off ferries, comparatively few visitors brought cars: these are not desperate necessities on an island only about 25km. long and nowhere 8km. wide. The lack of cars is one of the appeals of Bute.

Rothesay holds the impressive remains of one of the most outstanding medieval castles in Scotland. The Castle was certainly in existence by 1230, in which year it is known to have been stormed by the Norsemen (the breach they made can still be seen). It seems likely, though, that it was built about eighty years earlier. The existing remains date mainly from the end of the fourteenth century, with extensions by James IV (1488–1513) and James V (1513–42).

The Castle possesses a feature unique in Scotland: its 10m.-high curtain walls, originally fortified by four great drum towers (of which one still remains), enclose a *circular* courtyard. This courtyard is entered through an early-sixteenth-century fore-tower, which projects into the deep moat, still filled with water, that surrounds the site. From the courtyard, stairs lead to the great hall on the first floor.

Held by Cromwell's army from 1651 to 1659, the Castle finally fell in 1685, when it was sacked and burnt by a brother of the Earl of Argyll. Unoccupied for nearly 300 years, it is impressive yet.

Rothesay's popularity as a resort dates from the 1820s (the first steamboats were calling regularly in 1816). But the Castle was a favourite resort of the early Stewart kings in the late fourteenth century, and Robert III's son became Duke of Rothesay, the Scottish title of the heir to the throne ever since.

OPPOSITE TOP: *The impressive scenery of the Black Mount area, N and W of Bridge of Orchy*

OPPOSITE BOTTOM: *Rothesay, Bute*

63

Before the first visitors started to arrive, industry came to Rothesay around 1780. Richard Arkwright patented his water frame, which revolutionized the cotton industry, in 1769; James Kenyon of Sheffield induced some of Arkwright's men to go over to him, but as Arkwright held the patent for England, Kenyon had to move north of the Border. The first cotton mill in Scotland was established at Rothesay, and was followed by others. The mills lasted for about 100 years; but because of transport problems (a familiar story when industry on Scottish islands is discussed) all eventually moved to the mainland. By then, though, Rothesay was well established as a holiday centre.

The town (*pop.* 6,286) does well for its visitors: it is unquestionably the best-positioned major resort on the Firth of Clyde. Up on Canada Hill, where the eighteen-hole golf course was designed by James Braid, one of the most famous of 'golf architects', there are fine views

over the town and up the Firth. Just north of Rothesay is Kames Bay, a popular haven for yachtsmen, with Port Bannatyne, Rothesay's satellite village, at the northern end; the village, unfortunately, now looks across the water to the oil-related construction developments at Ardyne Point, as does Rothesay itself.

But there is more to Bute than the resorts. The island itself – which outside Rothesay has a total population of 1,670 – is wonderfully varied. Rich, well-farmed land in the south contrasts with open hill land to the north, and there are excellent views from nearly all of it.

Of the beaches, Ettrick's is the biggest – over 3km. long – and most popular, though it has not been improved by the modern café, refreshment kiosks, putting green, and the like. St Ninian's Bay and Scalpsie Bay, further south on the west side of the island, are very attractive, with the odd contrast that the first has yellow sands, while those of the second verge on red. From the

The Caledonian Canal at Corpach

road above Scalpsie are to be had the finest views on an island that does not lack scenery – a panorama that can range from the peaks of Arran to the distant hills of Galloway. Kilchattan, on the east side of the island, is a pleasant village with another good beach . . . and there are others.

For those who look for more than seaside-resort facilities, one of the advantages of Bute is its scope for walking. Even though much of the land is farmed, there are plenty of paths and tracks, and these include an 8km. nature trail from Rudabodach (Rhubodach) at the north end of the island and paths around Loch Fad, south from Rothesay: here, at Woodend, the actor Edmund Kean built a cottage in 1827.

For the angler there are coarse fishing for perch and pike in lochs Fad and Ascog, trout fishing on Loch Quien, and sea angling from Rothesay and Port Bannatyne.

There are two car ferries to Bute. The usual approach is by that from Wemyss Bay to Rothesay, a thirty-minute crossing; the ferry from Colintraive to Rhubodach takes five minutes – but from Glasgow you have to drive nearly 140km., about three times the distance to Wemyss Bay, to get to it. Either way, this delightful island is worth heading for.

Cairndow Strathclyde 4D4
Motorists coming down Glen Kinglas from the Rest and Be Thankful (see Arrochar) do not see this small village on the edge of Loch Fyne; those driving round the loch from Inveraray see only the entrance to it: Cairndow lies on a side road below the main A83, and is just a short line of whitewashed houses looking across a stony beach to the loch.

There is a hotel, of respectable antiquity: Wordsworth and his sister Dorothy stayed there in 1804, and another visitor was Keats, who having walked over the Rest and Be Thankful left a memento of his visit by scratching his name on his bedroom window-pane.

Beyond the hotel is Kilmorich church (the village was originally named Kilmorich). The original building was thirteenth-century; but today's version dates only from 1816, and is very attractive: a six-sided church with a square tower topped by spires, and with a most appealing plain interior. Adjoining the graveyard is a meadow with memorials to the Noble family, who bought the Ardkinglas estate in 1905; the entrance to the estate is just off the road past the church. While the house, built by Sir Robert Lorimer (who designed the National War Memorial at Edinburgh Castle), is not normally open to the public, for a small fee one can walk through the beautiful woods of Strone Gardens that surround it. Tall trees – the pinetum has what is claimed to be the highest tree in Scotland – rhododendrons, and exotic shrubs, as well as more native ones, grow in profusion here.

The road down the south side of Loch Fyne leaves the A83 a short way above the junction with the road to Cairndow. Some 3km. along it the road up Hell's Glen, by no means as fearsome as its name suggests, climbs to join that from the top of the Rest to Lochgoilhead (qv).

Another 12km. south along Loch Fyne, STRACHUR, the largest village in the Cowal district of Argyll, lies just inland past the well-known Creggans Inn. Here a miniature 'Great Glen' cuts through the hills of Cowal to the Holy Loch; although the mountains on each side rise to over 750m. above sea-level, the road from Strachur to Dunoon never rises higher than 54m., and for nearly 10km. runs beside placid Loch Eck (see Benmore).

Caledonian Canal Highland 8, 14, 15
Some 350 million years ago the plateau that was the base of today's Highlands split, and the huge mass of what is now the north-west Highlands, north from the Firth of Lorn to the Inverness Firth, 'slid' south-west for over 100km. Thus was formed Glen More – in the Gaelic *Glen More nan Albin* – running from Fort William to Inverness, and now usually known as the Great Glen (which is what Glen More means).

Along this split is more water than land, with three long narrow lochs – Lochy, Oich, and Ness – taking up about 72km. of the total length of 107km. For over 150 years these three lochs have been linked by the Caledonian Canal, built to avoid the long, often stormy, passage round the north of Scotland. Designs were first prepared for the Canal in 1773 by James Watt, whose estimate for the job, £165,000, considered excessive, stopped the project for thirty years. Thomas Telford was later commissioned to cut the canal, and work started in 1803. Nineteen years later it was opened, but found to be not deep enough; it was finally completed in 1847 – by which time it had cost £1,311,270. Ironically, much of its value was lost with the development of steam power, for which James Watt was so largely responsible.

In its 35km. length the Canal has 29 locks, the most remarkable being the series of 8 near Banavie, known as 'Neptune's Staircase'; the Canal reaches its highest point, about 35m. above sea-level, at Laggan Locks, just beyond the north-east end of Loch Lochy.

Campbeltown Strathclyde 3E5 *(pop.* 6,326)
Although on the same latitude as Alnwick in Northumberland, there are few towns more typically 'Highland' in atmosphere than this. Not even its most fervent admirers can call it beautiful, despite its attractive setting at the head of Campbeltown Loch; Campbeltown is an old grey town, with newer houses and estates lining the bay.

Campbeltown Loch is a magnificent natural harbour, protected by Davaar (Davarr) Island, and at the end of the last century some 650 fishing boats plied a prosperous trade in herrings here. The fleet, like the herring, is

now much reduced, and while some thirty boats are still based on Campbeltown, the catches are taken elsewhere.

Similarly, the thirty distilleries that used to be in and around the town have been decimated (it was said that people could smell Campbeltown before they got to it – no accident, perhaps, that there is a well-known song 'Campbeltown Loch I wish you where whisky'!). Coal mining was another industry; but that closed down in 1967.

With all this, though, unlike some other Highland towns, Campbeltown did not throw in its hand. A large creamery was established – accounting for the large number of dairy herds in the hinterland – and farming is usually as prosperous as farmers will ever admit to. Campbeltown is the market centre for this area; in addition, while not a seaside holiday resort, it does enjoy a certain amount of tourist trade – though this is not helped by the run-down of the Clyde steamer services and the almost complete disappearance of steamer trips.

Most visitors come to Campbeltown the long way round via Inveraray, 122km. away, which itself involves a longish run from Glasgow – from which one can fly in forty minutes to Machrihanish (qv), some 10km. west.

The local museum is generally praised – as happens in other small towns, not necessarily all Highland, where there is little else to see. Much is also made of a painting of the Crucifixion in a cave on Davaar Island, too typical of its date, 1887. It was done, in secret, by a local artist, Archibald MacKinnon. It has twice been retouched.

There is also a rather fine Celtic-style cross removed in recent years from outside the Town Hall to the head of the Old Quay. Its history is unknown, though it was probably sculptured in the fifteenth century.

There are many ways in which Campbeltown is a Highland place. One is in its treatment of death: funeral notices are quietly intimated in shops, black-garbed mourners often still follow on foot, and traditionally the funeral procession passes the 'Celtic' cross. There are other, more joyful, ways in which Campbeltown expresses its attachment to the Highlands. Its Gaelic Choir has for many years featured among the top prizewinners at the National Mod of An Comunn Ghaidhealach, the main body in Scotland for preserving Gaelic speech and culture.

The harbour, between the Old and New Quays, is as busily attractive as most working harbours are, despite the falling away of its fleet. South-east, towards KIL-KERRAN, are sand and shingle flats with fascinating bird-life, and at Kilkerran the neglected ruins by the

LEFT: *Campbeltown Cross (C 15?), front view*

RIGHT: *Campbeltown Cross, back view*

shore are of a castle built at the end of the fifteenth century. The name 'Kilkerran' stems from Ceann Loch Chille Chiaran, which in turn refers to St Chiaran, who was St Columba's tutor (*see* Iona). The name was later amended to Lochhead; and in 1667 it became Campbeltown in honour of the Earls of Argyll, who had then been given Kintyre.

Cannich Highland 14D4

Two long and lovely glens join near this village set in the almost equally beautiful valley of Strath Glass, through which the River Glass runs for over 25km. north-east to Beauly (qv).

Cannich has a hotel that has long been well known to salmon and trout anglers. In the past twenty-odd years the village has gained a number of houses – wellgrouped stone buildings – and now has many more than in 1952, when the Duke of Edinburgh inaugurated a large hydro-electric scheme that has its power station at Fasnakyle, some 4km. south-west up the river, at the beginning of GLEN AFFRIC. This major development by the North of Scotland Hydro-Electric Board aroused even more controversy than is usual with such projects. Many walkers averred that Glen Affric was the most beautiful glen in Scotland, and protested that this beauty was being violated. The scheme takes in Loch Mullardoch in Glen Cannich and lochs Affric and Beneveian in Glen Affric; between these two glens majestic Mam Soul and Carn Eige rise to over 1,180m.

From a power station at the eastern end of Loch Mullardoch (below which is Glen Cannich, no mean contender in the beauty stakes) water is piped through to another station beside Loch Beneveian (the level of Beneveian has been raised, resulting in tiny islets; the level of Loch Affric, further west in a horseshoe of steep mountains, remains unchanged). Both Cannich and Affric can be approached from the village; the road up Cannich has been re-made, and runs through rugged, wooded country. The road ends at the dam; but beyond it a track continues beside Loch Mullardoch and Loch Lungard, now one loch, then over the hills to Glen Elchaig and Dornie (qv) – a walk of nearly 50km.

Similarly, from Cannich, there is first a road and then a track through the mountains to the west. Fasnakyle Power Station is an outstanding example of the way in which, almost invariably, the Hydro Board did its best to meet conservationist ideas twenty years before 'conservation' became fashionable: to fit in with the surroundings, they built the station of golden-yellow sandstone. Beyond this, the road goes by the wooded Chisholm's Pass and the Dog Fall; the picturesque beauty of the latter would not perhaps have been uppermost in the mind of a famous fugitive of 1746, for around here, after Culloden, Prince Charles Edward Stuart was hunted.

The track continues after Loch Beneveian under the Five Sisters of Kintail to the south-east end of Loch

Cape Wrath

brilliant and gannets plunging into the waves are a common sight – they are as frequent here as anywhere off the mainland, coming, it is believed, from the nesting places at St Kilda (qv), Sula Sgeir, and Sule Skerry.

The only road to Cape Wrath starts from the west side of the Kyle of Durness, opposite the hotel. During the summer months a small boat takes passengers across, and a minibus then goes the 18km. across the uninhabited moorland of The Parbh. Because of the sandbanks in the Kyle, this ferry cannot operate at low tide and the return run, if the water is getting low, may mean a leap across to slippery rocks. But it is a worthwhile journey; and while the highest cliffs along this coast, rising some 260m. near Cléit Dubh, are hardly seen from the lighthouse, those nearer at hand are immensely impressive. Looking south from the low hill above the lighthouse one can see SANDWOOD BAY, to which there is no road: so rarely visited (*see* Rhiconich) and so beautiful that it is almost possible to believe the claim that there are mermaids there.

Carradale   Strathclyde   3E4

If there is not too much traffic on the road – and in summer, particularly weekends, there is a fair amount of it – the walk from one end of this village to the other, through woods and down to the harbour, is delightful. It is a 2½km. walk, for there are three separate parts of this village off the road down the east side of Kintyre.

At the junction of the main road – in the valley of the Carradale Water, which winds under steep, tree-clad slopes – as well as a shop with a café, the school, and the police station, there are the local Forestry Commission office and houses, and an interesting Forest Centre, which school children and local inhabitants, as well as the forestry staff, created. Although on a small scale, it has an aviary and a 'snake pit' (adders and slow-worms) and is worth a visit. From nature trails leading up the hill the chances of seeing wild goats and golden eagle are not unreasonable.

Further east is the older Carradale village, rather spoilt by new housing; east again are more houses, which have grown around the harbour: fishing and forestry, and catering for visitors, are the mainstays of the place.

South of the harbour, on the cliffs, from which viewpoint gannets and the triangular fins of basking sharks are commonplace sights, the site of Carradale's castle is indicated by grassy mounds. At the end of Carradale Point are more obvious remains of a much older settlement: an oval vitrified fort, probably built by 300 BC, stands on an island that can be reached on foot except at high tide. And at least a thousand years older is Brackley Cairn, a megalithic tomb, which, though ruined, is easily distinguished. But the beaches (Carradale Bay is only the largest of several), the superb views to Arran across Kilbrennan Sound, and the fishing are perhaps the main attractions of this area.

Duich (*see* Shiel Bridge); and from Cannich to Loch Duich, almost 50km.

The two glens, Cannich and Affric, have an odd feature in common; each, to the north, is dominated by a Sgurr na Lapaich. They are completely different mountains, one 1,150m. high, the other 1,037m.

Of the two glens, without any pretence of classifying the 'finest in Scotland', Affric is undoubtedly the more attractive: it is best visited in the early summer before the onslaught of midges.

Cape Wrath   Highland   18C1

The Norsemen called it Hvarf, 'the turning point': for here, off the north-west extremity of mainland Britain, their galleys sailing west would turn south.

Cape Wrath is as apt a name in winter for this exposed place, where the lighthouse stands over 120m. above the sea; but in summer the colours can be idyllic, not only from the sea pinks, primula scotia, and other flowers, but in the cliffs themselves, with pink veins running through the Lewisian Gneiss. The skies can be

Remains of the early-C18 bridge at Carrbridge

Carrbridge Highland 15H5

On the main road and rail routes from Perth to Inverness, this village has been a popular fishing and touring centre in the summer months for many years. In common with other Spey Valley resorts, most of its few hotels and guest houses used to close for the winter; but with the introduction of ski facilities on the Cairngorm – in the development of which some of its residents played a leading part – Carrbridge became virtually an all-year-round centre.

An extra attraction was added in the 1960s with the opening of the Landmark Visitor Centre, claimed to be the first of its kind in Europe. The main exhibition tells of man's struggle to survive in the Highlands; and in a multi-screen theatre twenty-minute films on the history, wild life, and other aspects of the Highlands are vividly projected.

Beside today's bridge over the River Dulnain is the arch of an older bridge, built in 1715 by the Earl of Seafield for the use of funeral parties going to Duthill on the road to Dulnain Bridge. To the west, General Wade's military road runs briefly up the picturesque Sluggan Valley before turning north.

Cawdor Highland 15G3

This attractive village beside the River Nairn has a

church with a small but unusual tower: the tower, with a corbelled, embattled parapet, carries a 'helmet' crowned by a pyramid; the church dates back to the fourteenth century. Also in the village is an old mill of 1635.

But the village is well known for more than these. Shakespeare's Macbeth was greeted as Thane of Cawdor, and traditionally Duncan was murdered at Cawdor Castle, one of the finest castles in Scotland, still remarkably unspoiled, and first opened to the public in 1976. This seat of the Earl of Cawdor has as its core a tall tower believed to date from 1396, and certainly built not later than 1454, when a royal licence to crenellate was issued. The tower is surrounded by a deep ditch crossed by a drawbridge. There were additions in the sixteenth and seventeenth centuries. There are pleasant gardens and extensive grounds outside the Castle. Cawdor is not the only castle in the area. Two km. west is KILRAVOCK CASTLE, again based on a tall tower, built in 1460, to which a five-storey block with a steep, gabled roof was added in the seventeenth century: other buildings followed later. This seat of the Roses of Kilravock was visited by Mary Queen of Scots in 1562 and by Prince

Cawdor church, showing the unusual tower

Charles Edward Stuart two days before Culloden. Another 2km. south is DALCROSS CASTLE, built in 1620 by Lord Lovat. This imposing building later passed to the chief of Clan Mackintosh; following a period of neglect it has now been restored and is lived in. Yet another castle in this area is CASTLE STUART, which stands on the north side of the main Inverness–Nairn road (the A96), about 4km. north-west of Dalcross. The Castle was built by the Earl of Moray in 1625.

Of the four castles, only Cawdor is open to the public, although the others may be seen from nearby roads.

Colintraive Strathclyde 3G1
Holidaymakers stay at this village – it has a couple of small hotels – on the Kyles of Bute; but many more go through, looking at it only while waiting for the car ferry to take them across to Rudhabodach (Rhubodach) at the northern end of the island of Bute, with Rothesay some 13km. away. Yet Colintraive is an attractive place, and the Kyles of Bute, the strait that does a sharp horse-shoe bend between the island and the mainland, a most picturesque waterway, with narrows almost blocked, west of Colintraive, by the small Burnt Islands. On the Bute shore two standing stones, the Maids of Bute, are a prominent landmark.

South-east from Colintraive, a dead-end road follows the coast to Strone Point at the mouth of Loch Striven (not to be confused with the Strone Point at the foot of Loch Long, *see* Dunoon), which bites deep into the hills. There are no roads up either side of the loch; here, as along the shores of the Kyles, there is a wealth of bird life, which includes rafts of eider as well as other duck.

Coll Strathclyde 6A3
If depopulation were to be used as a yardstick, this island should be a depressing place. In 1801 it supported 1,162 people; by 1891 the number had dropped to 522; today (1976) only about 150 people live there, and the population is not greatly swollen in the summer months by holidaymakers. There is only one small hotel – at Arinagour – though a few cottages provide accommodation and there are several areas for camping. Usually, there are two boats a week to Coll, from Oban, and at summer weekends there is an air service from Glasgow via Oban and Mull.

Yet there is nothing depressing about this 20km.-long island. Approached from the sea, its east coast is un-invitingly rocky; but once the small port of Arinagour – the only village on the island – is left behind, Coll is found to have fertile farms as well as rocky moors, and its west coast is nearly all shell sand, machair, and dunes (some of which have been piled up many m. high) facing the open Atlantic.

It is pointless to take a car to an island that has not much over 30km. of road, and when it is well under an hour's walk from Arinagour to the west coast. It does not take much longer to walk to the south end of the island, to admire the views across to Mull. BREACHAHA CASTLE is at this end: in the early fourteenth century Robert the Bruce gave this castle to Angus Og of the Isles; in the following century it was successively taken by Mac-Donalds, MacNeils, and MacLeans in the incessant battling between clans. By 1431 a branch of the Mac-Leans of Mull established this as their seat and, presumably, built the present castle: it stood for some 300 years before it became uninhabitable.

In 1750 the rather ugly sham castle nearby was built, and it was there that Dr Johnson and James Boswell stayed, stormbound, for some days in October 1773. This enforced stay gave Dr Johnson an opportunity to write at some length about the island in his *A Journey to the Western Islands of Scotland*. Some of his comments are as apt today as they were 200 years ago: even he, no angler, commented on the 'many lochs, some of which have trouts and eels' (the brown trout fishing on Coll is particularly good). He also commented that 'the inhabitants of Col [*sic*] have not yet learned to be weary of their heath and rocks, but attend their agriculture and their dairies' – equally true today.

'There is not much to amuse curiosity', said Dr Johnson. This may still be true; but there is a quiet fascination about this low island (its highest point is only about 100m. above sea-level) with its views to the east and the knowledge that to the west the next land is over 3,000km. distant.

Colonsay and Oronsay   Strathclyde   7C7

Once these were three islands, Colonsay being split in two by the then water-filled Kiloran Glen. Now for much of the day they are one island: at low tide it is possible to walk from Colonsay to Oronsay.

There is a car ferry to the small harbour of Scalascaig on Colonsay, though it is not primarily intended for tourist use: there are less than 20km. of motorable road. Despite this and its small size – 13km. long and 5km. wide – Colonsay does attract visitors, and even has an eighteen-hole golf course.

But there is much more than the attraction of being on a small island with views of nearby islands – including Mull, Jura, and Islay. Here are the exotic Kiloran Gardens, among the most beautiful in Scotland (open to the public from April to September), where rhododendrons, azaleas, and magnolias create a wonderful

Castle Stuart (1625)

ABOVE: *Cross at Oronsay Priory, seen from the W*
LEFT: *Memorial slab in C 14 Oronsay Priory*

display of colour, and bamboo and palm trees flourish. These are the gardens of Colonsay House, the building of which, in 1722, explains in part the disappearance of the once famous Kiloran Abbey, said to have been founded by St Columba (*see* Iona): in the eighteenth century, it seems, the stones were regarded as a useful quarry.

Colonsay and Oronsay were leading religious centres

Connel Bridge : the photograph was taken before it became a road bridge

hundreds of years ago; while there are only traces of most of the dozen churches that were once on the two islands, the roofless ruins of the fourteenth-century priory on Oronsay are worth a visit.

There are some fine raised beaches and magnificent cliff scenery on the west coast of Colonsay, and kitti-wakes, guillemots, and razorbills breed there. As a con-trast, the woods – delightfully unexpected on an island open to the Atlantic breakers – are notable for their wealth of smaller birdlife; as another contrast, hundreds of barnacle geese winter on Oronsay, off whose southern-most point is a favourite haunt of seals.

And with but one small hotel and a few bed-and-breakfast places, these islands do not get overcrowded!

Connel Strathclyde 4B2
With a couple of hotels and other limited holiday accommodation, this village 8km. north-east of Oban has as its main feature a remarkably ugly bridge, which for over sixty years was the cause of some intense ill-feeling.

When built by the Callander & Oban Railway Com-pany in 1898–1903, this bridge carried a branch line from Oban to Ballachulish; crossing the narrows at the mouth of Loch Etive, it was the only place for people to cross on foot – but the company refused to allow it. Eventually, in 1909, the company permitted a shuttle service by a char-à-banc with flanged wheels, and intro-duced a flat wagon on which cars could be loaded and

taken across for fifteen shillings – a not inconsiderable sum. Pressed to open a carriageway for vehicles, the company consistently refused – until a local man pro-posed to start a chain ferry, when it rapidly changed its mind, and built a carriageway alongside the railway. Protests at the extortionate toll charges – and idiocies like a shepherd having to take a flock of sheep over one at a time – continued until, amid general rejoicing, the line closed down in 1966, and the infamous Connel Bridge became a toll-free road.

At the time of spring low tides particularly, the Falls of Lora – actually rapids – can be seen *en route* for Benderloch, with views across Lismore Island to Mor-vern (qv). Unfortunately a large caravan site mars the south of Benderloch, and another monopolizes the best sands at the north end.

Near Ledaig, a hillock, many centuries ago, carried a fort said to be Beregonium, a seat of Pictish kings, and so named in George Buchanan's sixteenth-century *History of Scotland*. It is also held to be associated with 'Deidre of the Sorrows', a prominent figure in Celtic mythology.

Beyond Beregonium the road comes to the shores of Loch Creran, and halfway along this loch a minor road goes inland through Gleann Salach, pleasantly wooded with, at the top, a fine view over Loch Etive to Ben Cruachan. A right-hand turn at the bottom of this road leads to the ruins of ARDCHATTAN PRIORY, a Valliscaulian house founded in 1230. Here, in 1308, Robert the Bruce called a Parliament, said to be the last at which business was conducted in Gaelic. The Priory was burned by Cromwell's troops in 1654, but some good stonework remains. The ruins are mixed up with a modern mansion not open to visitors, but they may nevertheless be seen.

The road up Loch Etive ends at Bonawe quarries (see Taynuilt), which are not an object of beauty. LOCH ETIVE bites deep into the hills, and at its head, Kinlochetive, a road leads through Glen Etive to Glen Coe (qv). Along the lochside are neither roads nor paths: the loch can only be seen – and impressive it is – by boat trips from Taynuilt.

Conon Bridge   Highland   15E2

The bridge over the River Conon that gave this village its name was built by Thomas Telford in 1809, and sufficed for traffic on the A9 from Inverness to Dingwall and the north for over 150 years. But although it was strengthened to take more traffic, it proved insufficient to meet the demands of the 1970s and is now bypassed by a new bridge, which has to cope with the traffic to and from the oil construction centres on the Cromarty Firth.

West from the village there are pleasant walks beside the river towards Contin, some 8km. away. *En route*, just north of the river, is the site of Brahan Castle, and nearby is the village of BRAHAN, in a charming setting. This is the place linked with the seventeenth-century Brahan Seer, famous for his prophecies (see Strathpeffer). Summoned to the Castle by the Countess of Seaforth, who was worried about the long absence of her husband, he tactlessly told her that the Earl was at that moment making love to a French woman. Furious, the Countess had him seized, tried for witchcraft, and burnt to death in a barrel of tar at Chanonry Point near Fortrose.

Not 5km. south of Conon Bridge on the A9 is Muir of Ord, now fringing on an industrial estate, but once a centre for cattle, sheep, and horse markets. It is most notable for the roads out of it – to Gairloch, Ullapool, and other north-west Highland places, and to the Black Isle (qv).

Coylumbridge   Highland   15H6

Only some 4km. east of Aviemore, this village on the road to Loch Morlich is utterly different from its brash, commercialized neighbour on the A9.

Although a major hotel was built at Coylumbridge to take advantage of the developments at Aviemore (and was opened while the Aviemore Centre was still building), it fits into the Highland picture convincingly, as do the few other 'tourist developments' here. This is fortunate; for south of Coylumbridge, gained almost immediately by the B970 running south on the east side of the Spey, and by other roads and tracks from around Coylumbridge, is one of the most beautiful areas of the Spey Valley, the ROTHIEMURCHUS FOREST. This is one of the few areas where the native Scots pine still survives,

and is part of the Glen More Forest Park. It is a beautifully-wooded area lying under the westerly spur of the Cairngorms, which rises to over 1,100m. Its gem is LOCH-AN-EILEAN, around which there is a nature trail – details are obtainable from the small cottage 'Visitor Centre' at the south-west end of the loch. On an island are the stout ruins of a castle that was a fortress of the Wolf of Badenoch (see Grantown-on-Spey).

Coylumbridge is also the northerly end of the most famous mountain walk in Scotland, the LAIRIG GHRU, which goes through the great cleft in the hills between Braeriach (1,295m.) and Ben Macdui (1,313m.) and reaches a height of 838m. before dropping down to upper Deeside west of Braemar. The 'rough-walking' part of this track is over 30km. long, and near the top is the 'Shelter Stone', ringed by precipices some 25m. high: it is the only shelter on a route that alternates between rough rocks and high moor, the latter often sodden.

Six km. east of Coylumbridge lies Loch Morlich and the approach road to the chairlift (see Glen More Forest Park). Not twenty years ago this was a forest road, and beyond Loch Morlich only a track; now, with the development of winter sports and a vast increase in summer traffic – attracted by Aviemore and other tourist developments – it has been made into a fairly wide metalled road, very necessary for what it has to carry.

Crinan   Strathclyde   4A5

While there is a village of Crinan – an attractive one at that – at first sight the place seems to be nothing but boats. For this is the western end of the Crinan Canal, which cuts across the north of Knapdale (qv), linking Loch Fyne with the Sound of Jura.

This canal, 14½km. long, was built by John Rennie and opened in 1801, to save fishing vessels the long sail round the Mull of Kintyre. Its worth was enhanced with the opening of the Caledonian Canal (qv); and while it was never designed for big ships, it nevertheless carries hundreds of fishing boats and coasters, and as many yachts and powered pleasure craft, every year. Despite this traffic, it is said to lose the British Waterways Board £10,000 a year; but (though it may be no consolation to the Board) it brings very considerable prosperity to Crinan and to Lochgilphead and Ardrishaig at its eastern end.

For those without boats, a minor road from Cairnbaan, 3km. north of Lochgilphead, runs beside the Canal. It tends to be busy in summer; but it is possible to walk along the north side of the Canal; and walking, sailing, or cruising, it is a delightful journey, with the low, wooded hills of the Knapdale Forest stretching for much of the way above the south bank. The 'climbing' is negligible, for the highest point of the Canal is 27m. above sea-level, necessitating fifteen locks.

Three km. due north of Cairnbaan, the hill-fort Dunadd (see Kilmartin) stands on a hillock in the Moine

Mhor, the flat land between the main road to Oban and Crinan Loch. There is an extensive collection of standing stones and cairns in this area.

On the north side of Crinan Loch, opposite the village, DUNTRUNE CASTLE stands on a rocky outcrop by the cliff edge. Originally a plain Highland tower, built perhaps in the twelfth century (and thus among the oldest stone castles in Scotland), another tower house – just as plain – was added in the late sixteenth century. This was Campbell country, and the Castle was said to be haunted by the ghost of a Macdonald piper killed in the seventeenth century by the Campbells. The ghost, in comparatively recent years, was exorcized by an Episcopalian clergyman: whether effective or not, the Castle is now comfortably lived in and not open to the public.

A much earlier and less comfortable habitation is found at the northerly point of Crinan Loch. This is the circular Ardifuer Dun, an Iron Age fort, which stands, inexplicably, not on high ground but in a flat valley.

Cromarty Highland 15G1 (*pop.* 503)
Few small towns – and Cromarty is a very small town – have seen more changes in circumstance than this one.

At the northern tip of the Black Isle (qv), Cromarty lies on the south side of the narrows, the Sutors of Cromarty, that guard the sheltered waters of the Cromarty Firth, which have been a haven for ships for centuries. Cromarty was once a prosperous port as well as a fishing harbour; but this prosperity declined to such an extent that by the late seventeenth century it abandoned its status as a royal burgh, which in earlier days had given it the right to hold markets. After a hundred years of near-dereliction, the place was bought by George Ross of Pitkerie: he built the harbour and established cloth and other factories; but these, along with a brewery, flourished only until the railway was built along the west coast of the Firth. Cromarty's trade moved to Invergordon (qv), which was on the railway, and only the fishing remained.

More recently it has become a popular holiday place in the summer months. As well as a number of seventeenth- and eighteenth-century houses, there is the Court House of 1782, the cupola and clock of which have been a landmark since its building by George Ross, and the parish church, whose woodwork, erected in 1700, includes an ornate loft for the laird and a simpler one for

The Crinan Canal at Crinan

TOP: *Cromarty church: the 'simple' W loft*   BOTTOM: *Cromarty church: the 'ornate' E loft*

poorer folk. At the Fishertown the old cottages have been well restored, and there is a small craft centre there.

Cromarty has had two notable residents. One was the eccentric Sir Thomas Urquhart, translator of Rabelais; Sir Thomas was sheriff of this area. Exiled to the Continent when Cromwell came to power, he is said to have died with joy on hearing of the Restoration. The other was Hugh Miller, who was born in 1802 in a thatched cottage built in 1711 by his buccaneering great-grandfather John Fiddes. At the age of seventeen he became a stonemason; and for fifteen years this craft enabled him to make the geological observations particularly connected with the Old Red Sandstone quarries in which he worked. His health failing, he was forced to turn to lighter work and began writing – at first poems and legends, then theological works, which made him a centre of religious argument. His fame, however, came from the publication of *The Old Red Sandstone* in 1841, the year after he went to Edinburgh to edit an evangelical newspaper. His other works are forgotten, but this and subsequent similar publications established his importance as an early geologist. He shot himself on Christmas Eve, 1856.

Miller's birthplace at Cromarty, now cared for by the NTS, is an interesting museum of his life and work.

During the two World Wars the Firth was a haven for the Royal Navy. Then came North Sea oil: Cromarty looks across to Nigg Bay and the vast constructions around the largest graving dock in the world for the fabrication of steel production platforms. That, too, will end in due course; but early in 1976 planning permission was given for the construction of a large oil refinery at Nigg that could even undermine the North Sutor. Cromarty lies under the South Sutor, and will have a grandstand view of this development.

Culloden Highland 15G3

Twenty months after raising his standard at Glenfinnan (qv), Prince Charles Edward Stuart met his final defeat at Culloden Moor, some 8km. south-east of Inverness, on 16 April 1746.

It was a brief battle, lasting less than an hour; the Jacobite troops, hungry and in disarray after an all-night march, numbered some 5,000 men; the Duke of Cumberland had about 9,000 well-disciplined soldiers, including artillery and 800 mounted dragoons. The result was a massacre, the rights and wrongs of which have been argued ever since. Certain it is that after the battle the Government troops had no mercy for Prince Charles's Highlanders: the atrocities committed on the wounded and on prisoners earned the Duke the name of 'Butcher Cumberland'.

The battle, the last to be fought on British soil, is often represented as being between the English and the Scots; in fact there were more Scots in Cumberland's army than in the Prince's: the battle was between the old order and the new.

Whatever the rights and wrongs, however, a sadness still seems to brood over Culloden Moor. The scene has changed: in 1746 it was a bleak, treeless moorland; to-day, the surroundings are well-wooded and the roads to and through the battlefield bring up to 100,000 visitors a year to see the memorials to the battle. These memorials include the Well of the Dead, the Graves of the Clans, and a 6m.-high cairn erected in 1881. Much of the battlefield is now in the care of the NTS, which has a Visitor Centre at the site (there the story of the battle is told). Old Leanach Cottage, once a farmhouse, survived the battle, and now houses a museum.

Even were it not for the battlefield, Culloden would be of interest. Nearby are some quite notable archaeological remains – the Stones of Clava, a group of three chambered cairns, each surrounded by a stone circle. The line of the cairns suggests that they may have had an astronomical purpose; it also appears likely that the stone circles were erected c. 1600 BC around Neolithic cairns built much earlier.

Three km. north-west from the battlefield is Culloden House. It is said that Prince Charles stayed in the previous house on this site, owned by Duncan Forbes of Culloden, then Lord President of the Court of Session. That house was later burnt down; the present building, completed in 1783, is in Adam style and in 1975 became a hotel.

South-east from Culloden Moor, a minor road, the B851, goes up the valley of the River Nairn and in 4½km. joins the main A9. Going south on the A9 one comes to Daviot church, an attractive landmark with an unusual steeple. There has been a church here for centuries, but the present one was built in 1828.

Dalmally Strathclyde 4D2

With a hotel that can offer 10km. of salmon fishing on a tumultuous river, this village between the foot of Glen Orchy and Loch Awe ranks high for the angler as a place to stay in. But it is not only the fisherman with his eye on those beats on the River Orchy that makes this a lively centre throughout the holiday season. The river also attracts motoring families, who can drive up Glen Orchy, a beautiful valley between shapely mountains, picnic by its banks, and join the main road to Glencoe and Fort William at Bridge of Orchy (qv). The deep pools in the Glen can be admired, but they are not without hazard: one slip on the rocks can have – and has had – fatal results.

The mountaineer can start the ascent of 1,130m. Ben Lui – and get superb views of more mountains from the top – from a short way east of Dalmally: the path starts near Inverlochy where glens Orchy and Lochy meet.

The less energetic traveller can walk up the old road to Inveraray to the monument at the top, which commemorates the most famous of Gaelic bards, Duncan Ban MacIntyre, who was born at Inveroran, by Loch Tulla, in 1724. From the monument there is a fine view

The Stones of Clava, Culloden

along Loch Awe, to which the road drops down in under 3km.

Dalwhinnie Highland 9F3
The main road north from the Pass of Drumochter (qv) drops down to Dalwhinnie (in summer the occasional snowplough beside it is a reminder of the harshness of the area: in winter these snowploughs are in frequent use keeping the road open).

Dalwhinnie, which stands at 360m. among bare, high moors, and with the Cairngorm mountains too far away to make a scenic impact, has a distinct bleakness about it, though the pagoda-like towers of the nearby distillery add a touch of fantasy.

The village itself is now bypassed, the new line of the A9 lying on the east side of Glen Truim. From the village, near the distillery, is the road to Laggan (qv); it was across these forbidding moors that General Wade built his road over the Corrieyairack Pass to Fort Augustus.

South-west from Dalwhinnie, narrow LOCH ERICHT stretches for 25km. It is dammed at its southern end, and its waters taken through a tunnel to the power station on Loch Rannoch. Seen from around Dalwhinnie, Loch

Ericht is dark and forbidding; its main scenic feature is the fine peak of Ben Alder on the Highland side (the south-east shores are in the Tayside region). Here, hanging on the side of the mountain, in 'Cluny's Cage', a sort of hut hidden among low trees, the Highland chief Cluny MacPherson hid for nearly ten years after the defeat of Prince Charles's army at Culloden.

The BEN ALDER FOREST, the peaks in which rise to over 1,100m., is among the wildest and least accessible country in the Highlands: the only tracks are along the lochside from Dalwhinnie – for nearly 20km. before an ascent of Ben Alder can be started – or from Loch Laggan.

Dingwall Highland 15E2 (*pop.* 4,379)
For many years the administrative centre of the county (now the district) of Ross & Cromarty, Dingwall can claim a respectable history. The Norsemen founded it in *c.* 1034, calling it *Thing vollr*, or the 'Place of Parliaments': it was an administrative centre even then.

Macbeth is said to have been born here in 1040; William the Lion built a royal castle here at the end of the twelfth century; Robert the Bruce's queen was im-

prisoned here; and Dingwall was a stronghold of the
Earls of Ross until 1476. But there is virtually nothing
left to remind of these, or subsequent, incidents in a
stirring history. Even the pre-Reformation church was
destroyed when a citizen somehow set fire to it while
shooting pigeons, though the old Town House of 1730
remains.

It is as a centre of a rich agricultural district that
Dingwall flourishes, with notable livestock markets.
Until recently it was also notable for its traffic jams: the
main road north, the A9, went through the town and
turned awkwardly in the middle of the main street. Now,

happily, the town is bypassed: the summer holidaymakers going somewhere else, and the vastly increased
commercial traffic to and from the Cromarty Firth, all
year round, worrying it no longer.

Dornie Highland 14A5
Just south of the village of Dornie, where Loch Duich
meets Loch Alsh, lies EILEAN DONAN CASTLE.

When the A87 to Kyle of Lochalsh left the lochside at
Inverinate and climbed over the hill to Dornie, Eilean
Donan came suddenly into sight below, with the Cuillins
of Skye in the distance. But now that the road follows

Eilean Donan Castle, S of Dornie

the coast all the way the view at water-level is not so impressive: there is a viewpoint where the old road was, but the sudden effect is lost, and now, as often as not, Eilean Donan is pictured from just across the bridge west of the village, looking up Loch Duich to the Five Sisters of Kintail, a wonderful range of mountains rising to over 1,050m.

But whatever way it is looked at, Eilean Donan and its surroundings are the epitome of 'romantic' Highland scenery. The islet on which the Castle stands, now linked to the shore by a bridge, held a fort in prehistoric times; the present castle was built about 1230 to guard against Norse invaders. It had a stormy history thereafter, and finally fell in the abortive Jacobite rising of 1719. It lay in ruins for nearly 200 years until restoration started in 1912: it took twenty years to complete. The impressive

interior contains a memorial to the Macraes, who held the castle for the Mackenzies.

Dornie itself is only a small village, with a few shops, a hotel, and a small amount of other holiday accommodation, including some at Ardelve, across the bridge. From Dornie a minor road leads beside Loch Long to the foot of Glen Elchaig for the rough walk to one of the highest falls in Britain, the FALLS OF GLOMACH, which drop 113m. For the arduous ascent to these falls stout footwear and abundant energy are essential.

Dornoch Highland 21B7
Even before this spacious, if small, town was created a Royal Burgh in 1628, golf was being played along the links beside the sea. There are many ardent golfers who maintain that the game here excels that available any-

Loch Duich, looking S from Kintail towards Glen Shiel

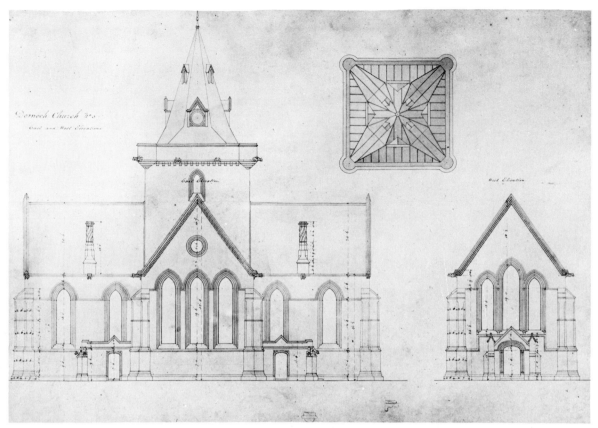

William Burn's drawing (1835) for the reconstruction of Dornoch's cathedral

where else in Scotland – not excluding the 'Old Course' at St Andrews. A leading golf writer in 1974 put the fourteenth hole at Royal Dornoch as one of 'the best eighteen holes in Scotland'; and added: 'At Dornoch you are in another world and the panoramic views in that part of the country must be seen to be believed'.

Golf had been played for nearly a century when the course became the scene of a less sporting activity. A rough stone marks where the last woman to be judicially executed for witchcraft in Scotland was tarred, feathered, and burnt to death in 1722. She was Janet Horn, accused of turning her daughter into a pony that was then shod by the Devil.

Dornoch's small cathedral, with a low tower and squat spire oddly out of keeping with the high roof, was begun around 1224 by Gilbert de Moravia, Bishop of Caithness, although it had been established seventy-five years earlier on the site of a Culdee monastery. It does not have the patina of age, however: badly damaged by fire in 1570, it was neglected thereafter; the nave was not rebuilt until 1835–7, and there was extensive restoration in 1924, which revealed some thirteenth-century

stonework. Sixteen Earls of Caithness are buried here; there is a statue by Sir Francis Chantrey of the first Duke of Sutherland, who died in 1838, and an effigy of the Bishop's brother, Richard de Moravia, who was killed in battle with the Danes at Embo, 3km. north, in 1248. The fire of 1570 also destroyed all but the tower of the Bishop's Castle, now part of a hotel.

The majority of Dornoch's visitors do not come for historic interest, or even golf, but for the long beaches stretching south from the town: the over-large caravan/camping site is easily left behind.

The road to EMBO is worth following, particularly in late spring/early summer, when it is brilliant with acres of gorse and broom. Embo also is disfigured, and its beaches restricted, by an extensive caravan site; as at Dornoch, fortunately, its holidaymakers do not move far.

Drumbeg Highland 18B4
The minor road dignified by the number B869 wanders and climbs round the coast from Lochinver to Kylescu, by bays with wonderful views. One of the most delightful

TOP: *The peaks of Quinag seen across Loch Cairnbawn*   BOTTOM: *Castle Urquhart, nr Drumnadrochit*

of these is near Drumbeg, a crofting township that has some good fishing lochs near to hand. From here there is a superb view of the long ridge of Quinag, rising to 810m., across Loch Nedd; seawards, you look across the scatter of islands in Eddrachilis Bay; and eastwards the road drops to the head of the loch to climb very steeply, with acute Z-bends, over to Loch Cairnbawn.

Drumnadrochit Highland 15E4
From this village at the foot of Glen Urquhart there is a picturesque road west up the glen to Strath Glass. Another road goes north up Glen Convinth over high moors to Beauly. But it is to Loch Ness that most eyes turn, for it is from this area that sightings of the 'Monster' are usually reported.

A more certain attraction stands on a promontory jutting into the loch east of the village. CASTLE URQUHART, once one of the largest in the Highlands, is in a superbly strategic position, with views along the loch almost to Inverness, 20km. north-east, and almost to Fort Augustus, 26km. south-west. It is believed there was a royal castle on the site in the twelfth century; but this would probably have been refashioned in the next century by Alan Durward, the first recorded Lord of Urquhart, who had vast possessions in Scotland and was brother-in-law of Alexander II. The Castle was too important strategically ever to be peaceful for long. Edward I gained control of it in 1296; in 1308 it was retaken by Robert the Bruce; and in the conflict between the Scottish Crown and the Lords of the Isles it saw warfare for over 200 years, enduring frequent repair, rebuilding, and strengthening.

By 1527, according to the historian Boece, the Castle was a ruin; but during the sixteenth century there was major reconstruction by John Grant of Freuchie, then Lord of Urquhart. By the end of the seventeenth century it was in ruin again: the local inhabitants found it a useful quarry – a practice that even the law courts could not stop – and in 1715 a storm did yet more damage.

Despite all this, the extensive ruins are well worth a visit.

Drumochter Highland 9G3
This is the main road and rail pass into the Highland region from the south. The road, the A9 from Perth to Inverness, originally built by General Wade in 1729, and redesigned by Telford a hundred years later, reaches a height of 463m.; the adjacent railway line tops the pass at a height of 457m.; then each drops down to the Spey Valley.

The scenery is drearily bleak except in winter, when the oddly-named mountains to the west, the Sow of Atholl and the Boar of Badenoch, each over 770m. high, are often snow-covered; they are an impressive sight. At this time of the year, too, large herds of red deer may often be seen feeding by the roadside, unworried by

traffic, which in summer months is too heavy for pleasurable driving – but there is no alternative for the motorist going from Perthshire to the Spey Valley.

Dunbeath Highland 20E4
Most of this rather attractive fishing village lies off the main road. Walk down to the harbour for a view of Dunbeath Castle (not open to the public): based on a fifteenth-century keep, this castle in a spectacular cliff-edge setting was built around 1633, but was considerably extended in the nineteenth century. In 1650 it was besieged by Montrose for three days before it capitulated – though Montrose, in his turn, was soon to suffer defeat at Carbisdale (*see* Invershin).

The village stands at the foot of the Dunbeath Water, joined just outside the bridge by other streams, which drain from the low hills west and north. Here, as all along the hinterland of this coast, are remains of brochs and other early settlements; the nearest, Dunbeath Broch, on a knoll only about 1km. from the town, is sadly neglected.

Some 3km. north-east of Dunbeath is the Laidhaye Croft Museum, housed in a low, thatched, eighteenth-century 'long-house'; the collection includes an interesting variety of domestic relics. Both cottage and adjacent barn are of cruck-roof construction.

A minor road from just south of Dunbeath leads over the hills for about 10km. to Braemore on the Berriedale Water: on the moors a granite cross marks where the Duke of Kent was killed when his plane crashed in 1942.

Dundonnell Highland 19B7
There is little more than a pleasant hotel and a youth hostel at this village set at the head of Little Loch Broom. But from here is the comparatively easy track up perhaps the finest mountain ridge on the Scottish mainland – AN TEALLACH, whose eleven red Torridonian Sandstone peaks stretch for 5km., and whose summit, Bidean a' Ghlas Thuill, is 1,062m. above sea-level. An Teallach means 'The Forge', and no doubt derives from the mists often seen rising smokily around the tops. In fine weather the ascent is a magnificent walk, in part up a glacial moraine; the ridge walk is not difficult for the reasonably agile and well-shod, and the views are superb. A possible bonus is the sight of a golden eagle soaring over the precipice.

Under the great cliffs of Sgurr Fiona, at a height of about 600m., the small loch Toll an Lochain lies in a horseshoe of great hills: it, also, may be reached by a path from Dundonnell.

'The Smiddy', the climbers' hut of the Junior Mountaineering Club of Scotland, close to the main road near Dundonnell, won an award made by the Association for the Preservation of Rural Scotland in European Architectural Heritage year (1975). It retains the forge, tools, and equipment from the old smithy.

Dundonnell House, built in 1769, has Japanese gardens and an aviary, and is occasionally open to the

public under Scotland's Gardens Scheme. From
Dundonnell, 'Destitution Road' leads to Braemore (qv).

Dunnet Highland 20E1

A 4km. crescent of sand, with dunes behind, runs south-
west from this village on the northern end of beautiful
Dunnet Bay to Castletown.

In the 1970s there was a proposal to establish oil construction projects in the Bay. Protests were followed by a
public enquiry, but by the time the Secretary of State
for Scotland had agreed to the proposal, the developers
had withdrawn and gone elsewhere. Dunnet Bay's sands
are left to holidaymakers.

Dunnet, though only a scattered hamlet, has a hotel
and a small white church with a saddleback tower, which
possibly dates back to the fourteenth century. Timothy
Pont, an early cartographer, was minister here from
1601 to 1608.

North from Dunnet, a minor road goes by St John's
Loch, with good trout fishing, to DUNNET HEAD, the
most northerly point on the Scottish mainland. It is
crowned by a lighthouse that, though standing over
100m. above the sea, is liable to have its windows shattered by stones hurled up in the fierce winter storms of
the Pentland Firth, one of the roughest stretches of sea in
Europe. In fine weather there are magnificent views
across the Firth to Orkney (qv) and along much of the
north coast. The lighthouse may be visited, and the cliffs
below it are the haunt of puffins and other sea birds; the
lochans on this promontory also have fascinating birdlife – including divers – and there is rich botanical
interest.

CASTLETOWN, at the other end of Dunnet Bay, is considerably larger (*pop. c.* 800): it was founded early in the
nineteenth century when local quarries started large-
scale production of flagstones. The small harbour built
to send these flagstones to Edinburgh, Glasgow, and
other cities remains, and reminders of this trade can be
seen in the frequent use of flagstones in Caithness for
walls between fields. An unusual feature of Castletown is
the trees planted at Castlehill, once the home of James
Traill (who started the quarrying industry): trees are not
a normal feature of the Caithness landscape.

Some 5km. east of Dunnet, CASTLE O' MEY, or Barro-
gill Castle, stands near the coast. Its building was
started in 1567 by George Sinclair, fourth Earl of Caithness; restored and improved, it is now owned by the
Queen Mother and is not open to the public, though the
gardens are occasionally open under Scotland's Gardens
Scheme.

Dunoon Strathclyde 3H1   (*pop.* 8,899)

For many decades, from the mid nineteenth almost to
the mid twentieth century, two Firth of Clyde resorts
were pre-eminent as destinations for holidaymakers
sailing from Glasgow. Dunoon's only rival was Rothesay
on the island of Bute (qv).

The first recorded holidaymakers to Dunoon went in
1779, hiring a wherry and taking most of a day to voyage
from Glasgow. They had to take all their provisions
with them; they ran on to a sandbank; and on arrival
they found that only the local minister spoke English:
the other inhabitants of this then rather miserable village
spoke Gaelic.

But by 1822 the first of many mansions and villas to
be built by Glasgow people at Dunoon was under construction. This was for Provost James Ewing, MP, and
was a mock castle called Marine Villa. In 1893 it was
transformed into the local Council Chambers: other
subsequent and similar villas round Dunoon's East Bay
and West Bay are now, mostly, hotels or guest houses.

Dunoon has no buildings of particular interest. Only
a few scattered stones remain of the Castle, which was
once the seat of the High Stewards (from whom came the
Stewarts) of Scotland. The statue on Castle Hill of
Robert Burns's 'Highland Mary' was erected in 1896,
110 years after Mary Campbell died at Greenock. She
came from near Dunoon; but whether the poet intended
to marry her, and the cause of her death, are questions
that still arouse controversy.

Along the coast from the town there are some 6km. of
promenade: north, the road goes beside the coast to
Kirn, Hunter's Quay, and Sandbank (long famous for
yacht building) to the head of the Holy Loch, disfigured by the USA nuclear-submarine base and,
latterly, with laid-up oil tankers. South, similarly, the
road goes along the coast, with houses all the way on the
landward side, and by Innellan, to Toward Point. Beyond this, at Ardyne Point, by the mouth of Loch
Striven, a big yard for the construction of concrete platforms for North-Sea-oil operations was started in 1973.

The views across the Firth of Clyde are pleasant
without being in any way outstanding. The same could
be said of Dunoon itself.

Dunoon is a well-known yachting and sailing centre.
But the main event of the year is the Cowal Highland
Gathering, a two-day event at the end of August, held at
the Sports Stadium (built to full international standard)
outside the town. At this, Highlandry is rampant; in
addition to full-scale Highland Games, including piping,
dancing, caber-tossing, hammer-throwing, and the like,
there is the March of a Thousand Pipers from the stadium
to the town. The 'thousand' is no exaggeration: in
recent years up to 1,500 pipers and drummers have
taken part, making this the most spectacular event in
the calendar of Highland Games in Scotland.

Dunoon, however, is wise enough to realize that its
visitors are likely to have considerably varying require-
ments; it will produce a leaflet on nature trails as readily
as an accommodation list; with Loch Eck and the South
Argyll Forest Park (*see* Benmore) just beyond the Holy
Loch, there is ample scope for walking and nature
interests.

One diversion enjoyed by generations of holidaymakers has, alas, almost completely disappeared. Dunoon was a major port of call for the cruising trips around the Firth of Clyde, an extensive programme of which was available into the 1960s. By 1976, however, the Caledonian-MacBrayne cruising fleet had been reduced to one vessel: a car ferry from Gourock is now the usual approach to the resort.

Durness Highland 18D2
This small village, which is, incidentally, the most northwesterly settlement on mainland Britain, is of considerable interest.

Not far south from Durness is a bare, rocky landscape, but around the village are more grass and less heather, and far fewer stones and boulders, for the basic rock here is an outcrop of Durness Limestone. It is this that accounts, also, for one of the features of Durness, the SMOO CAVES east of the village.

Seen from the cliffs above, the Allt Smoo River plunges down a hole and flows through caves below that it has scoured out of this softer rock. There are three caves, only the outer of which can be seen on foot: but this is immensely impressive, measuring 10m. high, 62m. long, and 40m. wide; and there is a great arch of an entrance, 16m. high. Access to the second cave, into which the waterfall from above descends, is difficult; the third is virtually impossible.

Just west of Durness is BALNAKEIL, where a ruined church of 1619 has a pre-Reformation font. In the churchyard a tombstone has an odd inscription to Donald Macmurchow; and Rob Donn, an illiterate Gaelic poet referred to by enthusiasts as the 'Burns of the North', is buried here.

A much more modern interest at Balnakeil is on the site of the World War II radar station, the ugly concrete blocks of which were, in the usual manner of HM Forces, left behind after their purpose was served. This unpromising place was improbably scheduled to be an industrial estate; as matters turned out, only craftsmen were interested and it became Balnakeil Craft Village, with potters, artists, and others in residence making and selling their wares.

From Balnakeil church it is a 5km. walk along the dunes to FAR OUT HEAD – an Anglicanization of the Gaelic *Fear Ard* (literally 'High Fellow'). From the headland, 100m. above the sea, are superb views across Loch Eriboll (qv) to Whiten Head in the east, to the Reay Forest hills in the south, and to Cape Wrath (qv) in the west; and round the headland itself are myriads of puffins, auks, and other seabirds.

The ferry (no cars), which is the start of a visit to Cape Wrath, goes from Keoldale, on the east shore of the Kyle of Durness, 5km. south of Durness.

Duror Highland 8B5
For some months after the regionalization of local government in Scotland, in May 1975, this village had

the novel experience of being both in the Highland and Strathclyde regions: the boundary passed through it. Commonsense prevailed in due course.

Nearby ACHARN was the home of James Stewart of the Glen, central figure in the Appin murder mystery. Colin Campbell of Glenure, known as the 'Red Fox', was government factor for Appin and pursued a policy of evicting Stewarts to replace them with Campbells. At Kentallan, just north of Duror, he was shot; and although one Alan Breck Stewart was suspected of the murder, as he could not be found James Stewart was arrested instead, taken to Inveraray, tried by a jury that included eleven Campbells, and hanged. Although almost certainly he was a victim of outstanding injustice, his story would probably have been lost among many such others had it not been for Robert Louis Stevenson's inclusion of the incident, however embroidered, in his *Kidnapped*.

Little is usually said of Duror beyond a recounting of this grim link: but it is a pleasant place with a good inn, Cuil Bay is within easy walking distance, and wooded Glen Duror goes under the steep slopes of the shapely Ben Vair ridge – Sgurr Dhonuill and Sgurr Dhearg, each over 1,000m. high.

Eriboll Highland 18D2
This small township is on the east side of Loch Eriboll, biggest of the three sea lochs that bite deep into the northern coast. Over 16km. long and more than 100m. deep in places, the loch was used as a naval anchorage in World War II – and became known to the crews as Loch 'Orrible.

Because of the loch's deep, sheltered waters there have been suggestions at times that the township should be developed as a major New Town; there have also been proposals to develop diatomite: the area has a considerable number of limestone outcrops. But the only road to the place is single track, twisting and exposed to bitter conditions in winter. So far even oil-plant developers have not been tempted to this wild, least inhabited area of Britain.

At the head of the loch, make suitable noises under 284m. Craig na Faoilinn and there will be some remarkable echoes. The north-east end of the loch is WHITEN HEAD – great cliffs, and caves that are the only place on the mainland where the Atlantic grey seal breeds. There is no access by road; but boat trips from Durness (qv) go there in the summer.

Eriskay Highland 22E3
Every morning (except Sundays) a mail ferry leaves Eriskay for Ludag on South Uist (qv), and it returns about half an hour later. That is the only regular service for Eriskay; but it is possible to hire a boat at Ludag. Eriskay is a bare and rocky island; but its main township, holding perhaps 200 people, who live mainly by fishing, is a colourful centre on the bay that bites deep into the

east coast: there is colour not only in the houses but in the lazybeds and grass that lie between the long ridges of rock around the bay. Here, as on Fair Isle (qv), the women knit unique patterns into shawls and jerseys, which are an Eriskay 'export' to the mainland: this is no decaying community, for modern fishing boats with local crews operate from here.

Eriskay has other claims to notice. It was here that Prince Charles Edward Stuart first landed on Scottish soil, on 23 July 1745, for the start of the most famous of the Jacobite risings (*see* Glenfinnan). It was here that Mrs Marjory Kennedy-Fraser collected folk songs (of which the 'Love Lilt' is the best known); and it was here that the S.S. *Politician*, carrying 20,000 cases of whisky, was wrecked in 1941, an incident that inspired Compton Mackenzie's *Whisky Galore*.

The island is full of interest; but, were there a path, the length of Eriskay could be walked in under an hour.

Evanton   Highland   15F1

This village was deliberately founded in 1810, on a piece of waste ground south of the River Glass, and hence has a neater appearance than many villages that have developed more spontaneously. The original settlement on the north side of the river, known as Drummond, has disappeared.

Although inevitably affected by construction developments for North Sea oil – Invergordon (qv), only 13km. further along the Cromarty Firth, offers more remunerative employment (though less security) than forestry and similar occupations – Evanton still has interest for the visitor. West from the village, a path leads off the road to a spectacular, 3km.-long ravine, the BLACK ROCK OF NOVAR; here the River Glass cuts through a gorge in which, at one point, there are cliffs 34m. high and only 5m. apart. The road west from Evanton continues almost to Loch Glass, under the northern slopes of Ben Wyvis (*see* Strathpeffer).

Above the main road north-west from Evanton is one of the odder monuments in Scotland – a replica of the Gates of Negapatam, which General Sir Hector Munro of Novar (1726–1805) had built on Knock Fyrish Hill to give work to local men at a time of poverty and unemployment.

At Novar Toll, between Evanton and Alness, the main road forks, the A9 continuing north-east at low level, and the 'top road', the A836, climbing over the hills to rejoin the A9 beside the Dornoch Firth, saving the detour round the coast by Tain. In summer this road is usually followed (in winter it is at times impassable) not only because it is a short cut but also because it gives some fine inland views. In recent years it has become even more desirable for the visitor who does not look for the ravages of industrialization.

Two km. beyond Novar Toll on the A9, ALNESS is a village that until recently consisted only of a string of undistinguished buildings along the road, with agri-

culture, forestry, and sawmilling as its main industries. Now it has become a dormitory town for Invergordon; the population has at least trebled, and a considerable amount of unimaginative local-authority housing surrounds the landward side of the village; Alness has also acquired the social problems such rapid expansion entails.

Fair Isle   Highland   23D8

Although not 5km. long and only about 3km. across, this island halfway between Orkney and Shetland has two widely-differing claims to fame.

On the one hand, there are the intricate, lovely patterns in the knitting done, with remarkable speed, by the women of the island. Where the inspiration for these designs originally came from is unknown: at one time it was said that the islanders learnt them from some 200 Spaniards whose galleon was wrecked here after its escape from the defeat of the Armada in 1588. The galleon was said to be the flagship of the Duke of Medina Sidonia; but while such a ship was certainly wrecked on Fair Isle, the likelihood of its crew having had such a knowledge of design is remote indeed. There is also the suggestion that the patterns are of Norse origin; but it is equally feasible to believe that they were the inspiration of the island women themselves. Whatever their origin, they are known far beyond Scotland and sought after, doubtless, by many who have but little idea where Fair Isle is.

The island's other notable asset is the Fair Isle Bird Observatory, about the origins of which there is no doubt. The Scots ornithologist George Waterston managed to scrape together enough money to buy the island and in 1948 established a bird observatory in a disused naval camp. In 1954 the island was taken into the care of the NTS, and in 1969 a new purpose-built observatory was established; this provides hostel accommodation for birdwatchers and naturalists.

Some 300 species of bird have been noted on the island; there are breeding colonies of great and Arctic skuas, and other breeding species include storm petrel, fulmar, shag, eider, kittiwake, razorbill, and puffin.

The NTS has done much to improve living conditions on Fair Isle. Crofters' houses have been brought up to modern standards with electricity, water, and drainage; the pier has been extended; and a radio-telephone link established. All this has been done in an attempt to arrest depopulation. Before 1939 about 100 people lived on Fair Isle; but this had dropped to not much over forty by the mid 1960s.

The island is also known as 'sheep island', and sheep form part of the crofting economy, which includes lobster fishing as well as knitting and weaving.

Twice a week in summer and once a week in winter the *Good Shepherd* does the three-hour trip from North Haven on Fair Isle to Sumburgh in Shetland, returning, weather permitting, the same day: gales may disrupt

Castle Tioram in the south channel of Loch Moidart

Cul Mor seen from the Lochinver–Ullapool road

the service at any time. The only other way to Fair Isle is to charter a seven-seater aircraft, for which there are arrangements at Sumburgh Airport.

Fearn Highland 21 B8

In the centre of the hammer-head peninsula that juts out between the Dornoch Firth and Cromarty Firth, Hill of Fearn is the hub of a flattish but very fertile farming area, notable for its high sunshine records in autumn and winter.

This peninsula is oddly isolated. Both the main road, the A9, and the railway approach it from the south-west, but each turns north-west to Tain (qv). Fearn station, where the turn is made, lies 2km. west of Hill of Fearn; and Fearn village is nearly as far east. Apart from a few houses, Fearn is but a church and its manse. But the church is noteworthy. In 1221 the Earl of Ross founded an abbey at Edderton, 7km. west of Tain; but attracted by the more fertile conditions to the east, this was moved to Fearn in 1298. It was not completed until 1543, by which time the Reformation was under way; its titular abbot, Patrick Hamilton, was one of the first Scottish martyrs of the Reformation, being burnt at the stake at St Andrews in 1528 for heresy. The abbey became the parish church; then, in 1742, during a service, the roof fell in, killing 42 people. The nave and choir of the abbey are still the parish church, though the north and south chapels are roofless.

The place that, before the Reformation, was called Abbotshaven, 3km. east of Fearn, is now BALINTORE, a fishing village with a good harbour popular with sea anglers. It has a sandy beach; and there is an even better one at the neighbouring village, not a km. away, of SHANDWICK, beyond which there are good red-sandstone cliffs, colourful in summer with wild flowers.

Some 7km. from Fearn and Balintore is Nigg (see Invergordon), where the inhabitants find there is more money to be made building platforms for North Sea oil than in fishing, farming, or looking after visitors.

Fort Augustus Highland 8D1

After the Jacobite Rising of 1715 a garrison was established at the head of Loch Ness, halfway between Fort William and Inverness, to keep the clans in check.

The first fort was built in 1729 by General Wade, who named it after William Augustus, Duke of Cumberland, the youngest son of George II.

Prince Charles's army captured it, after a two-day siege, in 1746 on their way to what was to be the fateful battle of Culloden; but two months later, with the Jacobite cause finally defeated, the Duke of Cumberland took possession. The fort was restored and extended, and remained a military garrison for over a century.

It is this fort that gave its name to the village, originally known as Kilchuimen. In 1867 the military forces were withdrawn for service elsewhere. The fort was eventually sold to Lord Lovat; and in 1876 it was pre-

sented to the Benedictine Order for the building of a monastery, which was raised to the status of an abbey in 1882. Features of the building, which can be visited, include cloisters of 1893 built by Peter Paul Pugin, son of the famous architect, and the school and clock-tower designed by Joseph Hansom (inventor of the hansom cab).

At Fort Augustus the Caledonian Canal (qv) enters Loch Ness down a 'staircase' of locks, at the foot of which is the 'Great Glen Exhibition', telling the story of the area – with a room devoted to the Loch Ness Monster.

Fort Augustus was the first place in Scotland to have a public electricity supply. It arrived in 1890, when an 18kw. water turbine was installed in a tumbledown building and used to generate electricity for the Abbey and part of the village.

South from Fort Augustus, Glen Tarff leads to the Corrieyairack Pass, 774m. above sea-level, on General Wade's famous road from Speyside to the Great Glen, a tough walk – nearly 35km. from Fort Augustus to Laggan Bridge – which may still be followed.

Fort George Highland 15G2

Barely 5km. separate Fort George and Ardersier on the peninsula that juts into the Moray Firth opposite Chanonry Point on the Black Isle. There could hardly be a greater contrast between two places so near to each other.

Fort George is one of the finest late artillery fortifications in Europe; it was built between 1748 and 1763 to replace an earlier Fort George built by General Wade in 1726. This latter was part of a chain of forts, including Fort William and Fort Augustus (qqv): it was destroyed by the Jacobite forces in 1746. Included in the present fort is the Regimental Museum of the Queen's Own Highlanders: the Fort was the depot of the Seaforth Highlanders until 1961, when they and the Queen's Own Cameron Highlanders were amalgamated.

The fort is immensely impressive. So, too, in another fashion is ARDERSIER, to the south. Until recently this was a fishing village but now it is a major centre for the construction of North-Sea-oil platforms, which reach high and hideous above the Firth. The sight of the one should not deter a visit to the other.

Fortrose and Rosemarkie Highland 15F2
(*pop.* 920)

Two small resorts, Fortrose and Rosemarkie, on the Inverness Firth coast of the Black Isle are not 3km. apart. They stand on either side of a narrow triangle of land pointing into the Firth, culminating in Chanonry Point, which itself is not 3km. from Fort George (qv) across the water.

The two small towns have much in common. Each has a couple of hotels, each has a holiday caravan site disfiguring its side of the peninsula. They share a golf

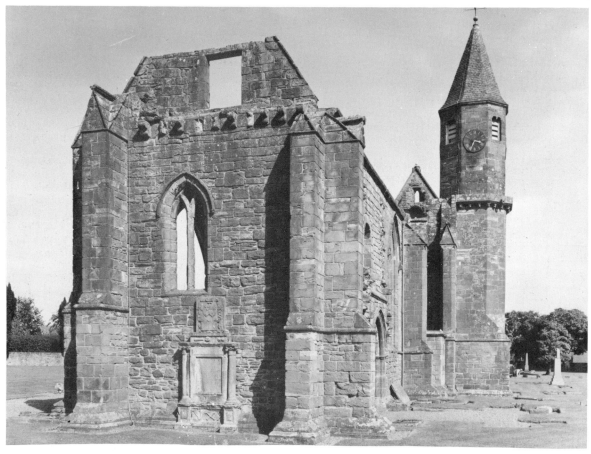

course, and shared their quincentenary celebrations in 1955. Rosemarkie is the more charming; its beach is surrounded by good rock scenery, with red-sandstone cliffs made famous by the geologist Hugh Miller, who was born at Cromarty (qv), 14km. to the north-east. Rosemarkie is also the older, despite the joint celebrations. The Celtic St Moluag founded a monastery here in 592; but when David I chose the seat of the diocese of Ross he placed it at Chanonry, now Fortrose, where the cathedral was built. Today's remains of that cathedral consist of the thirteenth-century sacristy and a beautiful vaulted south aisle, endowed in 1380.

The road south-east beside the Firth from Fortrose goes to Avoch (*pron.* Auch), a pleasant fishing village.

Fort William   Highland   8C4   (*pop.* 4,352)
Only a gateway – and that re-erected in 1896 away from its original site – is left of the fort that was originally built of earth and wattle in 1655 by General Monk, rebuilt in stone in 1690 by order of William III (after whom it was named), and strengthened by General Wade after the 1715 Jacobite rising.

Fort William was a strategic centre from which to control the turbulent clans; its position today makes it a major centre for touring. North-east, the A82 goes through the Great Glen to Inverness; or, off that road at Spean Bridge, one can go by Laggan to the Spey Valley. South-west are roads to Oban and to Glen Coe; west is the 'Road to the Isles' to Mallaig. As a further magnet for the traveller, Fort William lies under Britain's highest mountain, Ben Nevis (qv). 'The Ben' is not seen from the town, but there are superb views of it from Corpach, where a major pulp mill was opened in 1966. The mill has had at least one adverse side-effect: the building of a mass of uninspired housing around the town and an addition to the traffic problem, acute in the summer months when the town's many hotels and guest houses are filled to capacity. Some relief from traffic congestion in the town centre has resulted from the opening, in 1976, of a bypass beside Loch Linnhe.

The railway came to Fort William in 1864 (the fort was demolished to make way for the station). It has been allowed to survive. This accessibility by rail is one factor in current proposals to 'develop' Fort William as a skiing centre. It already has a Diving School – though this is not for holiday amusement, but to train divers

OPPOSITE TOP: *Fort George*
OPPOSITE BOTTOM: *Fortrose Cathedral*

BELOW: *Gairloch Harbour*

needed more than ever before in North Sea oil exploration.

The West Highland Museum in Cameron Square is one of the few interests in the town itself; it contains, among other things, a number of Jacobite relics.

Just north-east of the town is INVERLOCHY and the large aluminium factory and power house fed by the waters of the Lochaber Power Scheme, the pipe lines of which are seen on the mountain slopes. Old Inverlochy Castle, nearby, is the ruin of an impressive Comyn stronghold, dating back possibly to the thirteenth century. The modern Inverlochy Castle was the home of Mr J. W. Hobbs, who developed the 4,000ha. Great Glen Cattle Ranch off the road to Spean Bridge. Now the Castle is a hotel, much praised for its cusine, and priced accordingly.

Were it possible to bypass Fort William – a very large proportion of its traffic stops but briefly and spends but little – it would be a more pleasant place and its setting at the head of Loch Linnhe among good mountain scenery would be better appreciated. As it is, it has too much traffic, for which car parking must be provided: it pays the penalty for being what it is – a magnificent centre for touring.

Gairloch Highland 16F2

Even in the west Highlands, few places have a more superb setting than this village on the Gair Loch: the Torridon Mountains, Skye, and the Outer Hebrides are all to be seen, though the best view is from a few km. up the A832 towards Poolewe.

There are sandy beaches at Strathy – virtually part of Gairloch, and holding most of the hotels and other holiday accommodation – and beyond, off the B8021 to Melvaig, is the Big Sand, a huge sweep of fine beach, behind whose dunes is a very large, well-equipped camping/caravan site. All along this road – a private track continues beyond Melvaig to Rudha Reidh lighthouse – are views to the Hebrides.

To add to the beauty and the beaches, there are angling, sea angling, and one of the few golf courses in the north-west Highlands. South from Gairloch, off the road to Loch Maree, a minor road goes near the south shores of the Gair Loch to Badachro, Port Henderson, and South Erradale, to end at Red Point. While originally these places were crofting communities, they tend now to hold a high proportion of holiday homes. Beyond Red Point a track continues along the east side of Loch Torridon to Diabaig and Torridon, with more fine views, in this case of the Applecross Peninsula and Skye.

Delightful in summer, Gairloch's dependence on holidays results in a strong sense of desolation when the great majority of holiday places close down for the winter.

Garve Highland 14D2

At this village the scenery changes quite remarkably.

East of it, where road and rail from Inverness run beside Loch Garve, the high hills are richly wooded and beyond them is the pleasant farming country of Easter Ross. To the west, just outside Garve, the road divides. The A832 goes west, by Loch Luichart and through Strath Bran, with views of the Fannichs, the summits of which rise to over 1,000m. – though not dramatically – to Achnasheen for Kyle of Lochalsh or Gairloch.

The A835 goes north through Strath Garve before also swinging west, to run beside Loch Glascarnoch, at the foot of which is ALTGUISH, little more than an old coaching inn, which is now a hotel. It lies near the dam at the end of the loch, a reservoir built as part of the second stage of the North of Scotland Hydro-Electric Board's Conon scheme, which involved the building of five other main dams as well as this one – at Vaich, Fannich, Meig, Luichart, and Torr Achilty. The loch, 6½km. long, has certainly added new beauty to this empty country: a car pull-off at the western end of the loch gives the best easily-attained views of the area.

Glen Coe Highland 8C5

Although traversed by one of the busiest tourist routes in Scotland, from Glasgow to Fort William, this remains one of the most splendid glens in the country. In a distance of 18km. one passes from the bleak Moor of Rannoch through a narrow rocky pass, under high mountains – great rocky peaks split by ravines on one side, soaring steep slopes on the other – above a flat grassy floor, past a little loch, and to the shores of Loch Leven.

Strictly speaking, Glen Coe is only the lower part of this pass; but the name is generally applied to all of it. The gateway, from the south, is the Kingshouse Hotel, on a site where there was, for centuries, an inn. Across the road from the Hotel is the access to one of Scotland's three leading ski areas, with chair lift and ski tows for the slopes of Meall a' Bhuiridh, the 1,118-m. peak of the Clach Leathad (Clachlet) group.

With comparatively little accommodation in the vicinity, the Glen Coe slopes attract mainly weekend skiers, coming as often as not for the day only. So the chair lift runs regularly only at weekends and at Christmas, New Year, and Easter; at other times it can be chartered by groups; the skiing is said often to excel that on the better-known Cairngorm slopes.

A short distance beyond the approach road to the chairlift, a dead-end road goes down Glen Etive (see Connel), and towering above it is the forbidding mass of Buchaille Etive Mor followed by Buchaille Etive Beag: these are the Big and Little Shepherds of Etive, among the most challenging peaks in the country for mountaineers, and not to be attempted by the inexpert.

The main road down the Glen, under the Buchailles, goes through a narrow defile, near which is The Study (a corruption of the old Scots word *Stiddie*, 'an anvil'), a flat-topped rock under which the River Coe plunges

Buchaille Etive Mor in Glen Coe, with the R. Etive in the foreground

through a gorge, and from which there is a fine view of the Three Sisters of Glen Coe, outliers of the great Bidean nam Bian mountain. From there, too, can be seen the old road down the Glen; when the new road was opened in 1935 there was the usual outcry about spoiling a magnificent glen, though without the new road comparatively few people would have seen its magnificence.

Travelling down the valley – by the old road if you are walking – there are craggy peaks to the south, and great slopes soaring up to the rocky summits of Aonach Eagach to the north. Before reaching Loch Triochatan a well-known but not easy rock climb leads to Ossian's

Cave, allegedly the haunt of Ossian, the legendary third-century Gaelic bard. As the cave floor slopes forty-five degrees, the likelihood of occupation by *anybody* is remote.

Just past the loch, a side road leads to the Clachaig Inn and to Glencoe village. Behind the Inn a rock crowns a knoll: this is the Signal Rock, traditionally the place from which the sign was given to start the Massacre of Glencoe on 13 February 1692. The background to this much-told event in Scottish history is tortuous and tied up with the rivalry between the Campbells and the MacDonalds. William III had granted pardon to the clans who fought against him providing they took an

Part of the ridge between the summits of Bidean nam Bian, on the S side of Glen Coe

oath of allegiance by 1 January 1692; MacIain, chief of the MacDonalds of Glencoe, reached Fort William to take the oath by 31 December, but was told that this must be done at Inveraray. Delayed by the snows, he did not manage to reach there until 6 January. By 1 February 120 men under Campbell of Glenlyon arrived in the Glen, with demands that they be billeted, and with assurances that there was no hostile intent. They were given hospitality; but early on the morning of 13 February the soldiers turned on their hosts and some forty MacDonalds were slaughtered, including MacIain; probably as many again died from exposure as they tried to escape through the snow.

There is ample documentary evidence that the Massacre was planned: it includes letters from the Secretary of State for Scotland expressing the view that the 'thieving tribe' should be 'rooted out and cut off'.

There have been many such instances of brutality in Highland history; this one is particularly remembered, perhaps, because it was so deliberately planned and because the abuse of Highland hospitality was so flagrant.

Some 5,600ha. of Glen Coe are under the care of the NTS, which has an information centre in the Glen. At Glencoe village, just off the road to Kinlochleven, the Glencoe and North Lorn Folk Museum has relics of the '45.

Glenelg Highland 17F6
The road from Shiel Bridge climbs over Mam Rattachan (Ratagan) and runs down a long, narrow valley to the

Sound of Sleat and the village of Glenelg – whose name is probably the only palindrome in Scotland. It faces Kylerhea on the Isle of Skye, of which, much of the way down the glen, there are good views.

There is no other approach by land to this village; until recently many people who crossed this pass forked right for BERNERA, where, during the summer months, there was a car ferry across Kyle Rhea to Skye. The ferry ceased to run in 1975. Nevertheless, it is worth taking this road to see at Bernera the remains of the barracks built in 1722, where troops were stationed almost to the end of the eighteenth century.

The crossing from Bernera to Skye is less than 500m., as is the width of all of Kyle Rhea from here to Loch Alsh. Twenty thousand years ago Skye was part of the mainland, and was only finally separated by the action of a glacier flowing south from Loch Alsh. This was the main crossing for drovers bringing their cattle from

the islands to the mainland (*see* Road to the Isles). From the end of the sixteenth century four-day sales were held at Portree on Skye, and within half a century dealers were coming from the mainland to buy cattle: the animals were forced to swim the strait to Bernera, at low tide, roped head to tail in conveys of five led by a boat in which a man held a rope to the first cow's nose.

From Glenelg itself the road runs past the little-used pier to the foot of GLEANN BEAG, a lovely wooded glen up which a road goes for about 6km. to Balvraid: thereafter is private property. A short way up the glen are two of the most notable Iron Age brochs on the Scottish mainland; their walls still stand, in part, over 9m. high, and the entrances and galleries are still to be seen. These brochs are Dun Telve and Dun Trodden, named, it is said, after their builders, sons of the prehistoric lady who owned Caisteal Grugaig broch near Totaig, on the point opposite Eilean Donan Castle on Loch Duich (*see*

Bernera Barracks, N of Glenelg : N barrack-block from the SW

Shiel Bridge). Up Gleann Beag, beyond the end of the road, is Dun Grugaig, a fort that is earlier in date than the more developed brochs, which were probably built in the first century of the Christian era.

Glenfinnan Highland 8A3
A tall stone column, surmounted by the figure of a kilted Highlander, stands at the head of a long, narrow loch that has steep mountains sweeping up from its shores. This is Glenfinnan, some 25km. west of Fort William on the Road to the Isles.

It was here, on 19 August 1745, that Prince Charles Edward Stuart landed with seven men from the French ship *Du Teillay* and raised his standard as a rallying point for the clans. He had landed from France on the Isle of Eriskay, at the southern end of the Outer Hebrides, on 23 July; there, and later at Borrodale, on the shores of Loch nan Uamh, the clan chiefs tried to dissuade him from attempting to regain the throne of his grand-father, James VII and II. But eventually Cameron of Locheil was swayed; this persuaded others to follow suit, and some 1,400 men rallied to the Prince at Glenfinnan. Among them was Alexander MacDonald of Glenala-dale, in whose house the Prince stayed the night; it was one of MacDonald's grandsons, also Alexander, who had the statue erected in 1815 to 'commemorate the generous zeal, the undaunted bravery, and the inviol-able fidelity of his forefathers and the rest of those who fought and bled in that arduous and unfortunate enter-prise' – so reads the inscription (in Gaelic, Latin, and English) on the monument. In 1938 the monument was handed into the care of the NTS; the NTS visitor centre here, opened in 1966, tells the story of the rising.

The setting at Glenfinnan is superb, and is perhaps even more impressive in grey weather (as it was when the Prince landed) than in good. Loch Shiel runs between the mountains of Moidart and Sunart – rising to nearly 900m. – to Acharacle (qv). The islet on the loch is St Finnan's Isle, for centuries the burial ground of the MacDonalds of Glenaladale.

Glen More Forest Park Highland 15H6
With some 1,200ha. of forest and three times as much unplantable mountain and high ground, the Glen More Forest Park is an area for superlatives. It is usually approached by the road east from Aviemore by way of Coylumbridge; by the shores of Loch Morlich, its western boundary, there are a Forest Information Centre and, in the same area, a large camping/caravan site, a youth hostel, and a Scottish Sports Council training centre. The long ridge of Cairngorm, the south-east boundary of the Park, forms a magnificent backcloth. Beyond this ridge are four of the five mountains in Britain over 1,219m. (4,000ft.) high. Although they do not include the highest mountain in the country, Ben Nevis (qv), this is the largest mass of high mountains in the country.

In the area is the CAIRNGORM NATIONAL NATURE RESERVE – again, the largest in Britain; the Park itself has fair claims to be the richest in wild life, certainly in Scotland. And all this despite the heavy pressure of people, not only in the summer months but also in winter: this is the major skiing area of the UK.

LOCH MORLICH, a 'hole' left by a stagnant glacier after the main ice had retreated down to the Spey Val-ley (the granite mass of the Cairngorms was largely carved by glaciers), has a pleasant beach, which in-evitably attracts sailing craft, canoes, and the like, as well as picnickers, in summer.

But summer or winter, a main target is Cairngorm it-self, the fifth highest mountain in Britain (1,245m.) but quite the easiest to 'climb'. From Loch Morlich a good access road goes into Coire Cas, where, at 610m., there is a car park for 600 cars; as if this was not big enough (at times it is not), there is another car park for 300 cars at Coire na Ciste; there is a bus service from the Spey Valley centres.

At Coire Cas, as well as five ski tows, there is a chair-lift in two sections; from the top of these it is little more than a gentle walk to the summit of Cairngorm; and, weather permitting, there are magnificent views over Strathspey.

'Weather permitting' is not to be taken lightly: bad weather can come up at any time, and in winter Cairn-gorm often claims more than its fair share of deaths due to exposure.

The sub-arctic climate, allied with the variety of terrain lower down, makes the Glen More Forest Park a wonderful place for anybody who takes an interest in wild plants as well as birds and mammals. The fact that to see some of the best mountain flora, including moss campion and saxifrage, means scrambling away from the well-worn tracks will not deter the enthusiast. Over 200 species of flowering plants, and several hundred species of ferns, mosses, lichens, and fungi are to be found in the Nature Reserve.

Nor will the naturalist need telling that the best chance of seeing the capercailzie clattering through the woods, or catching a glimpse of a wild cat or blue hare or ptarmigan, or seeing the goosander on Loch Morlich, is early in the morning and well before the main holiday season. Among the smaller birds, this is the main area in Britain where the crested tit breeds; the crossbill, though its range is much wider, is more easily seen here than in most places; but the dotterel, which used to nest high up the Cairngorm, has been driven into more remote regions by the pressure of people. The most famous of Scottish birds, the golden eagle, still soars above the Park; but at ground level, and more likely to be seen, is the only herd of reindeer roaming semi-wild in Britain. The last reindeer in Scotland were hunted out of exist-ence in the twelfth century; today's herd stems from animals introduced in 1952.

There is only one motor road through the Park, that

from Loch Morlich to the Coire Cas. But there are a large number of footpaths as well as three forest trails and five longer treks.

Golspie Highland 21B6

There is no mistaking, here, whose land one is on. On the top of Beinn a' Bhragie, rising 380m. behind the town, is a huge statue of the first Duke of Sutherland, sculpted, as is that at Dornoch (qv), by Chantrey.

To the east, DUNROBIN CASTLE stands in a great park overlooking the sea. The core of this architectural extravagance is a tower built c. 1275: the original, earlier, keep was built by Robert, third Earl of Sutherland (hence Dunrobin, the 'mote or hill of Robert'). The Castle's present appearance dates from mid-nineteenth-century extensions, restored after a fire in 1915. The museum in the park contains a remarkable variety of exhibits, ranging from Pictish stones to relics of Queen Victoria, who stayed here. Of recent years, the Castle has held a boys' school.

In Golspie itself – which of course has a Sutherland Arms Hotel – the old bridge has a Gaelic stone that was the rallying point of the Sutherland 'clan'. Long before the time of the Sutherlands, however, the whole of this

coast was populated: Carn Liath broch, 2km. east of Dunrobin, is one of many prehistoric forts in the area.

Golspie is a pleasant resort, with a beach and a golf course, and Dunrobin Glen, north-west from the town, makes a very pleasant walk. The Orcadian Stone Company's workshop, in Golspie, is worth a visit. Six km. west, the A9 road and the railway cross the head of Loch Fleet on The Mound, an embankment over 900m. long, built by Telford in 1815–16. It not only obviated the need for a ferry but reclaimed some 160ha. of land. The minor road running along the south shore of Loch Fleet from here has fascinating birdlife.

Grantown-on-Spey Highland 12A4 (pop. 1,591)

This very pleasant small town can claim a longer experience as a holiday resort than most places in the Highlands. It was founded on a regular plan in 1776 by Sir James Grant of nearby Castle Grant, to replace the existing Castletown of Freuchie, which was too near to the castle for his liking. The intention was to develop it as a textile-manufacturing centre; but by the mid nineteenth century it had already become a place recommended by doctors for 'a change of air' – possibly encouraged by a visit in 1860 by Queen Victoria and

Carn Liath broch, E of Golspie

Prince Albert, duly written up in the Queen's *Journal*. A report of the 1890s extolling Grantown's salubrious character commented: 'In no other part of Scotland are there more octogenarians and nonagenarians to be met with'. The character maintains today: the well-built town has a wide, tree-lined square, and a fine setting by one of the most beautiful stretches of the Spey, with paths through pine and birch woods, and the Cairngorm mountains to the south.

The octogenarians and nonagenarians are not much in evidence in winter. This is a leading ski centre, with ski schools and the like.

For the rest of the year this stretch of the Spey is notable for its salmon fishing, there is a good golf course, and there is fine touring country to hand in all directions.

Some 10km. north, off the A939 to Nairn over the high Dava Moor, is LOCHINDORB, where an island holds the ruins of a stronghold, from 1372, of the 'Wolf of Badenoch' (Alexander, the son of Robert II), who terrorized the area in the late fourteenth century.

North-east from Grantown, the road to Craigellachie runs above a lovely stretch of the Spey and under the pleasant Hills of Cromdale; south-east is the high, colourful moorland road to Tomintoul, while other Spey Valley centres lie to the south-west.

West, just beyond Dulnain Bridge, the ruins of sixteenth-century Muckerach Castle, at one time a fortalice of the Grants of Rothiemurchus, are of interest. Castle Grant, near Grantown-on-Spey, dating back to the sixteenth century and with additions to designs by William Adam in 1750, is not open to the public.

Gruinard Bay   Highland   19A7

Coming north from Aultbea there appears quite suddenly a breathtaking panorama across Gruinard Bay, with its crescent of beach and its island, to the mountains of Coigach and, to the east, Ben Goleach, whose twin peaks look far more impressive than the 640m. height might suggest.

A minor road along the west side of the Bay goes to the crofting townships of Laide, Mellon Udrigle, and Achgarve on the Rubh Mhor Peninsula, while the main road goes through the unusually-named townships of First Coast and Second Coast to the beach, backed by woods, at the foot of the hill.

Soon after the road leaves the main Gruinard beach a track follows the Gruinard River to Loch na Seaige (Shellag) under the steep slopes of Sgurr Fiona of An Teallach (*see* Dundonnell). This may be walked; but one trip that cannot be made is to Gruinard Island, where, in World War II, experiments in germ warfare were undertaken and anthrax disseminated. It is said that 100 years may pass before 'Anthrax Island' is free of infection – a sad reflection in such a beautiful place.

Halkirk   Highland   20D2

This village, off the main road beside the River Thurso,

and some 10km. south of Thurso itself (qv), was built to a gridiron pattern at the end of the eighteenth century by Sir John Sinclair, one of the most far-sighted landowners of the period and a notable agricultural reformer.

The country is featureless but oddly fascinating under high Caithness skies, and the angling is well known: the Thurso is a salmon river, and within 4km. are lochs Calder and Watten, noted for trout, heavier here than further south.

BRAWL CASTLE, just north of the village, is in ruin: it may date back to the fourteenth century. Georgemass Junction, east of the village, is where the railway from Inverness divides for Wick and Thurso.

Harris   Highland   22   (*pop.* 2,696)

Although usually referred to as the island of Harris, this is merely the southern part of an island, the northern part of which is Lewis (qv).

Before local-government reorganization in Scotland in May 1975, Harris was in Inverness-shire, Lewis in Ross-shire. The boundary was not the *apparently* logical one cutting across the narrow neck of land, less than 1km. wide, between West and East Lochs Tarbert; it was further north, from Loch Resort to Loch Seaforth. In fact, the boundary did have a logic: it divided the basically flat, loch-ridden moorland of Lewis from the high, bare mountains that are a feature of Harris. These mountains, often the only indication of the Outer Hebrides that may be seen from mainland viewpoints – Lewis is too flat to stand significantly above the horizon – reach their peak in Clisham, almost 800m. above sea-level; but there are half a dozen others that exceed 600m. The mountains are in North Harris, a naked, almost forbidding landscape of grey rock. The rock is a reminder – more striking here than anywhere else in the islands – that the Outer Hebrides are made up of Lewisian Gneiss; carved, smoothed, and eroded over millions of years, there is little vegetation to cover this ancient rock.

South of Tarbert, South Harris has its mountains too; but here the landscape is more varied – though never lush.

The mountains reflect the forbidding side. But there is another. Keen climbers who ascend these mountains are rewarded with fine views; but more ordinary mortals can rejoice in some magnificent beaches on the west coast, and find colour of a different kind at TARBERT, an attractive place of white houses, with tweeds in its shops and boats in its harbour. Tarbert lies on that narrow neck of land between West and East Lochs Tarbert, and here the car ferries from Uig in Skye and Lochmaddy in North Uist dock. It is the main centre of the island, though might not have been but for the clash, half a century ago, of two irreconcilable interests. In 1918 a wealthy soap manufacturer, Lord Leverhulme, who founded Port Sunlight near Birkenhead, Merseyside, bought the island of Lewis and Harris and planned

Harris: the tomb of Alasdair Crotach in St Clement's church, Rodel

to build there a large canning factory for herring fished from the Minch. To make sure of retail outlets he opened a chain of fish shops – MacFisheries – but the setting up of the factory, at Stornoway on Lewis, met with opposition from crofters, who were not prepared to abandon their traditional way of life – mixing crofting with fishing – to concentrate on the fishing and so keep the factory working full time. Defeated, Leverhulme moved to the south of Harris, where, at a township called Obbe, he built piers, kippering sheds, roads, and houses for the workers. The name Obbe was changed to Leverburgh, but while Leverhulme found more cooperation here, the project was short-lived. He died in 1925, the island was sold and split into large estates, and today Leverburgh is a reminder of what might have been.

Otherwise, there is great beauty on this south-west shore of Harris, looking across islands in the Sound of Harris to North Uist. South-east from Leverburgh, the A859 from Stornoway ends at RODEL, where the small cruciform St Clement's church is the most outstanding ecclesiastical building in the Outer Isles. In the church-

yard there are some fine grave slabs; the church itself dates back to the early sixteenth century, and was built by Alasdair Crotach, eighth chief of Clan MacLeod, whose stately tomb records that he built it in 1528: he died in 1547. Much of the rich decoration in this church is said to derive from the monastery at Iona (qv); craftsmen from that island are said to have worked on it, and green marble from Mull is included in the ornamentation. The church seems strangely at odds with the Hebridean landscape, at its most typical if you follow the minor road – not really suitable for cars – along the south-east shores of the island. This road wanders by what seem innumerable bays and inlets: actually there are about thirty bays on this stretch of coast, which is only some 20km. as the crow flies from Rodel to Tarbert, but nearer 35km. if the road is followed, and very much longer if the coastline itself is adhered to. Logically enough, the area is known as The Bays. It is good for walking; and sometimes it is possible to hire a boat at one of the dwellings scattered *en route*.

The main road from Leverburgh follows the west coast

by some wonderful beaches, with views over the water across Taransay to North Harris, before it cuts inland for Tarbert, beyond the huge sands of Luskentyre Bay. The area around the bay is perhaps the richest crofting land in Harris; here too is a machair thick with flowers in summer and even possessing, rare indeed in Harris, a few trees.

The view in reverse, from North to South Harris, is as enthralling, and the pattern the same, if the minor road that branches west some 5km. north-west of Tarbert is followed. By bays and beaches it goes, with crofting settlements on the few places where the ground is flat enough; the hills behind hold red deer, and in early summer salmon leap the falls near Amhuinsuidhe. The small offshore islands are Soay More and Soay Beg – but not the Soay of the sheep: that Soay is part of St Kilda (qv).

The road ends at Husinish, with another wonderful beach and high cliffs beyond, looking across to the island of Scarp: even after World War II this island had some fifty people living on it, and a school for the children: now it is uninhabited.

From Tarbert, the main road goes beneath the bare grey hills to Loch Seaforth. There is a bridge across the river here. The long, narrow loch stretches over 10km. before it reaches the sea, and across the water is Skye. Across the bridge is Lewis.

Helmsdale Highland 21D5

A new, unlovely bridge carries the main road, the A9, from the south into this small fishing village at the foot of the Strath of Kildonan, up which the railway and the A897 road go towards the north coast. Until 1971 the gaunt remains of a castle, built in 1488, the scene of the poisoning of the Earl and Countess of Sutherland in 1567, stood on a headland above the village: it is now demolished.

North, the A9 climbs above cliffs and ravines to the

Ardvreck Castle, NW of Inchnadamph

high Ord of Caithness, boundary of the old counties of Sutherland and Caithness. Castle and counties may have disappeared, but up the Strath are dozens of reminders of early cultures – standing stones, stone circles, and cairns – on the moors on each side of the valley from Kilphedir, 5km. west of Helmsdale, to Kildonan, another 10km. up the Strath. There are more isolated relics further on. It is clear that this area was quite well inhabited for some hundreds of years BC. Few of the remains are notable in themselves; but the sheer number of them is impressive.

In 1868–9 the Strath was the scene of the 'Sutherland Gold Rush'. When gold was discovered here many prospectors went, in hope of a fortune, to pan the burns; but the gold found was never sufficient to justify the effort. Optimistic holidaymakers still occasionally indulge in panning.

Inchnadamph Highland 19C5

A hotel, a church, a house, and a cottage or two – these are Inchnadamph.

The hotel, as well as being a halt for the tourist, attracts two widely different types of enthusiast – the angler and the geologist. The former comes for the salmon and brown trout, and the remote chance of a gillaroo, a trout from Ireland almost unknown in Scotland. The latter comes because here is one of the most geologically intriguing areas in the country. Past the Skiag Bridge junction – where the road forks left for Lochinver, right for Kylescu – there is first an outcrop of Torridonian Sandstone, brown and purple rocks beside the road and up to a shoulder of Quinag; these rest on Durness Limestone. Then, within a km., is Lewisian Gneiss, one of the oldest rocks in the world.

This area is a tumult of rocks, caused by the vast movement westwards – the Moine Thrust – hundreds of millions of years ago. In more recent times, Ice Age glaciers shaped today's mountains, dumping gravel and boulders in the valleys and leaving the almost countless lochans (which today attract the angler). The peat came later, and the peat cutters later still (and they uncovered stumps of trees that had grown and died many centuries ago, when the climate was much more genial than it is today).

It is an amazing landscape, with peaks like Suilven (see Lochinver) rearing from the low, boggy moorland fretted with stretches of water: it is not a country for easy walking.

The geological story has not been fully worked out yet, though there is a cairn just north of Inchnadamph commemorating two geologists, Ben Peach and John Horne, who in the last two decades of the nineteenth century played the foremost part in unravelling the geological structure of the north-west Highlands.

On a point near the head of Loch Assynt are the stark ruins of ARDVRECK CASTLE, built in 1597 as a seat of the MacLeod of Assynt; here the Marquis of Montrose (see

Invershin) was imprisoned in 1650 after his capture and before being taken to Edinburgh and execution.

Some 5km. south of Inchnadamph, where the road crosses a stream coming down from Allt nan Uamh, is the southern boundary of the Inchnadamph Nature Reserve: in its steep sides are the caves where the bones of bear, reindeer, lynx, and lemming – all long vanished from the Highland scene, except in wildlife parks – together with traces of Stone Age man, have been found.

Further south, with grand views, to the west, of Suilven and Canisp, Ledmore is at the junction of the roads to Ullapool and Invershin, the latter going by Altnacealgach, a lonely inn famous as a base for brown-trout fishing.

But take the Ullapool road, and the near scenery changes again, with bright-green grass on both sides of the road indicating fertile land on limestone. In another 8km., past Elphin, a small crofting township, is Knockan Cliff, with a car park and viewpoint above the road; there is also a Nature Conservancy Council Visitor Centre. This is the start of an 80km. 'Motor Trail' designed 'to be read by a passenger while the car is moving' – a sad way to see one of the most remarkable wild areas of Britain.

Inveraray Strathclyde 4C4 (pop. 468)

There are few more pleasant small towns in attractive settings anywhere in Scotland than this 'planned' centre of whitewashed buildings on the shores of Loch Fyne.

It was about 1415 that Colin Campbell, who had his seat at Innis Chonnel on Loch Awe, built a castle here: it was soon to become the seat of one of the most prominent families in Highland history.

The Campbells started their rise to power in the eleventh century, though the first extant documentary evidence is of 1266. They gained much territory when Robert the Bruce gave Neil Campbell lands forfeited by the MacDougalls; they first became Earls, then, in 1701, Dukes, of Argyll.

In 1743 the third Duke decided to rebuild the castle, and to do so demolished the old village and built the present Inveraray a km. south. To rebuilt both the village and the castle he employed one of the most prominent architects of the day, Roger Morris, who had as his clerk of works William Adam, father of Robert Adam. Both Morris and William Adam died soon after the work was started, and Robert Mylne took over. He built the Argyll Arms hotel and the remarkable parish church: the latter is unique in that for many years services were held in one part of the building in English and in another, on the other side of a dividing wall, in Gaelic. The 'English' side of the church, beautifully cared for, is in use today; the 'Gaelic' side is used as a church hall.

Despite the prevalent story, the famous 'Appin Murder Trial' of 1752, when James Stewart of the Glen was convicted for the murder (which he almost

TOP: *Inveraray Castle before 1877 (when conical spires were added to the towers)*   BOTTOM: *Inveraray Castle before the fire of 1975*

Inveraray Harbour

certainly did not commit) of the 'Red Fox' Campbell of Glenure (*see* Duror), was not held in the old Town House: it was not built until 1753.

Every year tens of thousands of visitors go to Inveraray. Its castle is one of the most famous in Scotland: standing four-square in parkland it is one of the earliest examples of Gothic-revival architecture, marred by the conical spires added to its towers after a fire in 1877. Its exterior gives little hint of the magnificent Georgian decoration and the endless treasures inside; tragically, another fire towards the end of 1975 destroyed the upper storey of the castle; pictures and other works of art were lost and damage was estimated at over £1 million.

Behind Inveraray's Main Street is the Inveraray Bell Tower, built by the tenth Duke as a war memorial to the Campbells. Conceived in 1918, its ten bells rang only twice before they were silenced by World War II; now teams of enthusiastic campanologists travel long distances to enjoy change-ringing at Inveraray (there are only thirteen other places in Scotland where it can be

done). By 1967 the tower was in poor condition, but after renovation it was opened to the public in 1971. From the top is a panoramic view over Inveraray and Loch Fyne, looking across a beautiful stretch of water to mountain slopes.

Just up Glen Aray, north from Inveraray, a recent innovation is a fish farm, which may be visited. The road, the A819, climbs through beautiful woods to open moors, and at the summit is a superb view of Ben Cruachan above Loch Awe.

Towards the head of Loch Fyne from Inveraray one can catch a glimpse of Dunderave Castle, a stout tower-house dating from 1598, now very well restored and not generally open to the public.

South-west from Inveraray, though, are other places that may and should be seen. One is AUCHINDRAIN, a group of small houses and outbuildings that once were a multiple-tenancy farm lived in, 100 years ago, by seventy people, with their livestock under the same roofs. The cottages show the way of west-Highland farming

Nigg Bay

life in the eighteenth and nineteenth centuries, a subject further explained at a visitor centre that may eventually fit into the rural picture better than its newness now allows (1975). A craft shop, better than usual, and home baking, which has achieved a remarkable reputation in a short time, are other features.

Before reaching Auchindrain the road leaves the loch; but it comes back to it at Furnace, which took its name from the early-nineteenth-century iron-smelting works there. Now there are large quarries, which are about the only scenic blot on the whole stretch of the loch. In another 4km., the quarries forgotten, is more beauty: CRARAE LODGE GARDENS, open to the public daily from March to October; here rhododendrons and exotic trees and shrubs stand in a Highland glen, and

in a forest garden above (Forestry Commission) there are over 100 plots of spruce, firs, hemlocks, and many unusual trees. As in other places where gardens have been developed in the west Highlands, it remains a moot point which excels – the rhododendrons in spring or the trees in late autumn.

Invergarry Highland 8D2
This hamlet – a hotel and a few houses – stands on the west side of LOCH OICH, smallest of the three lochs in the Great Glen. Only 6km. long, the loch is a beautiful stretch of water, wooded along its shores.

Towards the southern end of the loch, beside the road, is the 'Well of the Heads' monument, erected in 1812 to commemorate a particularly unsavoury episode in

Highland history. This was the murder, in the seventeenth century, of seven brothers as 'summary vengeance' for their having murdered the two sons of Keppoch, head of a branch of the MacDonells. The man who disposed of the seven brothers was Ian Lom, the family bard, who washed their heads in the spring here before presenting them to the chief. The monument is unpleasant, quite inappropriate in relation to its setting.

At Invergarry there starts perhaps the most scenic, and certainly the most varied, road to the west coast, the A87 to Shiel Bridge and Kyle of Lochalsh. First it runs through pleasant woods beside the River Garry, then continues beside Loch Garry for about 8km. before striking uphill, above plantations, climbing round a shoulder of the hills and running above Loch Loyne to meet the Glen Moriston road east of Loch Cluanie. It runs beside this loch, past Cluanie Bridge – little more than a hotel – to Glen Shiel, then under the Five Sisters of Kintail – beautiful mountains – to Loch Duich. All the lochs *en route* are reservoirs for hydro-electric power. It is a magnificent drive.

But there are still many people who regret the passing of the old road from Invergarry to Cluanie Bridge – a road that was one of the 'Roads to the Isles' (qv). This continued beside Loch Garry – as it still does – to Tomdoun Hotel, where it climbed uphill, past the head of lochs Loyne and Cluanie. It was broken when Loch Loyne was dammed and its level raised; now there is no way through.

West from the Tomdoun Hotel, the minor road continues, and for some way can be motored along; but in its early stages at least it is far better walked, for only that way can the drama of the mountains ahead be properly appreciated. Some 6km. west of Tomdoun is a power station, near which is a track up Glen Kingie to the head of Loch Arkaig; the road goes on to the eastern end of Loch Quoich, among the great mountains of Knoydart, rising 1,000m. or more, and here there is a dam; the road continues alongside the loch to Kinloch Hourn, where it ends. A track through the hills goes to Arnisdale (qv) on Loch Hourn, but walking it is not encouraged. Perhaps it is better to see the superb views from lower Glen Garry, or from the road to Loch Loyne, than to travel too far into the mountains: their wildness has not been improved by the furniture and denudation of hydro-electric developments.

Invergordon Highland 15F1

Few places have seen such changes as this small town on the shores of the Cromarty Firth.

There was a castle here in the thirteenth century; but the town developed only after the estate had been bought, in the early eighteenth century, by Sir William Gordon of Embo, who changed its name from Inverbreakie to Invergordon. The name stuck, even though Sir William's son sold the estate.

The castle that replaced the thirteenth-century one

was destroyed by fire in 1801. The harbour was built in 1828, and two large wooden piers followed in 1857, to maintain trade with Aberdeen, Leith, and London. But six years later the railway arrived at Invergordon, and the harbour fell into disuse.

It was to be a temporary disuse. Invergordon stands beside one of the finest natural anchorages in Europe, and early in the twentieth century it became a naval base with a dockyard and other facilities. When World War I broke out it proved an invaluable anchorage for the Navy; but when that war ended its prosperity went away. The story was repeated in and after World War II – and, incidentally, because of the influx of the Navy this was one of only two places in Scotland (the other being Gretna, on the border with England) where the pubs were state-owned, and accordingly dreary.

The naval base was closed in 1956. To relieve unemployment, a grain distillery was built; then in the 1960s the Cromarty Firth region was chosen as a major growth point by the newly-established Highlands and Islands Development Board. With government encouragement, the Board was successful in persuading the British Aluminium Company to build an aluminium smelter behind the town.

Plans for further development – which ironically (in view of subsequent developments) included applications from petrochemical companies, which depended on crude petroleum being brought into the Cromarty Firth by tankers – became completely redundant with the discovery of North Sea oil. The deep, sheltered waters of the Firth, with flat, easily-excavated land nearby, created ideal conditions for the siting of rig- and platform-construction yards. So, from the waterside at Invergordon, there is now a view – looking across to Nigg Bay – of the largest graving dock in the world for the fabrication of steel production platforms; building started in February 1972. Over 300m. long and 180m. wide, the dock is over 15m. deep; and for years, to accommodate men working on it, two liners were anchored off Dunskaith Ness, at the eastern end of Nigg Bay. Other means for accommodating labour, the demand for which was enormous, included virtual shanty towns around Nigg and Invergordon, which once had looked across calm waters to the North and South Sutors of Cromarty, the high headlands that guard the passage between Cromarty Firth and Moray Firth.

The first construction development was of course followed by others and by other proposals, including one for an oil refinery, the plans for which were approved early in 1976.

The future for the construction yards, on this scale, is obviously limited: North Sea oil is self-evidently not inexhaustible. Before recent development, a plan supported by the Highlands and Islands Development Board was for a 'linear city', which would include the shores of the Cromarty Firth and give ribbon development from Nairn to Tain.

Invermoriston Highland 14D5

Like Invergarry (qv), Invermoriston is a hamlet consisting of little more than a hotel and a few houses standing back from a loch, in this case Loch Ness. Except, perhaps, to the angler, its main interest is the road that leads from it to Kyle of Lochalsh (qv).

'Early in the afternoon we came to Anoch, a village in Glenmollison, of three huts, one of which is distinguished by a chimney', wrote Dr Johnson in his *A Journey to the Western Islands of Scotland*, a journey that he made with James Boswell in 1773. They stayed at the hut with a chimney, which was an inn, dining and sleeping in a room lined with turf and wattled with twigs; and Dr Johnson did not exactly please his host by expressing surprise that there were books in the house. He made some amends by presenting the daughter of the house, 'not inelegant in mien or dress', with a book. The inn was at Aonach, some 15km. up GLEN MORISTON, on the north side of the River Moriston, west of Torgyle. Twenty-seven years earlier this glen – by no means as impressive as Glen Garry (*see* Invergarry), though well-wooded in its lower stretches – had received more desperate visitors. Some 8km. further west, near Ceannacroc Bridge, a cairn commemorates Roderick Mackenzie, who, pretending to be Prince Charles Edward Stuart, then on the run after Culloden, drew off the soldiers searching for the Prince, and was killed. Some 3km. up Glen Doe is the cave where Charles hid.

These events occurred around Torgyle because the old military road from Fort Augustus, still to be seen, emerged into the Glen there: the road runs through the high hills of Inchnacardoch Forest, climbing from Fort Augustus to over 370m.

Inverness Highland 15F3 (*pop.* 36,595)

Even 250 years ago Inverness was 'generally esteemed to be the capital of the Highlands'. Edward Burt, who accompanied General Wade on his pacification of the Highlands in the 1720s, made the comment in his *Letters from a Gentleman in the North of Scotland*, written in 1725–6. Dr Johnson, in his *A Journey to the Western Islands of Scotland*, made a similar observation.

In its geographical setting, it could hardly be anything else. Here the roads from Fort William, the Spey Valley, the Moray Coast, and the north and west Highlands meet. They are good roads today; but even in the centuries before General Wade started the road-building programme that opened up the Highlands, the natural routes through the glens and over the passes and along the coast came to this place: the vitrified fort on Craig Phadrig indicates that the district was inhabited as far back as the fourth century BC. The first *documentary*

Part of the old military road nr Invermoriston

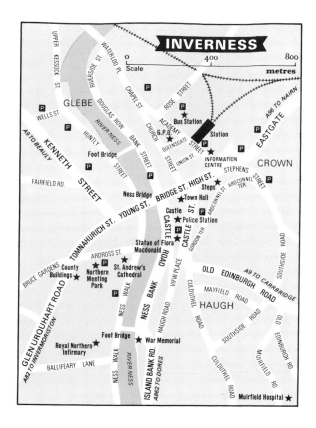

Inverness Castle

evidence of settlement comes from St Adamnan's account of St Columba coming to King Brude in 565 to seek his approval for monks from Iona to preach Christianity to the Picts. In the twelfth century David I made Inverness a Royal Burgh and built a stone keep on the hill where the present Inverness Castle stands. Mary Queen of Scots came here in 1562 and was refused admission to the castle; the governor was hanged shortly afterwards for his presumption. Cromwell's forces occupied the town in 1651 and built a large citadel. The Jacobites captured the place in 1715 – though not for long. Prince Charles Edward occupied it, after a two-day siege, in 1745, and in 1746, after Culloden, the Duke of Cumberland's troops took their revenge, pillaging houses and shooting prisoners.

Today's Inverness gives little hint of its long history. The Castle is a red Victorian building, of little interest: it houses administrative offices. Only the clock tower remains of Cromwell's citadel. To the essentially Victorian character of the town modern buildings of no distinction have been added; to build one large office block (occupied by the Highlands and Islands Development Board) the house where Mary Queen of Scots stayed was demolished. The few interesting buildings remaining include, in Church Street, Dunbar's Hos-

pital, built in 1688, and Abertarff House, of *c.* 1592, which now houses a Highland Craft and Information Centre.

Inverness has a wonderfully scenic setting – see it from Drummossie Muir, south on the A9; or, at less distance, from Castlehill. It stands on both sides of the River Ness (there is salmon and sea-trout fishing in the middle of the town), up which are several small islands linked by bridges. Loch Ness (qv) is less than 10km. south-west of the town.

Inverness is the Highland's major touring centre, and during the busy summer months Highland events are frequently staged. (It is, incidentally, one of the few places in Scotland where the kilt is worn by many men as normal, day-to-day garb.) As well as its holiday trade, the town has a limited amount of industry; but its prosperity rests as much on being the major shopping, distribution, and market centre for a very wide area. In this respect the 'Highland Capital' tag is legitimate, though the indefinable aura possessed by more genuine capitals is sadly lacking.

The River Ness comes into the narrows between Inverness Firth and Beauly Firth past a wasteland of timber yards, oil tanks, and the like. But the Caledonian Canal (qv) has left the river just south of the town, and

TOP: *Vitrified fort on Craig Phadrig, nr Inverness*   BOTTOM: *View across the R. Ness at Inverness*

at Clachnaharry are the last six locks for ships sailing across Scotland to the North Sea. From the peninsula between river and canal the Kessock Ferry runs a frequent, much-used, service across the narrows. Eventually there will probably be a bridge, desperately needed now because of the developments related to North Sea oil on the Cromarty Firth; but economic recession has postponed its building, and construction is not expected to begin before 1978. The ferry is worth taking, not only for access to the Black Isle (qv) and to avoid the main road via Beauly, but also for its fine views west up the Beauly Firth.

To North Kessock, a pleasant village on the north shore of the Firth, has been added an assortment of bungalows, for commuters and retired people; beyond this, along the minor coast road, the Black Isle Boating Centre at Coulmore Bay offers extensive facilities for sailing, canoeing, cruising, and water skiing.

With all these roads converging on it, its direct rail service to the south, its airport at Dalcross, and the explosion of industrial activity on the Cromarty Firth to add to its importance as a holiday, market, and administrative centre, Inverness has no doubts about its status. But its hopes of getting a Highland University have, as yet, met with little response.

Invershin Highland 19F6
This crofting township stands where the River Shin joins the River Oykell to flow into the Kyle of Sutherland. High on a mound nearby, CARBISDALE CASTLE, with its towers and turrets, is the only castle built in this century in Scotland; completed in 1914 for the Countess of Sutherland, it has been a youth hostel for many years.

Just north of Invershin, on the road to Lairg, is Inveran Power Station; and in another 2km., just off the road, are the Falls of Shin: here, from a platform built above the tumbling river, salmon can often be watched making seemingly impossible leaps up the Falls.

In this area, in 1650, the Marquis of Montrose, fighting for the restoration of the monarchy, was finally defeated; but – despite having his horse shot under him – he escaped up Strath Oykell to Assynt: three days later he was captured at Ardvreck Castle (see Inchnadamph).

There is a very pleasant road from Invershin up Strath Oykell; it runs beside the river, with well-wooded scenery almost as far as Oykell Bridge, beyond which there are fine mountain views from the moorland road.

Iona Strathclyde 7B5
Less than 1½km. separate this small island from the south-west tip of Mull. But in crossing the brief stretch of water you also cross the centuries – to the calm of the most venerated place in Scotland. It is a calm that, incredibly, is never shattered, however many people there are on the island; and in summer up to 1,000 people a day have been known to visit Iona.

Here in 563 St Columba landed from Ireland with

Iona: St Martin's Cross, E side

twelve followers and established a monastery from which he and his monks – the community grew fairly quickly – travelled over much of the Highlands, and to some of the islands, preaching Christianity. In 565 he travelled by way of Loch Linnhe and the Great Glen to meet the Pictish king Brude at a fort, traditionally Craig Phadrig at Inverness. He may or may not have converted the king, but he won Brude's agreement to missionary journeys, as a result of which the northern Picts were converted. Churches were established in many parts of the Highlands, and St Columba continued

Iona: St Martin's Cross, W side

Iona: the Cathedral from the W, with Mull in the background

his work for thirty-four years, from his landing on Iona, which was always his headquarters, until his death in 597.

His work continued, despite the differences between the Celtic Church and the Church of Rome. But in 794 Iona was sacked by the Norsemen. It was the first of many raids: the rebuilt abbey was destroyed again in 801, and in 806 sixty-eight monks were killed by the Norsemen at what is now known as Martyrs' Bay, just south of the pier where visitors now land. After this event St Columba's shrine was moved to Ireland; in 825 the

abbot of Iona was killed for refusing to say where the shrine was hidden (today, there is no trace of it). The island was then left in peace until 986, when it was plundered again, and the abbot and fifteen monks killed. Iona remained a religious centre, although its importance dwindled. In 1203 Reginald, son of Somerled, King of the Isles, rebuilt the abbey as a Benedictine monastery; but by the sixteenth century it had fallen into ruin.

When Dr Johnson visited Iona in 1773 he wrote: 'The man is little to be envied . . . whose piety would not grow warmer among the ruins of Iona'; but these famous lines need to be read in the context of his other comments. He found that the abbey had fallen into utter neglect: the bottom of the church was 'encumbered with mud and

rubbish', and the chapel of the nunnery was used 'as a kind of general cowhouse'.

In 1899 the Duke of Argyll presented the cathedral to the Church of Scotland, and some restoration was started; the first service for centuries was held in the Cathedral in 1910.

The appearance of the religious buildings on Iona today, though, is due more to the founding in 1938 of the Iona Community under the inspiration of the Revd George MacLeod (now Lord MacLeod of Fiunary). Not only are the buildings restored, but Iona is a living religious community, with ministers and laymen maintaining the abbey and sharing worship and work.

Walking up from the village, near which are the remains of the sixteenth-century nunnery, you come first to Reilig Oran ('Oran's Graveyard'). Until the eleventh century Iona was the burial place of Scottish kings: forty-eight are said to rest here, along with others from Ireland, Norway, and, perhaps, France. (Dr Johnson was not very impressed by this claim, and in any case the forty-eight cannot all have been 'kings of Scotland'. The first to be king of both Picts and Scots was Kenneth MacAlpin, who died c. 860; the last to be buried here was Duncan, murdered in 1040.) No trace of these tombs remains; the many sculptured stones to be seen at Iona date from the late Middle Ages. But close to the west door of the Abbey there survives a cobbled street – the Street of the Dead – along which burial processions went on their way to Reilig Oran.

Nothing remains, either, of St Columba's monastery,

Iona: the Cathedral interior looking E

Chapel, standing separately and said to have been built by St Margaret, wife of Malcolm Canmore, in about 1080.

Even were there no abbey, no hallowed history, Iona would still be worth visiting. It is no great distance to walk to the north end of the island, with its gleaming white sands washed by clear seas: a beautiful spot – yet the scene of the massacre of the abbot and his monks in 986.

On the west of the island, PORT BAN is a sheltered cove facing the Atlantic, with a 'spouting cave', where high plumes of water shoot above the rocks in rough weather. To the south, on a beach of coloured pebbles, surrounded by rocky, low cliffs, is the PORT OF THE CORACLE, where St Columba landed over fourteen hundred years ago.

On the way back to the village is another aspect of religion in the Highlands – a plaque outside the parish church that records that in 1824 the Government engaged Thomas Telford to design and build thirty-two churches and forty-three manses in remote Highland parishes. This church and manse were built in 1830 at a cost of £1,503.

At present (1976) there is talk of beginning a car ferry to Iona – running from Fionnphort – which, for an island that has less than 4km. of motorable road, is a lunacy hard to comprehend.

Islay   Strathclyde   2B2   (*pop.* 3,855)

For years two car-ferry operators have competed for the traveller's patronage between the mainland and Islay, going to different parts of the island but each starting, though from different points, on West Loch Tarbert. One, the State-controlled Caledonian-MacBraynes, gets a hefty subsidy; the other, Western Ferries, gets nothing – but still plies.

It was not the holiday trade that led to this competition. Although tourism is a useful part of Islay's economy, it is by no means the predominant one. Islay owes its undoubted prosperity more to farming and distilling (some of the great malt whiskies of Scotland come from here). These, in turn, owe their existence to the make-up of the island; much of it, geologically, is Dalriadan Limestone, which yields good farming land; and the peat, while not particularly deep, adds its tang to the water for the distilleries. Whisky is undoubtedly the island's most valuable export, used in many blends as well as being sold 'straight'. (Some of the straight malts, incidentally, are not sent out of the island.) But distilling only employs about 200 people; the several hundred farms account for more. Mostly they are dairy farms: Islay cheese is a speciality.

Few islands equal Islay for variety of birdlife: nearly 180 species have been recorded here, and of these ninety-seven were noted in just two days of winter bird-watching. It is said that one sixth of all the barnacle geese in the world can be seen at LAGGAN BAY and the choughs, a rarity in Britain, are comparatively common

the buildings of which would have been of wattle and daub with thatched roofs. Yet on a low hillock opposite the west door of the Cathedral are rough stones believed to be the foundations of a cell where St Columba slept.

Outside this west door are two great crosses: St Martin's, dating from the ninth century, and St John's, a replica of the original cross, which was blown down.

The Cathedral itself is a plain but serenely beautiful building of pink granite contrasting both with lighter sandstone and darker stones – so effective an interior that decoration would be out of place. In date it is very mixed: some pillars are of the thirteenth century, but much of the fabric dates from *c.* 1420. South from the sixteenth-century choir are pillars of *c.* 1500, with entrancingly grotesque medieval carvings on the capitals; yet all these, and later, periods stand happily together, the only jarring note being the rather presumptuous tomb of the eighth Duke and Duchess of Argyll.

The cloisters, north of the church, have two medieval arches but otherwise are modern; in the centre is a remarkable carving done by a Jew, Jacob Lipschitz, who had to flee four countries to escape Nazi persecution.

The oldest building is the small, restored, St Oran's

The Italian Chapel on Lamb Holm, Orkney

Looking from Applecross towards the Cuillin Hills on Skye

Islay: the C9 (?) cross at Kildalton

houses and cottages, though of no particular architectural distinction. Around here are most of the island's distilleries.

From Port Ellen the main road goes, dead straight for much of its way, to Bowmore, 16km. distant. Although at least a km. inland, so flat is the land here that it is possible to see much of the 11km. of beach along Laggan Bay: but do not be tempted to stop just anywhere on these sands – they are not always as firm as they look. This road also passes Glenegadale Airport, sixty-five minutes from Glasgow, including a twenty-minute stop at Campbeltown.

Perhaps it is some measure of Islay's prosperity that to see it a car is needed: there is little in the way of public transport (most of it represented by the postbus); distances between places are on the long side for any but the dedicated walker; and a cycle is not necessarily an alternative on an island facing the Atlantic winds.

Bowmore is really the central village of the island. It was the 'capital' of Islay in earlier days, and the 'Islay Parliament' – more a feudal court than a legislative assembly – met here from 1718 to 1843. Today's village, with its wide streets, was built in the mid eighteenth century: the main street leads up from the pier – the village stands beside Loch Indaal – to the parish church of Kilmarrow. This church is unusual in being circular in shape (allegedly so that no evil spirits can hide round corners). It was built in 1767, an inscribed panel on the tower records, by Daniel Campbell, 'Lord of this Island'.

From Bridgend, charmingly set among woods (not common on Islay), the A846 crosses the island to Port Askaig, with fine views across the Sound of Islay to Jura. Port Askaig is where one of the ferries from West Loch Tarbert docks, and it is the crossing point for Feolin on Jura. This is almost as far north as you will get with a car on Islay: after a 5km. road to Bonahaven Bay, with its distillery, there is only a path to Rubh a' Mhail point and lighthouse.

Loch Indaal almost cuts the island in two. Along its west shores are Bruichladdich, with another distillery, Port Charlotte, with the creamery whence comes Islay cheese, and, at the end of the point and looking across to Ireland, Portnahaven, above a rocky inlet sheltered from Atlantic breakers by two off-shore islets.

The pattern of the island villages varies hardly at all: pleasant well-built white houses by the water, chances for boating or sailing or sea-angling, good beaches not too far away (the west coast – despite Atlantic winds – is best for this), and bays reached by minor roads.

Islay has another attraction, too. There are not a few remains of prehistoric man, though none are outstanding. In historic times, being so near to Ireland, Islay became considerably more 'civilized' than places further north; from this period of Irish influence date the carved crosses on the island. The most famous is that at Kildalton: to see this cross, only equalled by those on Iona, take the road east from Port Ellen for 12km. The

on The Oa, whose cliffs and caves were once useful places for smuggling and illicit whisky distilling.

At the Mull of Oa, the south-west extremity of this broad peninsula, there is a monument, erected by the American Red Cross, to the 650 men who lost their lives on the troopships *Tuscania* and *Otranto*, the former torpedoed, the latter driven ashore, in 1918.

The Oa lies west of Port Ellen, the main centre of the island and a pleasant spot with its harbour and white

JOHN O' GROATS

cross is said to date from the ninth century, though this is disputed: its style would suggest a later dating. Whatever its age, the cross, standing nearly 3m. high, is a superb piece of carving; and it is only one of seventeen on Islay.

Past the approach to Kildalton the road ends at Ardtalla; here again there is a path along the coast to a lighthouse, at McArthur's Head, with good views to Jura.

Islay is a green and friendly island, and little 'developed' for the holidaymaker. Much of its interest – birds and beaches, sea views and crosses – it shares with other Hebridean islands; a difference, perhaps, is to be found in its quiet prosperity.

John o' Groats   Highland   20F1

Here, nearly 500km. from its start near Edinburgh, the A9 comes to an end. For those who would go 'from Land's End to John o' Groats', the distance is 1,405km. Once there, they will find but a few cottages, one or two inevitable souvenir places, a hotel, a little harbour, and a flagstaff and mound. The mound commemorates Jan de Groot, who came to Scotland in the early sixteenth century. He had eight descendants, joint owners of the land, who argued about precedence. To solve this an octagonal house, with a door on each side and an octagonal table inside, was built and everybody, it is said, was satisfied.

The house has long since disappeared; but Jan de Groot's gravestone is at Canisbay, 4km. west, at the simple but attractive church that is the most northerly on mainland Scotland.

John o' Groats, for all its end-of-the-road trumpery, is well worth going to for its scenery. Across the Pentland Firth, with the island of Stroma 5km. offshore to the north-west, and the Pentland Skerries east-north-east, are the Orkney islands; and just east of John o' Groats is DUNCANSBY HEAD with its lighthouse, an even finer viewpoint. South of the Head great rock pinnacles rise offshore: Duncansby Stacks, backed by fine sandstone cliffs pierced with deep gashes known as 'geos'. The Long Geo, with sheer 65m. walls, runs over 90m. inland; nearby is a natural rock bridge, The Glupe. Other stacks are known as The Knee, Tom Thumb's Stack, Little Stack, and Muckle Stack, the last rising over 90m. All can be seen by walking along the cliffs.

Jura   Strathclyde   2C1

Some 200 people and 5,000 red deer make up much of the population of Jura, perhaps the least-known of the larger Hebridean islands. Seen from Knapdale (qv), the three Paps of Jura – Beinn a' Chaolais, Beinn an Oir, and Beinn Shiantaidh, each rising over 730m. above sea-level – make a magnificent panorama across the Sound

RIGHT: *Early Christian cross at Kilmartin*

of Jura. But opportunities for exploring the island are not extensive: there is but one village, Craighouse, which has a hotel. There is a car ferry that takes ten minutes to cross the Sound of Islay from Port Askaig on Islay, and a bus runs from Feolin up the eastern shores of the island to Ardlussa. There the road, 37km. long and the only one on the island, stops. The last dozen km., further north, have deteriorated to a track; but it is one worth following to the north end of the island, for between there and the island of Scarba are the Strait of Corryvreckan and the infamous whirlpool (*see* Ardfern). The track, so far as it goes, should be kept to: the whole of north Jura is peat bogs and moorland, and no place in which to lose one's way.

All the western side of the island is uninhabited, and probably always has been. Its coast has some of the most remarkable raised beaches in Scotland, standing 30m. above sea-level; caves pit the high cliffs, and there is a wealth of seabirds, particularly round Loch Tarbert, which almost cuts the island in two.

This crofting island is tempting to the lover of deserted places; but away from the east coast it is not easy of access, even to the seasoned walker. Nor is the use of a boat necessarily the answer, with Corryvreckan to the north and the Sound of Islay, with notorious tide races, to the south.

Kilmartin Strathclyde 4A5

Kilmartin is a small village, with a church and an inn, in an attractive glen. It is also in the midst of one of the most fascinating areas on the Scottish mainland, with archaeological remains ranging in time from cairns of *c.* 3000 BC to sixteenth-century Carnasserie Castle.

At Kilmartin itself, in the typical west-Highland churchyard, are finely-sculptured grave slabs and a skilfully-carved Early Christian cross. One km. south-west of the village, across the Kilmartin Burn, are the Nether Largie cairns, the best of which, the South Cairn – one of the largest in the country – is a megalithic chambered cairn dating back to the third millennium BC. Nearby is the Temple Wood stone circle, thirteen of the original twenty stones erected in about 1800 BC still standing.

The South Cairn at Nether Largie, Kilmartin

Many more standing stones and stone circles, cup-and-ring markings, and other ancient remains, in various states of preservation, are to be found in this area.

Some 6km. south of Kilmartin, a farm road leads to a hillock standing up from the flat Moine Mhor (the 'Great Moss'). Excavations have shown that here was a Dark Age fort on the site of an earlier, Iron Age, settlement. This is more than just another fort. It is DUNADD, the 'capital' of Dalriada, established in the sixth century by the Scots from Ireland. It does not require a

great deal of imagination to see the entrance to this fort in the deep gully, or to identify the two lower enclosures and the citadel at the top, where the imprint of a human foot, a carving of a boar, and a basin are carved out of the rock. According to tradition, the footprint is that of Fergus, the first king of Dalriada; each successive king placed his foot in it as part of the installation ceremony.

CARNASSERIE CASTLE stands on a green hill just west of the junction of the roads to Loch Awe and Oban, north of Kilmartin. Although partly blown up in 1685

Kilmartin: Temple Wood stone circle

when Argyll made the mistake of backing Monmouth's rebellion, this castle, built in the 1560s, is still worth seeing.

It was the home of John Carswell, Bishop of the Isles, an eminent scholar who published the first book ever printed in Gaelic, a translation of John Knox's *Liturgy*, in 1567.

Kilmelford   Strathclyde   4A4

While Kilmartin (qv) is to be explored for its archaeological and historic remains, the attractions of Kilmelford, 21km. further north by road, are scenic.

The road from Lochgilphead crosses the head of Loch Craignish (*see* Ardfern), then comes to the coast, with magnificent views to Shuna and Luing across Asknish Bay, at the north end of which, on the point at the end of Loch Melfort, are the coastal gardens of ARDUAINE. These are open from April to October, with attractive displays of rhododendrons, azaleas, and magnolias at the appropriate seasons. Past this, the road goes along the south shore of Loch Melfort, a charming inlet looking almost landlocked by the islands beyond its mouth. The new road then goes almost due north above the old Pass of Melfort, a ravine down which runs the River Oude. Below the new, the old road can be seen following the river: it is worth walking when the sun is well up. At the top of the Pass the river takes a sharp turn east to drain Loch Tralaig, one of the largest of over a dozen freshwater lochs in the area east of the road; all of these lochs have a good supply of salmon and trout. The road continues down Glen Gallain, and in 3km. crosses Glen Euchar, where salmon essay the leaps up the River Euchar, to Loch Scamadale. Kilninver and the approach to Seil Island (qv) are a few km. further on.

Kilmun   Strathclyde   4D6

No stretch of water is more inappropriately named today than the Holy Loch, where the USA has its depôt

Dunadd Fort, 6km S of Kilmartin: the rock carvings are (left to right) a human foot, a boar (under glass), and a basin

ship for nuclear-powered submarines – which are also often to be seen there – along with a huge dry dock and other erections suitable only for an unholy purpose.

This naval activity is concentrated near the pier at Kilmun, on the north shores of the loch; but it does not appear to detract from the appeal of the village of Kilmun or of Strone, on the point of the loch, or of Blairmore, a short way up Loch Long. Each of these was once a separate village; but they are now more or less one.

The Holy Loch probably takes its name from St Mun, who in the early seventh century built a small monastery here: nothing remains of it but the name Kilmun, the 'Church of Mun'.

Beyond Kilmun church, the Forestry Commission's Kilmun Arboretum is a collection of forest plots containing a remarkable variety of foreign trees, including the best collection of Australian eucalyptus in Scotland. There are over 12km. of paths to walk around.

From Strone Point, the road continues up the west side of Loch Long, but ends at ARDENTINNY, a neat enough village in a delightful setting of hills and woods, but looking across the loch to Coulport, a hideous reminder of the Polaris establishment on the Holy Loch.

Loch Long, the easternmost boundary of the Cowal Peninsula, has seen much traffic since King Haakon sailed his galleys up to Arrochar (qv). Oil tankers have been among the most recent visitors, bringing their cargoes to Finnart, 10km. further up the loch and on its eastern shore. From there the oil goes by pipeline for nearly 150km. to Grangemouth on the River Forth. The Finnart storage tanks, however, are not in view at Ardentinny, where the road leaves the loch and goes through Glen Finart to Loch Eck. There are pleasant farms and woods for much of the way; but at and over the pass, and along the road down to Whistlefield, Forestry Commission planting has not improved the scenery.

Kincraig Highland 9H1
This Spey Valley village lies on the traffic-ridden A9, which it is fortunately easy to leave for a delightful walk across the bridge to see Loch Insh, small but one of the most charming lochs in the district. Here, atop a mound, Insh church stands on a site said to have been used continuously for worship since the sixth century.

Just beyond Insh, the road forks west to FESHIE-BRIDGE. Here – not surprisingly – there is a bridge over the River Feshie; it crosses a fine gorge, and there is a picturesque track up the glen. General Wade planned a road here to link Speyside with Deeside; but it was never constructed. For many years, more recently, the building of this road has been urged, to make a 'round trip' for motorists; fortunately, the high cost of this project is likely to render it impossible for many years to come – if ever.

Near Kincraig is the HIGHLAND WILDLIFE PARK, where in extensive, reasonably natural surroundings may be seen creatures that used to live in the Highlands, such as wolves, wild boars, beavers, and brown bears, along with many that are still to be seen (though not by any means without a large amount of luck), including such as the wild cat and the capercailzie.

Kingussie Highland 9G2 (*pop.* 1,040)
Although St Columba (or one of his monks) is believed to have founded a chapel here, and there was a Carmelite friary founded by the Earl of Huntly at the end of

Ruthven Barracks, Kingussie

Liathach, W of Kinlochewe, seen across Loch Clair

the fifteenth century, nothing remains of either. The main attraction of this Spey Valley village (officially a 'small burgh') is the Highland Folk Museum at Am Fasgadh, founded in 1935 by Dr Isabel F. Grant; it is one of the earliest and still one of the most fascinating of the numerous (perhaps too numerous) folk museums now in Scotland.

Outside the village are the gaunt ruins of Ruthven Barracks, in use for less than thirty years. They were built in 1718, on a site that was the motte of fourteenth-century Ruthven Castle, to keep the Highlanders under control after the 1715 rising. Following their defeat at Culloden in 1746, fugitives from Prince Charles's army gathered at these barracks, hoping Charles might lead them again. But instead he sent a message telling them to seek their own safety.

James Macpherson, whose claim to have 'translated the works of Ossian' earned him a final resting place in the Poets' Corner of Westminster Abbey, was born in 1738 at the clachan of Ruthven, of which nothing now remains. Kingussie today is a popular holiday centre for the Spey Valley.

Kinlochewe   Highland   14B2

West from this characterless village at the junction of the roads to Gairloch and Torridon is a vast area of magni-

ficent mountains, an area with an outstanding collection of flora and fauna. This is the BEINN EIGHE NATIONAL NATURE RESERVE, covering over 4,000ha. The nine-peak ridge of Beinn Eighe reaches 1,009m. Adjoining this mountain is Liathach (*pron.* Leeagach), with seven tops rising to Spidean a' Choire Leith, 1,053m. high; and to the west Beinn Alligin, 921m., stands above upper Loch Torridon: this is the Torridon Estate, which in 1967 was taken into the care of the NTS.

A notable feature of Liathach and Beinn Eighe is the white quartzite that tops the former and comes almost to road level in the latter. These are Cambrian rocks whose strata were laid down some 600 million years ago; they rest on Torridonian Sandstone probably 150 million years older, which in turn is on beds of Lewisian Gneiss, dating back some 2,700 million years. It is hardly surprising that this area, subsequently eroded and carved by glaciation – of which there is much evidence – fascinates geologists.

The barren slopes of these two mountain groups are also rewarding to the botanist, who will find a wide variety of plants clinging to the rock ledges, often making spectacular alpine rock gardens on the tiered sandstone cliffs.

Here, too, is wildlife ranging from the largest to the smallest in Britain – the animals from the red deer to the pygmy shrew, the birds from the golden eagle to the goldcrest. Other animals include wild cat and pine marten; other birds peregrine, merlin, raven, greenshank, ptarmigan, and ring ouzel.

On the Loch Maree road north-west from Kinlochewe the Nature Conservancy Council has a visitor centre at Aultroy Cottage, where much fascinating information is to hand. But to see the animals and birds the Nature Trails in the Reserve, and other tracks among the hills, must be followed; walkers should of course be properly shod and clad.

Past Aultroy is LOCH MAREE, which many claim to be the finest of Scottish inland lochs, its only likely rival being Loch Lomond. But Loch Maree is infinitely wilder than its even longer competitor further south, and, by the motorist, can be seen much better.

Towering above the south-east end of Loch Maree is shapely Slioch. And in the loch itself is a cluster of islands; one of the smallest of these is Isle Maree, said to have been a sacred place for pagans over 1,300 years ago, and holding the scant remains of a chapel, possibly built by St Maelrubha, who died in 621, and an ancient graveyard. The island is best seen from a track that follows the north-east shore of Loch Maree, under Slioch and by Letterewe: there is a right-of-way for much of the loch's length.

Kinlochleven Highland 8C5

Before the bridge across Loch Leven was opened in 1975 many motorists travelling to and from Fort William elected to go round the loch rather than wait for the ferry. It involved an extra 21km. driving; but it usually took no more time than waiting for the ferry, and was infinitely more rewarding scenically.

Along the south side of the loch the road climbs and swoops with good views across to the mountains of the Mamore Forest, rising, at Binnein Mor, almost to 1,130m. For first-time visitors it is usually a disagreeable surprise to find that Kinlochleven, at the head of the loch, is not a picturesque village but rather a small industrial town, with rows of great pipes laid up the hill behind it.

At the beginning of the twentieth century Kinlochleven did not exist; but in 1908 an aluminium works was established, gaining its power from hydro-electricity generated by water coming from the Blackwater Reservoir high in the hills $6\frac{1}{2}$km. to the east. About 1,000 people are employed at this works.

Until a few years ago Kinlochleven was certainly a depressing place; but extensive re-painting and tidyingup operations have taken place since, and while nobody can pretend that the town is picturesque, it has certainly made the best of what it is. Cheerfully colour-washed houses might seem inappropriate in such a setting; but in a town that for some four months of the year gets no sunshine, so deeply set is it among great mountains, colour is welcome.

South-east from the town, the old military road to the head of Glen Coe climbs to 533m. over the DEVIL'S STAIRCASE – an 8km. walk, not as fearsome as its name suggests. North-west from the town this same military road continues round the western end of the Mamore ridge to Fort William, 20km. away. In 1975 the British Aluminium Company opened up two walks into the hills behind the town, one leading to the Grey Mare's Tail waterfall, and one by the riverside. The main road along the north shore of Loch Leven is comparatively level, and before reaching North Ballachulish there is a splendid view up Glen Coe.

The fastest way from one side of Loch Leven to the other, now, is undoubtedly the bridge; but the journey to Kinlochleven, with adequate time and light, is well worth making.

Knapdale Strathclyde 3E1

This large area of land lying between the Crinan Canal

Eilean Mor, off Knapdale: effigy in the C12 chapel

and West Loch Tarbert is comparatively little known to the tourist. The roads do not 'go anywhere': all are narrow, none go round the area, and only one runs across it. The few hotels are small and other accommodation is very limited; the visitor, if he tours the area at all, tends to base himself at Lochgilphead, Ardrishaig, or Tarbert.

Yet there are few more beautiful seascapes in Scotland than that seen from Knapdale's west coast, looking to the Paps of Jura across the Sound.

From Bellanoch, beside the Crinan Canal, a minor road goes south to fork, shortly, into two dead-end roads that then run down opposite sides of Loch Sween. Each has its own kind of beauty. The right fork runs between lush woods and narrow Caol Scotnish, a branch of Loch Sween, before coming to a wider bay. This is TAY-VALLICH, a small place with a long beach; across the narrow neck of land is Carsaig Bay, with views to Jura from a level sward. Tayvallich – which is pronounced Tayviallich, stressing the second 'a' – has some new holiday houses: but they are not unpleasant.

It is some 11km. from Tayvallich down the peninsula, where, at the head of Loch na Cille, the road branches right for Keills, with the roofless but otherwise well-preserved remains of an eleventh-century chapel. Here there is a remarkable collection of carved slabs dating back to the fourteenth and fifteenth centuries (but sadly worn by weathering); nearby is a high Celtic Cross almost as old as the chapel.

Another minor road goes down the east side of Loch na Cille to Danna Island (there is a causeway across). Looking down the Sound of Jura, Gigha, off Kintyre, is visible, and, lying very low on the horizon, Rathlin Island off the north coast of Ireland. Much nearer is the island of Eilean Mor, with other reminders of the religious settlements here many centuries ago: these include the remains of a twelfth-century chapel and a cell built 500 years earlier by St Carmaig. The island is but 3km. from Dana, but can only be reached by hiring a boat.

The other road from near Bellanoch runs along the east side of Loch Sween, with Forestry Commission houses *en route*, to CASTLE SWEEN, the massive ruins of which stand above a beautiful bay. This small bay, unfortunately, no longer has the loneliness it deserves: a very large caravan site adjoins it and does nothing whatever for what is almost certainly the oldest stone castle on the Scottish mainland: it was probably built by Somerled, King of the Isles, around 1150.

Towards the end of the peninsula, at Kilmory Knap, fourteenth-century MacMillan's Cross stands nearly 4m. high near the Chapel of St Maelrubha, ruined but containing some thirty late-medieval sculptured stones, many well preserved. A short way beyond Kilmory, the road ends.

South Knapdale can be circled by taking the minor road running along the north-west side of West Loch Tarbert from Tarbert. It runs through woods and beside the loch until it cuts across a low headland to Loch Stornoway, with standing stones at its head, where, in spring, flocks of wild geese congregate.

Apart from a collection of more medieval sculptured stones at Kilberry Castle, there is nothing of note along this western shore to the head of Loch Killisport. Nothing, that is, except small fields and occasional woods, rushes and a mass of wild flowers, and eider duck and waders along the shore.

After the road leaves Loch Killisport, a road – little more than a track – doubles back for Ellary, a private estate, whose owners have done much to care for ST COLUMBA'S CAVE, on the west side of the loch. This cave, in a rock bluff, stands above a ruined chapel, probably dating from the twelfth century, and round it once ordered gardens have been allowed to grow beautifully wild. The cave is as much a chapel as a dwelling, with an altar, bowls carved in the rock for holding water, and a small cross. It is quite possible that St Columba did use this cave, either before or after he went to Iona in 563.

From Loch Killisport the road climbs over high moorland, past Loch Errol, to drop down to Loch Fyne south of Ardrishaig. The once bare beauty of much of this shapely moorland, from which there are fine views back over Loch Killisport to Islay and Jura, is being rapidly destroyed by extensive Forestry Commission plantings.

Kyle of Lochalsh   Highland   17F6

Here is the end of the road, and of the railway also, from Inverness, and from here the car ferry to Kyleakin on Skye operates.

The strait Kyle Akin, not 1km. wide, separates the island from the mainland; according to tradition, it is named after King Haakon, who anchored here during his voyage to the Firth of Clyde, before his defeat at the Battle of Largs, in 1263. On its south shore, opposite Kyle of Lochalsh, are the slight remains of Castle Moil, a small thirteenth-century keep said to have been built by the daughter of a Norse king to exact toll from ships using the strait. She would have made a fortune in our own time, as, during the holiday season, this is one of the busiest sea crossings in the country, the car ferries running shuttle services to ferry visitors to and from Skye; in addition there is a constantly increasing commercial traffic. For some years there have been proposals to build a bridge across the strait, but the cost has so far prevented it.

Kyle of Lochalsh, although itself rather undistinguished, has magnificent views of the jagged Cuillin Hills. And Kyle is a good touring centre, not only for Skye but also for boat trips along the Sound of Sleat and to Toscaig on the Applecross Peninsula.

Thirteen km. east, along the north shores of Loch Alsh, is BALMACARA, where the NTS has an estate of some 2,500ha. covering most of the peninsula: the

Sunset over the Red Hills seen from Kyle of Lochalsh

visitor centre and woodland garden at Lochalsh House are well worth visiting.

Kylescu Highland 18C4

Here traffic from Ullapool to the far north crosses Loch Cairnbawn just west of where that loch forks to become lochs Glencoul and Glendhu. The car ferry for the short crossing to Kylestrome tends to be busy in summer but until 1976 there was the consolation, almost unique, that it was free. For that year, however, the new District Council imposed tolls in the knowledge that as the alternative was a drive over 160km. long they were unlikely to face diminishing traffic.

From here there are splendid views of Quinag (811m.) and Glasven (714m.), to the south. The latter has nothing of the drama of the Quinag ridge, but has the distinction of holding Britain's highest waterfall, Eas-Coul Aulin, which has an unbroken drop of 200m. The falls are not easy to get to: there is no track along the side of Loch Glencoul, only steep grassy slopes above sheer

Looking W along Loch Laggan

cliffs, and the falls are a further 1½km. beyond the head of the loch. From the summit of the road south of Kylescu there is a scanty track that leads by Loch Ganvich towards the head of the falls: but, again, it is not easy going.

Laggan Highland 9F2

Laggan Bridge and Loch Laggan are only 10km. apart; but between them is the watershed between the Spey Valley and the Great Glen.

At Laggan Bridge, an iron structure, the road from Newtonmore crosses the Spey, which, fed by countless streams, has come from Loch Spey, 20km. east, down a long, lonely glen. It is a glen seen now only by the hardened walker who follows General Wade's road to Fort Augustus: Laggan Bridge is the last village he will see for well over 30km.; although a very minor metalled road goes east for about a third of the distance, the real

wilderness is further east, with the 774m. Corrieyairack Pass to surmount.

Today's road from the Spey Valley to the Great Glen, the A86, cuts through the mountains by Loch Laggan and Loch Moy to Spean Bridge. It follows Strath Mashie briefly; but after the Mashie Water, flowing to the Spey, is crossed, it is but 2km. before the road comes to the River Pattock, flowing east into Loch Laggan; going through pleasant woods, the watershed is almost unnoticed.

Loch Laggan, beside which the road runs for about a dozen km. (with, in places, good views of the Ben Alder Forest mountains), is bigger than it used to be. The Lochaber Power Scheme pre-dated the operations of the North of Scotland Hydro-Electric Board: between 1931 and 1943 a big dam was built at the south-west end of Loch Moy, virtually linking it to Loch Laggan and increasing the length of the latter by over 5km. From here,

The dam on Loch Laggan

the water is piped to link with that coming from Loch Treig.

East of Laggan Bridge, off the road to Newtonmore, Cluny Castle was the home of Cluny MacPherson (*see* Dalwhinnie), and there are many MacPherson graves in Laggan churchyard. The Newtonmore road goes above the north bank of the Spey: above its south bank a minor road goes from Catlodge, just east of Laggan Bridge, to join the A9 south of Newtonmore. Beside this road there is a stone said to mark the exact geographical centre of Scotland: but in so intricately-shaped a country there are, not surprisingly, other places that lay claim to this distinction.

Lairg Highland 19F6

This village at the foot of Loch Shin is a meeting point for the roads from Bonar Bridge and Dornoch, and from there roads radiate into the north-west Highlands. 'All roads meet at Lairg', it is claimed locally.

Loch Shin, stretching 27km. north-west (but only at one point more than 4km. wide), is now harnessed for hydro-electricity and is a well-known angling loch.

Roads and fish, and the fact that Lairg is a reasonably attractive stopping-off place for tourists, make the village a holiday place; but the biggest congregation of bodies is in August when the sheep sales are held here; there are about a quarter of a million sheep in the Sutherland hills, and Lairg is a major market.

The area north of Lairg is rather featureless moorland. Here, and around Rogart, some 15km. east, are many remains of Iron Age hut circles. ROGART is the centre of a flourishing crofting community. The beautiful Rovie Lodge gardens here are normally open to the public between mid July and the end of September: the herbaceous borders and water garden are notable features.

Latheron Highland 20E4

The village of Latheron is at the junction of two main roads, the A9 to Wick and the A895 to Thurso, the latter built as a single, planned operation in the late eighteenth century by Sir John Sinclair (*see* Thurso).

Just south-west, a road goes down from the main road to the coast: this is Janetstown, also known as Latheronwheel, where the steepish road ends at a small and charming natural harbour carved out of the steep cliffs.

The area is rich in prehistoric remains. At the main road junction there is a massive standing stone, over 3m. high, with a smaller one nearby. North-east of Latheron, between Forse House and Upper Latheron, is the Wag of Forse, excavated in 1939 and in 1946 to reveal a massive circular drystone enclosure with remains of stone long-houses: it is probably early Iron Age.

Further north, just south of Loch Stemster, is a remarkable collection of thirty-six thin stones and stumps in a 'U' formation: the Standing Stones of Stemster, dating possibly from Neolithic times; their purpose is uncertain.

These are only some of the many reminders of long habitation in the area; the remains of most, though, are scant: the stones have often been 'quarried' for later building.

Lewis Highland 22 (*pop.* 14,959)

There are two facets to Lewis. One is the island itself, flat or undulating low moorland, scattered with lochs and lochans – and where not actually water, often sodden – with a long coast holding many beaches and cliff-surrounded bays. The other is its capital, Stornoway.

These two aspects of this Outer Hebridean island have little in common. But Stornoway has not always been in such sharp contrast to the rest of the island. Although created a 'burgh of barony' by James VI (James I of England), it was no more than a poor fishing hamlet then. At that time there was a MacLeod castle there – soon after taken by the Mackenzies – but not much else; and the castle was largely destroyed by Cromwell's troops in the mid seventeenth century. It was not until the latter part of the eighteenth century that the town started to develop its natural harbour, and by the beginning of the twentieth century it had become the main centre of the Scottish herring industry. Lord Leverhulme tried to extend the fishing interests, but failed because of the clash of interest between him and the inhabitants (*see* Harris).

Gradually the fishing failed; and the depression of the early 1930s, competition from boats that could land their catches at harbours directly linked – by road or rail – with the markets, such as Mallaig and Oban, and, finally, the outbreak of war in 1939, which, as in 1914, took away the young men to the Navy and the Merchant Navy (the islands have always been a major source of such supply), left only a remnant of the industry.

As the fishing failed, after World War I, the tweed-weaving industry developed. The Harris people had been hand-weaving tweeds for centuries (Harris tweeds were first sold in London in the 1830s). Stornoway became the main centre for spinning yarn and finishing the world-famous tweed, which was protected from infringement by a judgment in the Court of Session (the supreme law court of Scotland) in 1964. This judgment laid down that the 'orb' trademark of Harris Tweed could only be used if the cloth was 'made from pure virgin wool, produced in Scotland, spun, dyed and finished in the Outer Hebrides, and hand-woven by the islanders at their own homes in the islands of Lewis, Harris, Uist, Barra and their several appurtenances, and all known as the Outer Hebrides'. During the 1960s there was a tremendous boom in Harris Tweed: over 5 million m. were produced annually, some three quarters of it being exported. But change of fashion and the impact of man-made fibres caused a slump in the early 1970s. To counter this, in 1975 proposals for streamlining the industry were put to the weavers: these included the introduction of power-driven looms housed in small 'factories' of up to twelve units each, which would produce double-width cloth, compared with the single width of the handlooms. As Lord Leverhulme found fifty years earlier, the islanders were by no means happy that the traditional pattern of working should be changed, and in April 1976 the weavers emphatically rejected the proposed change. Between 1970 and 1975 the number of weavers dropped from 1,329 to 630; but it is believed that there will always be a demand for the hand-woven tweed.

In the meantime, however, a new industry has appeared on the Stornoway horizon and has brought new prosperity to the town. In August 1974 the Scottish Development Department (a branch of the Scottish Office) listed Stornoway as a 'preferred development zone' for North Sea oil, and construction work started at Glumaig, on the south side of Stornoway harbour, on fabrication work for rigs and production platforms and on the development of a service base. (It is somewhat

ironic that the Secretary of State, while expressing the view that 'Stornoway should be developed in preference to allowing development pressure to fall on the west coast of the mainland of Scotland', at about the same time allowed the 'development' of Kishorn – *see* Applecross.)

So, for the third time, as one industry slumps in Stornoway another takes its place. It is quite typical of this lively town, which, contrary to expectation, presents a colourful picture. West of the town, Lewis Castle, built in the 1840s by Sir James Matheson (who was largely responsible for other local developments of that period), was later given to the town by Lord Leverhulme and is now a technical college; it stands in extensive parkland and its masses of rhododendrons are a delight in early summer.

East from Stornoway, the Eye Peninsula is connected to the mainland by a neck of land hardly wider than the road that runs along it; here are some of the beaches that attract the holidaymaker to Lewis.

The rest of Lewis presents a very different picture. The

Lewis: the Standing Stones of Callanish

old 'black houses' have largely disappeared or, as in so much of the western Highlands, been hideously re-roofed with corrugated iron to serve as storage sheds. The crofters, mostly, live in unimaginative new local-authority houses: usually they do their best to brighten them up with gay paint on doors and window frames; but often, too, when there is space – and that there certainly is on Lewis – it is easier to dump unwanted material than to clear it away. While the houses are no different from their many suburban counterparts on the mainland, more incongruous are the piles of peats stored beside them. Lewis does not pay exorbitant prices for coal, and there is virtually no wood: the population dig their fuel from the moors, the peat many m. deep laid down perhaps 9,000 years ago.

The peat is now about 3m. deeper than it was some 3,500 years ago when prehistoric man erected the STANDING STONES OF CALLANISH. Only the tops of these stones were showing when Sir James Matheson undertook their excavation; today they stand up to 4½m. high, and are second in importance only to Stonehenge – and vastly more impressive in their loneliness – although, incredibly, in 1975 it was suggested that a 'housing scheme' should be extended to the fringe of the area. At Callanish an avenue, over 8m. wide and 80m. long, lined with nineteen standing stones, leads to a circle of thirteen stones; and from this circle more rows of stones fan out. Built, probably over a long period, between 2000 and 1500 BC, the purpose of Callanish remains a mystery. It could have had a religious function (though a suggestion that a chambered cairn inside the circle was an altar for sacrifices is probably over-fanciful); it could have been for astronomical purposes, though the geometrical explanations for this are rather over-complicated. Whatever the reason for Callanish, it is immensely impressive.

The road from Callanish goes north by the shores of East Loch Roag and in about 10km. a side road leads to the other major archaeological remain on Lewis, the DUN CARLOWAY BROCH, the best-preserved Iron Age broch in the Western Isles. Though partly cut away now, it shows the double wall and galleries that were a feature of these buildings; in one place the walls are still nearly 7m. high.

There are various reminders of the past on the road from Carloway to the Butt of Lewis. At Shawbost a museum created locally in a Highland-village competition in 1970 shows the old way of life in Lewis, and nearby is a restored Norse watermill. At Arnol a 'black house' has been turned into a museum, and shows what these traditional dwellings were like: low buildings of rough stones without mortar, roofed with thatch, and with a peat fire in the centre – with no chimney to let the smoke escape.

At the oddly-named Europie, almost at the northern end of Lewis, is Teampull Mholuidh (the church of St Moluag), the walls of which were built in the late twelfth century. It was restored in 1912 and is used for services by the Scottish Episcopal Church. That form of worship is, in Lewis, unusual: the island is a major stronghold of the Free Church of Scotland and even in Stornoway, for all its bustling, near-cosmopolitan air, the Sabbath is a day when the only activity should be church-going. In recent years the Church's strictures have been increasingly ignored by a younger generation no longer prepared to tolerate them; but tradition dies hard.

There is on Lewis an abundance of brown-trout fishing, though for salmon and sea trout the opportunities are more restricted. Stornoway is a leading sea-angling centre, catches including blue shark as well as the more usual conger, halibut, cod, and skate.

Many people are attracted to Lewis by the island's immense sense of space: the very desolation of its moors, the emptiness of its remoter beaches, are compelling.

Loch Awe Strathclyde 4B4

For centuries the Campbells completely dominated the area of Argyll around Loch Awe and Loch Fyne. The clan sprang from the Campbells of Lochawe, whose castle stood – and still stands in ruin – on an island, Innis Chonnel, near Portinnisherrich on Loch Awe.

The main road through Dalmally to Oban runs alongside Loch Awe's most scenic stretch, which, in fact, is a branch of the 37km.-long loch.

During the Ice Age the glaciers that covered what is now Loch Awe moved in a south-westerly direction towards today's Firth of Lorn. When the glaciers melted, the glacial moraine became fertile land (now studded with archaeological remains) between Ford, at the foot of Loch Awe, and Crinan. Loch Awe drains to the sea through the Pass of Brander, through which, also, go the main road and the railway.

Going west from Dalmally, perhaps the most striking view to be seen from the loch is visible almost immediately: on a flat marsh rise the high ruins of KIL-CHURN CASTLE, with the great mass of Ben Cruachan as a backcloth. The castle was built c. 1440 by Sir Colin Campbell of Glenorchy, whose family subsequently became Earls, then Marquesses, of Breadalbane. To Sir Colin's original keep, other buildings were added in 1693; but within fifty years the castle was abandoned. One of its towers was blown down by a great gale in January 1879 – the same gale that blew down the Tay Bridge to Dundee – but it is still a moving sight.

Round the head of the loch, and just past the village of Lochawe, an odd church stands above the loch: St Conan's Kirk. A small, simple church was completed here in 1886 by Walter Douglas Campbell; but he was not satisfied with it, wanting something nobler. He started on a new building in 1907; but it was not completed until 1931, long after his death. To build it, boulders from the hill were rolled down, split, and shaped on the spot. The end result is an odd mixture of

Kilchurn Castle on Loch Awe

126

styles, with ornate, often inappropriate, features inside and out.

Further on is the approach to the most remarkable power station in the country, built *inside* Ben Cruachan, and opened in 1965. From a reservoir created in a corrie 401m. above sea-level, two long shafts take water down to the power station, excavated out of solid rock, and about the height of a seven-storey building. Water is pumped up from Loch Awe – usually at night and at weekends when the demand for electricity is lowest – and is supplemented by water from the catchment area of the Ben through 16km. of tunnels and piped aqueducts. Visitors are welcomed at the power station, and taken from the roadside in minibuses through a km.-long road tunnel, to see where 450 million units of electricity are produced annually.

West from the power station, road, rail, and river crush together through the narrow Pass of Brander before dropping down to Taynuilt.

The long loch itself hardly lives up to the scenic beauty promised from, say, the memorial above Dalmally. The road along the south-east shores is too narrow and twisting for either motoring or walking with pleasure; too often the views of the loch are hidden by trees and bushes, and there is a plethora of 'No' signs – no parking, no camping, no picnics. It is a fine fishing loch, though. Near the pleasant hamlet of Portinnisherrich is a fine view of the ruins of the Campbell castle. Ford, at the south end of the loch, is a resort for anglers, and from here another road runs along the north-west shores of the loch through New York (a derelict house and pier) and Dalavich, a forestry village, to Kilchrenan, where the churchyard has some interesting old stones.

As a change from the monotonous conifers along this road, it is refreshing to take the minor road to Ardanaseig, where, from April to October, beautiful gardens are open to the public; here there are magnificent views across the loch to Ben Cruachan and the peaks east leading up to Ben Lui. Offshore are the small island of Inishail, with the ruins of a thirteenth-century chapel, and the even more diminutive island of Fraoch Eilean, where there are castle ruins of about the same age. From Lochawe, boats can be hired to visit these islands – and a boat is probably the best way to see Loch Awe.

Lochcarron Highland 14A4

This village is but a string of houses along the shores of Loch Carron; it is, however, a very long string, with the houses spread out, though with many intervals, along nearly 5km. of road. The houses – small and pleasant – look across a beautiful calm loch; for although Loch Carron is a sea loch it is sheltered by Skye; and the upper loch, above the narrows at Stromeferry, is normally even more placid.

At the end of the eighteenth century, although there were only a few crofts where Lochcarron now stands, there were often many more boats on the loch than are seen today. Vast shoals of herring came into the sea lochs along this coast; and hundreds of boats would be out for them or, at the end of the day, lying up overnight. Although the herring started to dwindle in numbers around the 1820s, the village of Lochcarron began to expand about ten years later, and for many years it was a prosperous fishing port.

But the herring have gone now; so have the commercial fishing boats, though there is some casual sea angling from the village.

Lochcarron is a popular holiday place in summer; but it is not entirely given over to the visitor. There are a number of working crofts, and there is a weaving mill south of the village.

Just south of the main part of the village, the road, which has come south-west from Achnasheen for 34km. (following the railway for most of the way), turns inland up the hill for Shieldaig (*see* Torridon); it is possible, though, to continue by the lochside – enjoying beautiful views – to a point opposite Stromeferry, which until 1970 was one of the Highlands' major bottlenecks: it was quite possible, at the height of the season, to wait for three or four hours to take the ferry across – and there was no alternative if heading south. Now, just short of Stromeferry, the road from the A87 between Dornie and Kyle of Lochalsh goes along the south side of Loch Carron. It was not an easy road to build: in some stretches retaining walls, sometimes covered with metal 'netting' to prevent landslides, had to be built. Sections of the road are single-track, and there are some steepish hills; but the hours of frustration it has saved are countless, and it gives pleasant views across the loch, although the hills opposite are not particularly distinguished.

At the north jetty for the now-vanished ferry are the scanty remains of Strome Castle, of unknown date but destroyed in 1602 – indeed, so scant are the remains that one wonders why the NTS accepted the ruin in 1939. Beyond the Castle there is a road, climbing and dipping, to Ardaneaskan, with superb views to Skye.

But these views, and possibly even Lochcarron, are not secure; for Kishorn, a brutal violation of one of the most beautiful stretches of coast in Scotland (*see* Applecross), is just round the corner.

Lochgilphead Strathclyde 4B6 (*pop.* 1,200)

While there is no obvious reason why it should be particularly attractive, this small town has an appeal that grows the longer you stay in or around it.

Lochgilphead is a well-built place of white or colour-washed stone houses, and even its local-authority housing does not spoil it too much. Backed by low hills, its main street, running back from the road round Loch Gilp, is pleasantly wide; there are some shops, a couple of hotels, a moderately-sized caravan site, and a cinema; and that is about all.

The view down Loch Gilp, a 5km.-long inlet off Loch Fyne, may explain some of its appeal; though the low

Suilven seen from the Lochinver–Ullapool coast road

hills along each side are in no way dramatic, the hills of Arran, seen from the head of the bay, stand up on the southern horizon. The shores of Loch Gilp have more stones than sand; and in spring particularly there is a wealth of bird life – not only the mute swans, which always seem to be in the bay, but a large number of waders as well.

Lochgilphead's appeal has unfortunately not communicated itself to Ardrishaig, Lochgilphead's neighbour, not 3km. down the west shore of Loch Gilp.

Lochgilphead was a small village, and Ardrishaig even less, until the opening in 1801 of the Crinan Canal; the considerable traffic of fishing boats and, particularly, pleasure craft on this canal adds considerable colour and life to each.

Just north of Lochgilphead is one of the most interesting areas for archaeological remains on mainland Scotland (*see* Crinan and Kilmichael). South is Knapdale (qv) and Kintyre (*see* Tarbert), and Loch Fyne stretches to the north-east. Nowhere is the scenery startling, nowhere can one be more than a few km. from water. Everywhere the views are appealing, and the nearest popular tourist resort is a good 40km. away.

Lochgoilhead Strathclyde 4D4
Although Loch Goil, one of the most beautiful of the sea lochs off the Firth of Clyde, is only about 6km. from Ardentinny at the end of the road up Loch Long from Dunoon, it cannot be reached that way. The only approach is from Arrochar, by the main road, the A83, up

to the Rest-and-Be-Thankful: at the top a single-track road turns west and, after a brief climb, descends through spruce woods and open hill grazings to Lochgoilhead, a village (as you might guess) at the head of Loch Goil.

Where this pleasant village, once called Kinlochgyll (which means the same thing), now stands there is reputed to have been a church as early as the seventh century. Even the present building is of respectable antiquity, having first been mentioned in the early fifteenth century; there have, though, been additions to it since then. Beyond the churchyard is a curious sundial, standing over 3m. high and dated 1626; but the markings have been obliterated by time. The village itself was enlarged in the nineteenth century by the influx of prosperous Glaswegians, as the villa development testifies.

The road down the loch continues along the loch's west side, looking across to 'Argyll's Bowling Green', the rugged peninsula of Ardgoil separating Loch Goil from Loch Long. (The road down the east shore goes only a short way.) It goes as far as CARRICK CASTLE, standing on a rock jutting into the loch. Built in the fifteenth century, this castle is said to have been a hunting seat of Scottish kings. Before it was 100 years old it came into the hands of the Campbells of Ardkinglas (successive generations of that family, incidentally, have been buried at Lochgoilhead church since the building of Carrick).

Behind the Castle, along the lochside, a small village with a hotel has in recent years developed as a holiday centre. It is in a delightful setting, more open than Lochgoilhead, with good outdoor sporting facilities.

The Loch Goil area has an extensive and fascinating assortment of wild life, ranging from the golden eagle – not often seen – and the wild cat to a considerable heronry, with schools of porpoise often plunging along the loch.

Retracing towards the Rest-and-Be-Thankful, the road forks in about 4km. down Hell's Glen, which by no means lives up to its name, to come to Loch Fyne south of Cairndow (qv).

Lochinver Highland 19B5

This village at the head of Loch Inver is a busy fishing port and, in summer, an even busier holiday centre. Lochinver's attraction for travellers lies, in considerable part, in its being the only place with any amount of accommodation close to the beautiful sandy coves around the crofting townships of Achmelvich, Clachtoll, Stoer, and Clashnessie, the last two lying each side of the Stoer Peninsula.

The road to these places plunges and twists between the sea and loch-strewn moors. Achmelvich is reached by an even narrower track down to the bay; the others are beside the road and have suffered from their popularity: at Clachtoll the machair has been destroyed and the beach has been eroded, by cars bringing caravans

and by campers allowed to pitch indiscriminately. By the time some control was imposed, the damage was done. Achmelvich Bay is little better in this respect. But all the townships, nevertheless, retain a sizeable measure of their beauty.

Lochinver itself is a charming place; from near it, and from the A837 to Loch Assynt, are magnificent views of the fantastic Sutherland peaks. The most remarkable of these mountains is Suilven, the 730m. twin peaks of which rise almost sheer from the moor. Suilven is not seen from the harbour; but just inland it rears like a huge thin pillar. This, with nearby Canisp, is Torridonian Sandstone resting on a platform of Lewisian Gneiss, some of the oldest rocks in the world. They, with Cul Mor and Ben More Coigach and other isolated peaks, are seen from the road that runs south from Lochinver to Inverkirkaig (there is a good waterfall near here) and eventually joins the road to Achiltibuie.

Loch Ness Highland 15E5

Perhaps 350 million years ago a great geological fault split the Highlands: a deep rift now known as the Great Glen or Glen More nan Albin. Loch Ness runs for nearly a third of its length, from south of Inverness to Fort Augustus. Not one km. shorter than the longest inland loch in Scotland (Loch Awe – qv), Loch Ness is never more than 2km. from shore to shore, which stops its being the 'biggest' in Scotland: it is only three quarters of the area of Loch Lomond.

It was the long waterway of Loch Ness that made the Caledonian Canal (qv) possible; it was the new road built along its north-west shores in the early 1930s that helped bring it prominently into the news, not only in Britain but in much of Europe and America as well. The existence of a 'monster' in Loch Ness was not, though, first reported by the newspapers of the 1930s but by St Adamnan, Abbot of Iona (d. 704), who in his *Life of St Columba* referred to an *aquatilis bestia* in the loch. Since then there have been further references to 'monsters' in Loch Ness and, indeed, in other Highland lochs; press reports on the subject first started in the 1870s.

The opening of the new road and the corresponding increase in the number of people travelling by the lochside brought many reports of sightings, by local people (many of whom firmly believe in there being some sort of unexplained beast in the loch) as well as visitors.

In the early 1960s the Loch Ness Phenomena Investigation Bureau was established and, through this and other bodies, scientific devices, including underwater microphones, sonar, infra-red cameras, and miniature submarines, were brought into the search. More fuel was added to the fire of controversy in 1975 when photographs purporting to show the monster were shown in the House of Commons, and many leading figures, including Sir Peter Scott (who devised the name *Nessieteras rhombopteryx* for the creature), expressed their belief in its existence. Other people and bodies were as

vehement in their disbelief, 'explanations' for the monster ranging from remains of a Viking boat to gas from
decaying matter breaking the surface of the water. The
Secretary of State for Scotland solemnly assured the
House, not for the first time, that he would consider giving himself powers to provide 'protection' for the monster, if required.

But whether 'Nessie' is one of a family of prehistoric
reptiles whose ancestors were trapped in Loch Ness when
it became landlocked, or whether it is a tree trunk, a
seal, a giant eel, wave shadows, or any one of many
suggested explanations, is not yet known. The seemingly
obvious ways of finding out, such as sending down
divers or dragging, are impracticable with a loch that

Lybster Harbour

plumbs to 300m., is always bitterly cold, and contains dark-brown peaty water, impenetrable to eye or camera beyond a m. or so.

While the hills on either side of Loch Ness are by no means among the most dramatic in Scotland, the loch makes a pleasant waterway for day cruises from Inverness; cabin cruisers may be hired for longer periods. There are good views of the loch almost all the way on the main A82 from Fort Augustus to Inverness. Between Invermoriston and Drumnadrochit a roadside cairn commemorates John Cobb, the racing driver who lost his life in an attempt on the world water speed record in 1952.

On the south-east side of the loch the military road built by General Wade follows the lochside between Foyers and Dores; Foyers was the scene of the first commercial hydro-electric scheme in Britain: developed to supply power for an aluminium smelting works, it began operations in 1896 and continued to give service for another seventy years; in 1975 the North of Scotland Hydro-Electric Board opened its second 'reversible pumped storage' generating station here (the first being

at Ben Cruachan on Loch Awe): this is remotely controlled from Fort Augustus.

Luing *see* **Seil**

Lybster   Highland   20E4
As at Latheron, Dunbeath, and other places along the A9 coast road to Wick, the interest at this village is divided between a picturesque harbour under cliffs and archaeological remains inland.

Although there is a hotel on the main road, the village itself lines the side road down to the coast at Skail on Lybster Bay; both east and west of this road, off the A9, are minor roads, sometimes just tracks, leading down to the wild, rocky shore, which contrasts strongly with the low, rolling moor, dotted with small farms and fields, often with dramatic skies, to the north and west of the main road.

One of the most mysterious of 'ancient monuments' is seen at Mid Clyth, where a track leads 1km. west from the road to the HILL O' MANY STANES. Here are almost 200 stones in twenty-two parallel rows; they are no

Hill o' Many Stanes, Mid Clyth, nr Lybster

great size – none over a m. high – and are believed to date from neolithic times or the Bronze Age; their purpose – as so often – remains a mystery.

About 3km. east of Lybster a lonely road goes virtually dead straight for 15km. over the moors and between low hills. Just off this road, 11km. north from the main road, are the Grey Cairns of Camster, two megalithic chambered cairns dating back over 4,000 years. One is a long-horned cairn with two chambers; the other, more rounded, has a single chamber approached by a passage.

Machrihanish Strathclyde 2D5

With a beach 6½km. long and a golf course that has been described as possessing one of the best eighteen holes in Scotland, this village on the west coast of Kintyre can be assured of summer custom.

Machrihanish cannot be described as picturesque. It had a colliery, Drumlemble, which closed down in 1967. It has a few houses let in summer, closed in winter, and a few council houses. But nobody comes here for the village: the main attraction is the long, wide beach, with Atlantic rollers endlessly coming on to it, and with the links behind.

Coming from Campbeltown (qv) in summer, once the oil tanks at the NATO buildings *en route* are left behind, the view to Machrihanish can be brilliantly colourful. The bay, though, is well south of the protection from Islay: in winter the gales can be fierce.

Mallaig Highland 17E8

Today's Road to the Isles (qv), the A830, comes to its end 77km. west of Fort William and plunges downhill to the harbour at Mallaig, a town of plain whitewashed

ABOVE: *One of the Grey Cairns of Camster, nr Lybster*

BELOW: *The harbour at Mallaig*

houses. Its attraction is due in large part to its harbour, the most important fishing centre on the west coast of Scotland; to see the fishing fleet land its catch is a fascinating sight.

From here the car ferry sails to Armadale on Skye (passengers only in the winter months), and there are steamer services to other Hebridean islands, of which there are magnificent views from the bay. Even these views are excelled by those from other points beyond the east side of the bay: from Mallaigvaig at the end of Loch Nevis and, above all, from Carn a' Ghobhair, over 550m. above sea-level and looking across Loch Nevis, Knoydart, and Loch Hourn to the mountains of Kintail in the north, to Ardnamurchan in the south, and to the Cuillins in the west.

Of the many boat trips available from Mallaig, take, in particular, one to Loch Hourn and Loch Nevis, perhaps the two finest sea lochs in Scotland.

Melvich Highland 20B2

This scattered village above the estuary of the River Halladale is a good place from which to see some magnificent cliff scenery – and the sea birds that go with it – and the nuclear power station at Dounreay, 11km. east.

All the coastline here is good, with small bays standing under high cliffs, the finest of which are at Bighouse, seat of the Mackay family, on the east side of Melvich Bay, and at Portskerra on the minor road that goes out to the point and loops back.

West of Melvich, another small village, STRATHY, lies just inland from its bay, and beyond it, pointing a finger over the Greenland Sea to the North Pole (even if it is about 3,500km. away, there is nothing in between!) is Strathy Point, its cliffs holding many caves, and more tumultuous seabirds. The most recent lighthouse to be built in Britain stands at the head of this point; it went into operation in 1958.

There is more than the mainland scenery to view; to the north-east the mountains of Hoy and the lower islands of Orkney are easily seen; and there is more for the nature-lover than birds: Strathy Point is well covered with wild flowers, notable among which is *Primula scotica*, which only grows along the north coast and in Orkney; and in just over 12km. up the Strathy Water is Strathy Bog, a national nature reserve of some 48ha.

East of Melvich, REAY is another village above another charming bay. Reay has a church typical of the Caithness district; it was built in 1739 and has an outside staircase to its belfry; the plain pulpit and loft have changed little since they were built.

Dounreay Castle, with a sixteenth-century tower, lies 3km. north-east. But DOUNREAY today means the first experimental nuclear power station in Scotland. Seen from the rocky coastline east from Sandside Bay, below Reay, the contrast, between sea surging up these rocks and the power station, seems almost a fantasy: the contrast between the power station and the bleak moors behind is nearly as remarkable. Built in 1954, the power station has had its ups and downs, and has more than once been threatened with closure; but its work continues. The station itself cannot be visited; but by the

Reay church, nr Melvich, showing the outside staircase to the belfry

St Mary's Chapel, Crosskirk, E of Melvich

roadside the UK Atomic Energy Authority has an exhibition explaining its work.

For a further contrast in this fascinating stretch of countryside, travel another 5km. north-east to CROSS-KIRK and the ruins of St Mary's Chapel. Only the chancel and the roofless nave remain; but this rudely-constructed building is one of the oldest in north Scotland, having been built in the twelfth century.

South from Melvich, long Strath Halladale goes for 34km. across formless moorland to Forsinard Hotel, popular with anglers, who have eight lochs as well as the River Halladale for their sport. Here the railway from the south strikes east, and in about 12km. there is ALTNABREAC, just a railway halt amid desolate moors:

road ended at Millhouse beside Loch Moidart, only a track continuing round the coast; now it is a wonderfully scenic run for the motorist.

Near the head of Loch Moidart, Kinlochmoidart House, where Prince Charles Edward Stuart stayed before sailing up Loch Shiel to Glenfinnan to raise his standard in 1745, was destroyed after that event, to be replaced by the present house. Near it, and seen from the road, a line of seven beech trees commemorates the 'Seven Men of Moidart' who landed with the Prince (one tree that was blown down was subsequently replanted – and is noticeably smaller). The road climbs up Glen Uig, and from a car park at the top a track leads west to a hilltop. The track gets lost more than once – low cliffs and colourful, though wet, bog tend to interrupt progress – but the views of Eigg and Rum from the top are magnificent.

Almost the same views, although from a lower level, may be had by taking the footpath via Samalaman Bay to Smearisary: a rough track, which, unfortunately, does not deter cars from trying to follow it, eventually turns into a narrow path that can be traversed only on foot. In high summer and good weather only the midges detract from the splendour of the view. The broken remains of crofts (only one 'working croft' remains) remind that this was once a more populous district than it is today. Glenuig, too, is little more than a hotel, and the bay and pier here are more used in summer by pleasure craft than lobster fishermen.

Commercial fishing, though, comes into its own on Loch Ailort, which the road follows from Glen Uig. At Inverailort, near the head of the loch, an experimental fish farm for breeding salmon and trout was started in 1966, and has proved successful. The power boats going round the enclosures may at times introduce a slightly jarring note: but this development is infinitely less alien to the Highland scene that some of the more recent incursions of tourism and industry.

Morar Highland 6E1

North from Arisaig the road to Mallaig passes an unlovely power station beside the River Morar, which links Loch Morar and the sea. The Morar is probably the shortest river in Scotland – about 2km. long – and it flows from the deepest inland water in Britain: the huge weight of an Ice Age glacier gouged out a hole that even today reaches a depth of 328m.

A narrow but metalled road runs its wooded way along the north side of the loch as far as Bracora, after which a path, well worth walking, goes to the end of the loch. (Loch Morar is 20km. long and, at its widest point, less than 3km. across.) The path then climbs up a ravine to a small lochan with a large name – Lochan Gaineamhaich.

With its depth, it is not surprising that Loch Morar is reputed to hold a 'monster'; 'Morag' can claim documentation as can her more famous sister 'Nessie' of Loch

the only road to it – and that a very minor one – comes from Westerdale, 15km. away to the north-east. Altnabreac is interesting only as the scene of an experiment by the North of Scotland Hydro-Electric Board, conducted over twenty years ago, to produce milled peat for electricity generation. The idea was sound – it has been successfully done in Ireland and Russia – but it was not then economically viable.

Moidart Highland 6E2

Bounded by Loch Ailort and Loch Eilt to the north-west and by Loch Shiel south and east, this area of peaks and glens has but one road – that from Acharacle by Loch Moidart and the Sound of Arisaig. Until 1966 this

Torosay Castle, Mull

Ness. Of more interest to many people is that Loch Morar and its river are good for salmon and sea-trout angling.

Inevitably, there are a few holiday houses along the road; equally, there is attraction for the small-boat fraternity at the peak of the season; but the people who stay in and around the village of Morar tend to go to the Silver Sands (*see* Arisaig).

Morvern Highland 6E2
Only a stretch of land not 10km. wide prevents this big peninsula being an island. Its other boundaries are Loch Linnhe, the Sound of Mull, and Loch Sunart; and, like the other similar areas in this south-west part of the Highland region (Sunart, Ardgour, Moidart, and Ardnamurchan), there are few motorable roads in it. The road approach is from Ardgour; the alternative is the car ferry from Fishnish Point on the island of Mull to Lochaline, but it is not the cheapest of ferries, and one has to get from Oban to Mull, a similar expense, in the first place. The short trip across the water does, though, give excellent views along the Sound of Mull, and, to the east, approaching Lochaline, Ardtornish Castle stands dramatically on a point. This ruin of a

fourteenth-century stronghold of the Lords of the Isles is in fact more impressive from the ferry than close at hand. But there is a fine view, looking back to Mull, of an infinitely more imposing castle – Duart on its great headland.

LOCHALINE itself is more flourishing than picturesque. A bed of sandstone, discovered in 1925, proved invaluable when war broke out in 1939 and Britain's supply of silica, needed for the manufacture of optical glass and scientific instruments, was cut off. The Lochaline sand, mined from over 40km. of tunnels, is extracted in vast quantities – over 60,000 tonnes a year – and is treated at Lochaline before being loaded by conveyor belt on to steamers.

The Forestry Commission's timber operations at Lochaline do not add to the attraction of the area, either.

But Lochaline is easily left behind; there is a road along the north side of the Sound of Mull, with impressive views across to the island; it goes as far as Drimnin, 18km. along the coast, although a track goes further towards Aulitson Point, looking across to Tobermory Bay.

North from Lochaline, KINLOCHALINE CASTLE is a fifteenth-century square tower in a prominent setting on a knoll looking down the valley and across the Sound of Mull. A previous castle on this site was the seat of Clan MacInnes, vassals of the Lords of the Isles; but in 1390 MacInnes and his five sons were murdered at Ardtornish, and the lands were given to MacLean of Duart (*see* Mull). It is assumed that the MacLeans built the present castle; but which castle was given the local name of 'Butter Castle' is not known. The tradition for the name is the most unlikely story that the masons were paid in butter.

While the hills of Morvern are scenically not particularly striking, from the road between Kinlochaline and Sunart Ben Resipol (846m.), a landmark for much of this area, can often be seen.

Mull Strathclyde 7D5 (*pop.* 1,499)
Some 50 million years ago there was tremendous volcanic activity off the west coast of Scotland, which affected the geological make-up of Britain as far south as Yorkshire. Mull was at the centre of this activity; and its effects can be seen today, even after all the subsequent earth movements and the gouging of the rocks during successive Ice Ages, the last of which retreated from this area only about 12,000 years ago.

Around Ben More (966m.), the highest peak on the island, are the basalt terraces that resulted from lava flows (the terraces, incidentally, make this one of the most infuriating mountains to descend, with endless diversions around the low rock cliffs). This pattern is repeated over much of the island, though on the lower hills the terraces are grassy.

When the last of the ice was retreating, Mull was still part of Morvern (qv). Now it is split from the mainland by the Sound of Mull, up which you sail from Oban to Tobermory, the main centre on the island. When it became an island, and having slowly raised itself – released from the huge burden of ice – to its present level, the result was a remarkably indented coastline, with a total length – tracing all its bays and sea lochs and inlets – of some 500km.

Lava, in the millions of years since it covered the ancient gneiss, has broken up into good soil. So Mull, though it has its quota of wild moorland, has also much luxurious vegetation, many green fields and delightful woods, and is the most varied and colourful of all the larger Hebridean islands.

While tourism is important to the economy of Mull, the island is not as heavily visited as Skye (qv). Perhaps this is because it has not the 'romantic' appeal, nor the dramatic grandeur of the Cuillins, perhaps because there is not the same amount of holiday accommodation, perhaps even because it costs about seven times as much to go by boat, with or without a car, from Oban to Craignure as it does from Kyle of Lochalsh to Kyleakin.

Although there is a car-ferry service between Fishnish on Mull and Lochaline on Morvern, it is to Craignure that most visitors, if they have cars, travel. Until

recently most of them headed promptly for Tobermory or some other selected holiday spot; now a 62-bed-roomed hotel tempts more to use Craignure as a base. Craignure is a straggle of a village, busy when the ferries are in, welcoming, and somewhat dominated by its necessary car park at the pier.

In 1976 Mull got its first railway – a miniature one, running all of 2km. from Craignure to the imposing Victorian Torosay Castle, part of which, along with the 4½ha. of Italian terraced gardens, with a walk lined by statues, is open to the public.

While Mull has not much more than half the land area of Skye, distances are often longer than anticipated. From Craignure to Fionnphort, at the westernmost end of the Ross of Mull (the long peninsula at the south end of the island), it is 64km. This is the route that has the most frequent bus service on the island: Fionnphort is the embarkation point for Iona (qv). Yet even on this route there are but four buses each way daily: there are many more direct coach trips heading for the 'Sacred Isle', but these tend to bypass some beautiful places off the road.

Six km. south of Craignure, approached by a minor road from near Lochdonhead, Duart Castle enjoys a dramatic situation, standing high on a rock above the Sound of Mull, with magnificent views from its ramparts. The first buildings of this stronghold of the chiefs of Clan MacLean were probably erected about 1250. Residential quarters were built inside the massive curtain wall in 1633. The Castle was stormed by the Earl of Argyll in 1691, and after the risings of 1715 and 1745 it was garrisoned by English troops. After their departure in 1751 the Castle fell into ruin, and was uninhabited until 1912, when its restoration was started by Sir Fitzroy MacLean: the rowan tree in the courtyard was planted by him on his hundredth birthday. The Castle, now home of Lord MacLean, former Chief Scout of the Commonwealth, is open to the public.

South from Lochdonhead, at Ardura, a minor road has at its junction a monument to the Gaelic poet Dugald MacPhail (1818–87); this road goes beside Loch Spelve and Loch Uisg to Lochbuie and another monument – a high stone pyramid 'Erected by Lochbuie and his Highlanders to Commemorate the Coronation of their Majesties King Edward VII and Queen Alexandra. God Save the King and Queen; 9th August, 26th June 1902'; to which some wag has added '*Sic Transit Gloria Mundi*'. There is a similar pyramid commemorating Queen Victoria's Diamond Jubilee.

From the nearby shores of Loch Buie, Colonsay (qv) can be seen. Around the head of the bay among the trees are the high ruins of the ancient seat of the MacLaines of Lochbuie, a branch of Clan MacLean, who held it for nearly 600 years. The castle was deserted in 1752, when the nearby mansion was built; neither is open to the public.

Walking through woods by the west shore of Loch

Buie, a rough path continues under caves and cliffs, some with the perpendicular basalt columns reminiscent of Staffa (qv), to Carsaig, which can also be approached by a high moorland road from Pennyghael. There are superb views of high cliffs from Carsaig's harbour; and in these cliffs, after 5km. of rough, stony walking along the beach, is some of the most remarkable natural rock sculpture in Scotland – Malcolm's Point, with more basalt columns and, beyond, the Carsaig Arches, a huge arch, nearly 20m. high and wide, through a headland, with rock columns, a deep cauldron, and a 36m.-high spire gashed by a deep 'window'. As a bonus on this magnificent coast, you may see wild goats or golden eagles.

From Bunessan, an attractive village on a deep bay and with a little-used harbour, a road crosses the moors to Uisken, a small crofting centre with a wide beach. There are other beaches on this south coast of the Ross: but there are no roads to them.

TOBERMORY is the only 'town' on Mull; in 1974 it had 647 inhabitants. A century ago it had twice that number; but in this respect it is more fortunate than the rest of the island, which has a population level only a quarter that of a century ago. Yet there is nothing depressed-looking about Mull or its 'capital': Tobermory is the most picturesque of the Highland ports, its gaily painted eighteenth-century cottages on the main street around the harbour wall looking across a sheltered bay, in which lies a Spanish galleon, storm-driven north after the destruction of the Armada in 1588. The galleon took refuge here, and it is generally believed that it is the *Florida*, treasure ship of the Armada. The crew were at first hospitably received; then, for some reason, one Donald MacLean was taken prisoner and kept as a hostage. He escaped, and set light to the ship's powder magazine, blowing up both the ship and himself. Many attempts have been made to recover the treasure, but only a few small cannon (one is at Duart Castle), coins, and other trivial items have been recovered: the remains of the *Florida* are many m. below the sea, deeply buried.

In 1788 the British Fisheries Society started to develop Tobermory as a fishing port, and it was then that the houses around the harbour were built. There is no fishing now: in the nineteenth century the vast shoals of herring disappeared. But there is no lack of boats; sheltered behind Calve Island, Tobermory Bay is an admirable haven for sailing dinghies, yachts, and other craft. There are cruises available to Ardnamurchan, Mingary, and Loch Sunart, as well as the regular service (no cars) to Kilchoan in Ardnamurchan.

South from Tobermory there are forest trails; north from the town you can walk through charming woods to the lighthouse on the Rubha-nan-Gall; but only minor roads and tracks go to this northern end of the island.

The road west from Tobermory twists and climbs over low hills, and in 10km. comes to Dervaig, claimed to be Mull's 'prettiest village'. It probably is; but its main

claim to attention is that here is the smallest professional theatre in Scotland. The Little Theatre was started by Barrie and Marianne Hesketh in the 1960s: the weather has to be very bad if there are not full houses – which means about forty people – in the summer; and during much of the winter the company tours extensively, from the south of England to the north of Scotland.

Further west, a minor road goes to the pier at Croig, with beaches nearby and summer motorboat trips to the Treshnish Isles and Staffa; and a 2½km. walk to the point is rewarded with wonderful views to Coll and the Small Isles.

This is the pattern on all the west coast of Mull. Seldom anywhere on the road that winds to the head of Loch Scridain are there not wonderful views of water and islands. Calgary Bay (Mull's emigrants gave the name to Calgary, Canada) has the whitest shell sand on

Mull: scenery nr Clachandhu, on the coast opposite Inch Kenneth

the island; along the shores of Loch Tuath there are views across to Ulva and Gometra; and from the pier near Laggan Bay are trips, again, to Staffa and the Treshnish Isles.

Around Loch na Keal is much sandy sward, popular with campers: permission to pitch may be had from the estate office near the head of the loch. From the head of this loch it is only about 5km. across the island to Salen, another holiday centre on the Sound of Mull. From here, going along the road to Tobermory, in 3km. the heavy ruins of Aros Castle, once a stronghold of the Lords of the Isles, stand on a bluff above a bay; here, too, is a road across open moorland to Dervaig.

But going along the southern shores of Loch na Keal, the scene changes dramatically as the road turns south opposite Inch Kenneth (where there are ruins of an ancient chapel and a graveyard with sculptured slabs).

Now the road hangs between high cliffs and the sea, and huge boulders lie on the beach and the hillside.

There is no road approach to the Ardmeanach Peninsula, at whose westernmost end is Burg, 800ha. of rough ground high above the sea, owned by the NTS. Here, on the north side of Loch Scridain, embedded in the lava that created this beautiful island, are the hollow remains of a fossil tree that grew perhaps 50 million years ago.

Nairn Highland 15H2 *(pop.* 5,890)
Until the reorganization of local government in Scotland in 1975, Nairn was the 'capital' of the small county of Nairnshire, which looked east to Elgin for its administrative headquarters rather than west to Inverness. Created a royal burgh by William the Lion at the end of the twelfth century, Nairn was historically where Highlands and Lowlands met. James VI (James I of England) used to boast that he had a town so long that the people of one end did not understand the language spoken at the other: at the south-west end of Nairn Gaelic was spoken (Dr Johnson, during his tour of 1773, heard it here for the first time); but English was spoken at the north-east end. Though there has been no Gaelic spoken for a long time, Nairn was taken into the Highland region in 1975.

Nairn, which has good sands, is a popular seaside resort; it is also well known for its golfing facilities.

Three km. east of Nairn the pleasant village of AULD-EARN was the scene of a battle on 9 May 1645, when the Marquis of Montrose defeated a Covenanter army twice the size of his own forces (1,500 foot and 200 horse). On the hillock where he raised his standard for Charles I stands a massive seventeenth-century doo'cot (dovecote). This is the Boath Doo'cot, presented to the NTS in 1947; the plan of the battle is on display here.

Nethybridge Highland 12A5
The River Nethy, which gives this country resort its name, rises, 823m. above sea-level, at The Saddle on the east side of the Cairngorm ridge. It flows almost due north through the Abernethy Forest, then turns west to join the Spey beyond Nethy Bridge.

It was the river that was the reason for an early industry here, though little trace of the industry remains today. It stemmed from the enterprise of Aaron Hill (1685–1750), a Londoner and a notable public figure of his time: he was a poet and playwright, a translator of Voltaire, and manager of Drury Lane Theatre. Among various commercial and industrial schemes he started – most of them failures – was timber felling on the upper part of the Nethy: timber was floated down the river to the Spey, then, in rafts, to Garmouth on the Moray coast. It was a flourishing industry until the end of the nineteenth century, though the transport of timber cannot always have been reliable; the Nethy, normally placid enough, is subject to violent spates: in two major floods, in 1829 and 1850, Nethybridge was flooded and all the flat ground between it and the Spey, 3km. away, became, temporarily, a loch.

For anglers, who provide much business for the hotels in this village, it is the salmon, sea trout, and brown trout of the Spey that are the principal attraction. The place is popular, too, for country holidays, and in winter for skiing. Tracks lead from the village into Abernethy Forest (see Boat of Garten), and from the 'back road' from Nethybridge, which joins the A839 Grantown–Tomintoul road, there are fine views of the Cairngorms.

Newtonmore Highland 9G2
This most southerly of the Speyside resorts owes its attractive appearance, in part, to having been chosen in the early 1960s as a Highland village to be 'tidied up', in a scheme in which Sir Hugh Fraser (later Lord Allander), the inspirer of the Aviemore Centre, was involved. As a result, the overhead wires, which had disfigured the streets, were put underground, and assistance was given for house-painting and other improvements.

Before then, in 1952, the village achieved some distinction as being the first place in Britain where pony-trekking was developed as an organized sport, from the Balavil Arms Hotel: it is still a centre for this pastime.

With the development of skiing on the Cairngorms Newtonmore became a holiday centre for much of the year, most of its numerous hotels and guest houses remaining open over the winter; it has successfully avoided brash development, although, of course, it has to try to cope with the heavy holiday traffic in summer and increased commercial traffic throughout the year.

This is MacPherson country, and at the southern end of the village is the Clan Museum, whose exhibits include a 'Black Chanter' of pipes played at a battle in Perth, famous in clan history, and a green banner under which it is claimed the clan never met defeat.

North-west of Newtonmore lie the Monadhliath mountains; their highest point is Cairn Ban (941m.), to which a track leads up Glen Banchor from the village. From these slopes are fine views of the Cairngorms to the east and to the mountains of Badenoch to the south.

North Uist Highlands 22E1 (*pop.* 1,818)
This Outer Hebridean island is about 20km. long by 26km. across. But the measurements can give no indication of the land area: the eastern half of North Uist is so fretted with lochans, so riven by long sea inlets, that the island is often said to be as much water as land. Little can be done with such land, and it is the western part of the island that sustains the crofting community of North Uist.

The only centre for the island, however, is on the east coast: LOCHMADDY. The place gets its name, it is said, from islets in the bay, which, if imagination is strong enough, could be said to resemble dogs: the Gaelic for

dog is *madadh*. Lochmaddy is the port for North Uist, a car-ferry service doing the two-hour journey from and to Uig on Skye daily (except Sundays) during the summer, less frequently in the winter.

A reasonable road follows the roughly triangular coast of the island, and at the south links with Benbecula (qv). Although so water-ridden, North Uist has a few hills, reaching their peak at Eaval, on the south-east of the island. This rises to 347m.; but the way to it is so tortuous – it is almost an island – that it is better looked at across the lochans and waterways. Marrival (231m.), in the centre of the western part, is more accessible.

To the angler all this water means salmon, sea trout, and brown trout. To the ornithologist the immense attraction is BALRANALD NATURE RESERVE, on the westernmost extremity of the island: it is a wonderful place scenically, with sweeping white sands, dunes, and machair. The Reserve was established by the Royal Society for the Protection of Birds to safeguard the red-necked phalarope, which breeds here; but there are other waders, as well as duck and seabirds, to watch. Visitors should contact the warden at Hougharry.

In addition to this reserve, on the lochans and other waters on the island wild geese, whooper swans, and a fair variety of duck are to be seen; and from Balranald you look out to a little scatter of five uninhabited islands – the Monachs, which are also a Nature Reserve: barnacle and white-fronted geese winter here, and the grey seal breeds. There is no regular service to these islands, and permission to visit them must be sought.

To the archaeologically-inclined, North Uist is rewarding. While not as imposing as those on Lewis and the Northern Isles, Dun Torcuill broch, on a loch just off the road some 6km. north-west of Lochmaddy, is worth seeing. Just south of the road, 9km. west from Lochmaddy, Barpa Langass cairn, dating back to Neolithic times, is not dissimilar to the Grey Cairns of Camster (see Lybster). There are many other cairns and standing stones; but North Uist is famous, archaeologically, for its 'wheel houses', round dwellings where partitions like spokes of a wheel divide the house into rooms. The remains to be seen in various places on the island unfortunately do not indicate the scope nor the degree of civilization reached by their inhabitants in the early centuries of the Christian era.

More substantial remains are those of Teampull na Trionaid – the church of the Trinity – whose ruins may well date back to the thirteenth or early fourteenth century. They stand on the Carinish Peninsula at the south end of the island.

For all its isolation – or perhaps because of it – North Uist has supported man for a long time.

Oban Strathclyde 4B2 (*pop.* 6,410)
Only the peculiar quirks of the planning mentality can explain why the resort that for generations was known as the 'Charing Cross of the Highlands' is now in the

Strathclyde region. Oban is essentially Highland in atmosphere and in its superb setting on the Firth of Lorn, with magnificent seascapes beyond Kerrera Island to Mull and across Lismore to Morvern.

From its harbour, the finest on the west-Highland coast, car ferries link with Mull, the Small Isles, and the Outer Hebrides. And Oban is one of the few holiday centres in the Highlands that have direct train links with Glasgow. As a result of these assets Oban's winter population more than doubles during the holiday period.

Although some 5,000 years ago Stone Age man was living in caves where the town's main street now runs, Oban's character is Victorian, having been built mainly between 1869 and 1884, following the arrival of steamboats in about 1850 and in anticipation of the railway reaching it: the railway took fifteen years to build and passengers did not arrive until 1 July 1880.

Dr Johnson and James Boswell found 'a tolerable inn' at Oban in 1773; 200 years later they would have found about thirty hotels and much other accommodation to welcome them, some much more than 'tolerable'. None draw the eye by their architectural distinction: the dominant buildings in the town are the odd 'McCaig's

Folly' and the eyesore of a distillery chimney. The first, an approximate imitation of the Colosseum at Rome, is a round unfinished tower, condemned by purists but adding a pleasant touch of fantasy to the Victorian scene. Its building was due to John Stuart McCaig, an Oban banker, who laudably had it erected in the 1890s to give work to unemployed masons and, less laudably perhaps, as a memorial to his family. When some £5,000 had been spent, McCaig died, and the work was never completed: after decades of neglect it now holds gardens and is floodlit at night. The distillery chimney is presumably a necessary adjunct to a valuable industry.

But the main feature of the town, unquestionably, is its harbour, which as a venue for fishing fleets is rivalled on the west coast only by Mallaig (qv). In its sheltered situation Oban enjoys a mild climate, the rains tending to precipitate further east and north.

Another scenic attraction is the view from Pulpit Hill, above the south harbour, looking across the bay, with Lismore stretching up Loch Linnhe and the wide panorama of Mull and Morvern.

At the northern end of the town, on Corran Esplanade, are the Corran Halls of 1965, with a 1,000-seat concert hall and a restaurant. Among other

Oban, showing 'McCaig's Folly'

Orkney : Skara Brae

entertainment offered in Oban is the Argyllshire Gathering in August, a well-known date in the Highland Games Calendar.

Near the Corran Halls is the pink-granite Roman Catholic cathedral of St Columba, the work of Sir Giles Gilbert Scott; and north from the Esplanade is the Clach a'Choin, a tall rock pillar to which the legendary giant Fingal is said to have tied his dog. Nearby, DUNOLLIE CASTLE stands on a crag above the sea: there were forts on this site as far back as the seventh century, and today's imposing ivy-clad ruin dates back to the twelfth or thirteenth century. This was the seat of the MacDougalls, descendants of the Lords of Lorn who at one time claimed to control a third of Scotland: the Brooch of Lorn, said to have been torn off the cloak of Robert the Bruce during a skirmish in 1306, was held here for many years, but is now in safe custody elsewhere.

A km. or so further on is Oban's main beach, Ganavan

Sands: a fine beach with fine views, but also equipped with a large car park, tearoom, children's playground, and the like.

Another MacDougall stronghold, GYLEN CASTLE, stands on Kerrera Island, which can be reached by ferry from Oban. This ruin, in a wild and striking setting on a rock pillar, dates back to 1587; the remains are impressive, although it received rough treatment in 1647, during the Covenanting wars, when it was captured and burnt, and its MacDougall defenders slaughtered.

More impressive than either of the two castles described, though, is DUNSTAFFNAGE, off the road to Connel north from Oban, an exceptionally fine and well-preserved thirteenth-century stronghold with immensely thick curtain walls still standing nearly 20m. high. Flora MacDonald was imprisoned here in 1746 for her part in helping Prince Charles Edward Stuart to

Orkney: Ring of Brogar

escape – before being sent to the Tower of London. While the Castle had its quota of sieges and attacks, it survived until 1810, when the interior was destroyed by fire. Renovation has taken place in recent years, and the Castle can be visited. Traditionally, Dunstaffnage stands on the site of a seat of the Dalriadic kings, who are said to have held here the Stone of Destiny (now in Westminster Abbey), on which they were crowned. This claim is also made for Dunadd.

Orkney Highland 23 (*pop.* 17,462)
Like Caithness and the coastal areas of Easter Suther-

land and Easter Ross, Orkney is 'Highland' only in that it is one of the seven crofting counties. These islands have little in common with the Western – or any other – islands, except Shetland, and even in the reorganization of local government in Scotland in 1975 Orkney, Shetland, and the Outer Hebrides were given the special status of 'Islands Areas', to a certain extent outside the Highland region.

Orkney's culture is Norse, not Celtic; the speech owes nothing to the lilting Gaelic; the farming is arguably the best in the country; the scenery, with one outstanding exception, the Island of Hoy, is low and green and infinitely colourful with wild flowers in summer. Gaunt castles hardly exist; yet Orkney has one of the most notable cathedrals in Scotland and is by far the richest area in Britain for prehistoric remains.

When North Sea oil, inevitably, impinged on the community, it was confined, so far as possible, to one island, where the storage tanks are set low so as hardly to intrude, and where housing and conditions for the workers are so good that they need not go elsewhere.

Orkney was obviously attractive to settlers even in prehistoric times. The Old Red Sandstone, which is the predominant rock type, smoothed by countless centuries under ice, resulted ultimately in green pastures ideal for the purposes of the neolithic herdsmen. There were no animals to prey on their flocks, and the distance from the mainland kept them reasonably secure, for many centuries, from raiders. They lived in communities, as is shown at Skara Brae, on the west coast of Mainland (the main island of Orkney), where, below ground level but open to view, are ten stone huts with walls still standing 3m. high. Set beside a sandy beach, this village, built of the flagstones that are a feature of

Orkney: Stones of Stenness

The Cathedral of St Magnus, Kirkwall, Orkney

Orkney, and whose 'houses', linked by passages, have stone 'cupboards' and central hearths, was finally buried in a great sandstorm, and not discovered until 1850.

From the Skara Brae period, the second millenium BC, come the incredible burial places to be seen on Orkney. Of the 'stalled cairns', the largest – 35m. long – is Midhowe Cairn, on the Island of Rousay; here there are twelve compartments, separated by pairs of upright flagstones, each containing slab benches on which the dead were laid.

But perhaps the most remarkable burial place is MAESHOWE, the finest megalithic tomb in Britain. It is contained in a huge mound just off the main road from Kirkwall to Stromness; through a passage 12m. long you enter a central chamber, 5m. square, built of immense stone slabs often as long as the walls themselves. It is difficult to reconcile the superb craftsmanship of the masonry with the primitive stone and flint tools that were used.

Not 3km. from Maeshowe, almost beside the Loch of Stenness, are remains of another type of monument of the period: the four Stones of Stenness, standing 2–5m. high; and, nearby, the magnificent Ring of Brogar, where some twenty-seven of the original monoliths in a circle still stand up to $4\frac{1}{2}$m. high; the moat that surrounded them is now dry, but is very obvious.

In Orkney over a score of these cairns, standing stones, and brochs, dating from the second millenium BC, are in the care of the Department of the Environment.

The Vikings came to Orkney in the eighth century,

first raiding then settling, and within 200 years they were masters of much of north and west Scotland. A reminder of this period is visible at Maeshowe, where, in the twelfth century, they broke in at least three times and engraved on the walls the largest collection of Runic inscriptions to be found anywhere. But the major Norse monument is the magnificent red and yellow sandstone cathedral of St Magnus at Kirkwall, founded in 1137 by the nephew of the treacherously murdered Earl Magnus of Orkney. It is in use today; and from its tower you can look down on the remains of the Bishop's Palace, built about the same time, and Earl Patrick's Palace, extensive remains of 'the most mature and accomplished piece of Renaissance architecture in Scotland', built for Earl Patrick Stewart in about 1600.

The Norse link with Orkney was broken in 1468, when Christian I of Denmark and Norway pledged the islands for 50,000 florins, the dowry of his daughter Margaret when she married James III of Scotland.

There are sixty-seven Orkney islands, less than thirty of which are inhabited. Mainland, the largest, has a bigger land area than all the others put together, and its two main centres, Kirkwall and Stromness, hold over a third of all the islands' population.

It is at STROMNESS (*pop.* 1,681), probably, that you arrive on the car ferry from Scrabster near Thurso. The town's narrow main street from the fine harbour weaves between rows of houses, a street of stone flags and no pavements, with closes running off it.

From here you can take a boat to the mountainous ISLAND OF HOY, with spectacular cliffs: St John's Head is the highest perpendicular cliff in the UK, rising 347m. above the sea. Further south the extraordinary Old Man of Hoy is a rock pillar rising 137m. Hoy has more than superb rock scenery: it has a huge block of sandstone, the Dwarfie Stane, out of which a burial chamber was quarried in about 2000 BC; and, in contrast, a rich variety of flowers, including rare alpines.

From Stromness it is 24km. to KIRKWALL (*pop.* 4,814), which has, like Stromness, a narrow, twisting, stone-flagged street, in this case connecting the Cathedral to the harbour. Tankerness House, a first-rate example of a merchant-laird's mansion, dating from the sixteenth century, houses a fascinating museum of Orkney life.

South from Kirkwall is SCAPA FLOW, a magnificent natural anchorage, about 140sq.km. in area, and famous in both world wars. When the German fleet surrendered in 1918 some seventy warships lay here, until on 21 June 1919 nearly all were scuppered or beached by their crews. About forty of them had been raised by 1939,

Earl Patrick's Palace, c. *1600, Kirkwall, Orkney*

TOP: *Old Man of Hoy, Orkney* BOTTOM: *The Italian Chapel on Lamb Holm, Orkney (*see also *colour plate facing p. 110)*

when Scapa Flow again became a naval anchorage; but a submarine penetrated the defences in October 1939 and torpedoed the *Royal Oak* with a loss of 833 lives. To prevent more attacks causeways were built linking Mainland with South Ronaldsay; later, these causeways, the Churchill Barrier, were surfaced to make a road, which now makes it possible to drive from Mainland by Lamb Holm, Glimps Holm, and Burray Island to South Ronaldsay. The barriers were built by Italian prisoners captured during the North African campaign; and on Lamb Holm they built the beautiful 'Italian Chapel' out of nissen huts, plaster board, concrete, and scrap.

For the visitor some of the other Orkney islands are comparatively easy to visit by regular boat services. Those who live on them, of course, have boats themselves. A light-aircraft service operates from Kirkwall to several of the islands, among which is WESTRAY, where Gilbert Balfour, Master of the Household to Mary Queen of Scots, started to build Noltland Castle; it was never finished, though what was is impressive enough. This island is an outstanding one for another major interest of Orkney – huge gatherings of seabirds on the cliffs, as well as corncrakes, duck, snipe, and many other species.

EDAY, also reached by air as well as sea, has similar birdlife interest; but, then, so has all Orkney, where on many a cliff you have to look out for 'bonxies' (great skuas) diving and can watch gannet plunging into the sea.

A small boat can take you across to WYRE, off the north-east of Mainland, to see Cubbie Roo's Castle, probably the earliest stone castle in Scotland: the *Orkneyinge Saga*, written in the thirteenth century, records its building, in about 1145, by Kolbein Hruga. Originally a small square tower, other buildings were added later.

On the coast opposite Wyre is the BROCH OF GURNESS, an Iron Age broch tower with a complex of other buildings, all surrounded by a moat. This site must have been occupied for over 1,000 years, for there are also late-Celtic and Norse buildings.

NORTH RONALDSAY, most northerly of the islands, can be reached by air as well as by boat; here, in addition to rich bird life and an Iron Age broch, seals can usually be seen on the rocks and beaches.

In the north-west corner of Mainland is BIRSAY, where on a tidal island is the Brough of Birsay, a ruined Celtic church with remains of later Norse dwellings beside it. A magnificent Pictish sculptured stone was discovered here, but, as the guide will tell you somewhat bitterly, it was taken away to the National Museum of Antiquities in Edinburgh: it was replaced with a replica. South from this spot, looking across the bay, are the 85m.-high

OPPOSITE: *Broch of Gurness, Orkney*

cliffs of Marwick Head, where a tower commemorates the sinking, by mine, of the *Hampshire* on 5 June 1916: Lord Kitchener, Secretary of State for War, was drowned, with most of the crew.

Wherever you go, Orkney is intensely attractive. But it does not live on the holiday trade nor, though visitors are welcome and have increased in numbers very substantially since the introduction of roll-on, roll-off car ferries, does it rate tourism too highly. It is fine farming country, both for beef and dairy cattle, and the farms are well mechanized. Despite all the water around it, fishing is second to farming as an industry – but Orkney lobsters are exported as far as Paris and Scandinavia, and the shellfish fleet is expanding. Boatbuilding, food processing, distilling, and a not inconsiderable craft industry are other occupations followed in this group of islands; it is to be hoped that they will also be able to cope with the demands of North Sea oil, an industry that has so far made itself felt only on the island of Flotta, a southern barrier of Scapa Flow.

Oronsay *see* **Colonsay**

Plockton Highland 17F5
Few Highland villages have a more beautiful setting than this former fishing centre on an inlet of Loch Carron. Unlike most settlements in the north-west Highlands, it faces east; so its views are not to distant islands but across the bay to wooded crags, with a foreground, in summer, of fuchsias and iris and sub-tropical plants. Early on a summer morning, with a light haze softening the bluffs, it is ethereally lovely.

At the time of the annual regatta, or any time in high summer, it can be busy with yachts and boats, for which it is a popular anchorage. No longer a fishing village, neither can it be said to be truly a crofting place; it has in a sense become – since the end of the 1960s – a victim of its own beauty: over half its houses have been taken over as holiday or retirement homes by 'outsiders' who can afford to pay prices far beyond the reach of the villagers.

From just north of the village street there are views to the Applecross and Torridon mountains; but these can no longer be called 'good': they look across Loch Kishorn, now holding construction facilities for the North Sea oil programme (*see* Applecross), which may well change the character of Plockton again.

Poolewe Highland 16F2
At the head of Loch Ewe, this is an area of small crofts, but the village relies heavily on the tourist industry in the summer, with a couple of hotels, a few guest houses, and a camping/caravan site operated by the NTS – which was so keen to make sure that the caravans would not be seen from the road that accordingly the campers and caravanners do not see the fine view down the loch.

Poolewe stands on quite a narrow neck of land. The

Poolewe : view from the Inverewe Gardens

head of Loch Maree is not 5km. to the south-east, and there are good views of the loch from the path by Tollie, off the road south from the village. Further along this road, past Loch Tollie, are superb views over Gair Loch to Skye and the Outer Hebrides. From Poolewe, too, a minor road, the B8057, goes alongside the west bank of Loch Ewe for 15km., past small townships and some beaches, to the end of the peninsula.

The almost unique attraction at Poolewe is the Inverewe Gardens (NTS), open throughout the year. The incredible thing about these gardens is that they were established on Am Ploc Ard ('the high lump'), a mass of red Torridonian Sandstone exposed to every gale, with acid black peat as the only soil, and only stunted heather and one dwarf willow for vegetation. Out of this, in 1862, Osgood Mackenzie determined to establish a wild garden. As a start, soil had to be carried in, in creels, to provide beds for the plants. Today,

magnificent Monterey pines, Australian tree ferns, rhododendrons, and exotic shrubs from many parts of the world attract some 100,000 visitors every year.

Portmahomack Highland 21C7
At the end of the nineteenth century over 100 men and boys were employed in fishing from the harbour, a harbour that had been improved by Thomas Telford early in that century. There is still fishing; but some of it is sea-angling by holidaymakers.

For those residents for whom fishing and the holiday trade are insufficient remuneration, Nigg (*see* Invergordon) is on the other side of the peninsula, 15km. away.

Beyond the church at the southern end of the bay are long sand dunes, known locally as the Sands of Gaza because they are said to resemble a desert. Beyond that, however, holidaymakers should not venture from the land: the sand bar that guards the entrance to the

Dornoch Firth around the islets of Innis Mhor and Innis Beag – known locally as 'Grizzen Brigs' – is dangerous.

At the end of the peninsula, north from Portmahomack, there stands on Tarbat Ness the second-highest lighthouse in Britain, with good views across Moray Firth and Dornoch Firth; a rocky, cave-indented coast runs down the east of the peninsula from Wilkshaven to Rockfield.

Portnacroish   Strathclyde   8B6
On an islet just offshore from this village stands a strong tower that for position as well as appearance rivals the better-known castle of Eilean Donan (*see* Dornie). This is Castle Stalker, originally built in the thirteenth century but as it appears today dating from *c.* 1450, when it was owned by the Stewarts of Appin and used by James IV as a hunting seat. Prior to 1966 it had become a picturesque ruin; but under a new owner it is now re-roofed and habitable. It is not normally open to the public; but the view of it from the road, looking across Loch Linnhe to the hills of Morvern, is breathtakingly beautiful.

Portnacroish stands on the north shore of Loch Laich, an inlet off Loch Linnhe. Just round the head of Loch Laich, a minor road goes to PORT APPIN, an attractive collection of small houses, with a pier from which a ferry plies to the island of LISMORE. It is a trip worth taking: the buildings on this island include the small church at Kilmoluaig, near Clachan, originally built in the thirteenth century as a cathedral, but destroyed at the Reformation; the rather plain parish church is its choir, re-roofed in the eighteenth century. There are also ruins of an ancient broch and of two early castles. But the joy of a visit to Lismore is to walk along the island for excellent views of Morvern to the west and Benderloch to the east.

From Port Appin it is delightful to follow the road, under low cliffs and through occasional woodland, round to the shores of Loch Creran, which bites between the hills of Appin and Benderloch.

The old railway (*see* Connel) crossed the loch at the narrows, but the road still has to go round the head of it, from where Glen Creran goes further into the hills. This glen is devoted to forestry; but a minor road goes up it as far as the foot of Glen Ure, where Colin Campbell, the 'Red Fox' of the Appin murder mystery (*see* Duror and Inveraray), lived.

Rhiconich   Highland   18C3
The last village on the road to Durness, a lonely 25km. away, Rhiconich stands at the head of Loch Inchard. It is no more than a very few houses and a hotel, and from it runs one of those small dead-end roads that yield glorious views of the Hebridean scene without having any particular focus.

There is a brief road, turning into a track, along the south side of Loch Inchard. Along the north side the road wanders to KINLOCHBERVIE, which, despite its

remoteness, is a busy fishing harbour – the most important on the far-north-west Highland mainland. It is a double harbour, set on a narrow isthmus with piers on either side, the buildings between; the nets are often to be seen hung up to dry on high poles. The catches are nearly all whitefish.

Despite the harbour, Kinlochbervie is quiet enough, for few of the fishermen live there; mostly they come from the east coast of Scotland, to which they depart as soon as the catch is landed. Visitors at the hotel are away, too, as a rule: they are fishermen also – but for brown trout in the inland lochs, or for salmon or sea trout. There are sands below Oldshore More, further north-west; and a car can be taken as far as Sheigra, where a track continues to Sandwood Bay. But this is a rough track over peat hags – peat stacks will be seen around and beyond Sheigra – and the return walk covers some 13km. So Sandwood Bay sees few visitors, though one, witnessed by a local shepherd, is said to have been a mermaid. More prosaically, seals frequent this coast as they do so much of the west-Highland shoreline.

Some 5km. south from Rhiconich, LAXFORD BRIDGE stands at the head of Loch Laxford, a beautiful long sea loch. Laxford Bridge is what it purports to be: a bridge, and nothing more. There is no village, no hotel, although the River Laxford is a famous salmon river (as the Norse element of its name implies). Immediately south of the Bridge the road forks, west for Scourie (qv), east by lochs Stack, More, and Merkland to Loch Shin and Lairg (qv), 60km. away – a road often followed by brown-trout anglers.

Road to the Isles   Highland
17E8   (Mallaig) – 8C4 (Fort William)
Named highways – the Great North Road, the Golden Road to Samarkand, for example – hold promise of magic. Often, the reality is bitterly disappointing; but that at least cannot be said entirely of the Road to the Isles, which, today, is the A830 from Fort William to Mallaig. It starts prosaically enough, crossing the River Lochy just north-east of Fort William, then with views of housing schemes (though with views backwards of Ben Nevis) before Corpach, and then the paper mill. There are pleasant stretches along Loch Eil, but you have travelled 30km. before the scenic grandeur comes at Glenfinnan (qv), looking down Loch Shiel. West from there, the road that was notoriously bad not forty years ago is now wide and fast enough to cloud the fact that the scenery is no more than pleasant until the drop to Loch Eilt. After that, as the road passes the head of Loch Eilt and the charming Loch nan Uamh, the scenery is often superb, with Hebridean views above and beyond Arisaig. This is tourism's Road to the Isles, with Mallaig and ferries to Skye and the Small Isles at the end of it. But the name is a very recent tag.

The traditional Road to the Isles – or, perhaps more

OPPOSITE: *Portnacroish: Castle Stalker, off the Appin coast*   ABOVE: *Saddell Castle (1508): view from the S*

correctly, the Road from the Isles – ran much further north. Until the railway from Inverness to Kyle of Lochalsh was opened the main crossing between Skye and the mainland was from Kylerhea to Bernera, just outside Glenelg: here, where the Sound of Sleat narrows into Kyle Rhea to join with Loch Alsh, was the best place for bringing cattle across. Black cattle were for centuries the main export of Skye, and were made to swim across the strait before starting on their long journey to the cattle marts at Crieff, Falkirk, or other places in central Scotland. Skye was also a 'gathering ground' for cattle exported from North and South Uist, and possibly other Hebridean islands. Once at Glenelg the cattle drovers found their way south by diverse tracks; but there were two main routes. They might turn south, then east along the north shores of Loch Hourn to Arnisdale, and over the hills to Loch Quoich and Loch Garry to join the Great Glen at Invergarry. Or they might go east over Mam Rattachan to Shiel Bridge, then up Glen Shiel to Loch Cluanie. Today's A87 runs along the north shores of this loch; but the old drovers' road turned south-east to Tomdoun in Glen Garry – a track now blocked by the raising of Loch Loyne for hydro-

electric generation. Or, from Loch Cluanie, the drover might go along Glen Moriston to Fort Augustus and the Corrieyairack Pass to join today's A9, the Great North Road, over Drumochter into Perthshire. Those who went to Fort William would go by the old road through Glencoe and thence to Killin.

There is no road today from Loch Hourn to Loch Garry, and General Wade's road over the Corrieyairack Pass (*see* Fort Augustus and Laggan) is for seasoned walkers only. Otherwise, there are roads today that more or less follow those used as Roads from the Isles for over 300 years. But the A830 is not one of them.

Rosemarkie *see* **Fortrose**

Saddell Strathclyde 3E4
South from Dippen, near the junction of the road to Carradale, the road along the rocky east coast of Kintyre climbs up hillsides and drops to valleys, with not a few acute bends, time and again. After 8 or 9 rather tortuous, but scenically very pleasant, km. it drops to Saddell, now a small village, where in 1164 Somerled, King of the Isles, was buried. He was a tempestuous

character, probably half Celtic, half Norse, the fore-runner of the Kings (later Lords) of the Isles and the progenitor of Clan Donald (later the MacDonalds). The Cistercian abbey at Saddell, which he may have started, was completed by his son Reginald (or Ragnall) and was an important religious centre for some centuries. Little now remains, and what there is is sadly neglected: carved grave slabs lying on the ground (one of which is traditionally – but probably only traditionally – that of Somerled) are cracked and moss-covered.

A road leads down to Saddell Bay, at the western end of which Saddell Castle lies under a steep, tree-covered hillside. Built in 1508 by the Bishop of Argyll (the date appears on the wall), this castle is an oblong keep four storeys high, crowned with parapets. Above the entrance is a carving of the Galley of Somerled. The castle has been restored to a certain extent.

It was at Saddell that Somerled's descendant, Angus Og, welcomed Robert the Bruce in 1306, after the latter's defeats and flight following the murder of the 'Red Comyn'. Bruce's Stone, marking the place where he landed, is just off the road above Ugadale Point, 4km. south of Saddell. Here, above a rocky bay with good views to Arran, are slight remains of a dun; more, and better preserved, ruins stand on a point across the bay: Kildonan Dun, an Iron Age fort built between 100 BC and AD 200 and occupied – though not continuously – for seven or eight centuries after that.

St Kilda   90km. W of Harris

Almost the only way to get to stay on these famous but remote islands, some 90km. west of Harris, is under the auspices of the NTS, which owns St Kilda and organizes working parties there in the summer; NTS cruises also occasionally go there.

St Kilda, actually four islands and three stacks, has been uninhabited, except for a small Army unit associated with the South Uist rocket range, for nearly half a century. The main island is HIRTA, which has in Conachair the highest sea cliff in Britain, rising 426m. sheer above the water. On this island is Village Bay, once the main settlement of St Kilda, where working parties now renovate the ancient cottages and carry out other restoration work. Across the Bay, making a natural breakwater, is the craggy island of Dun.

SOAY is the 'Sheep Island', where the small, long-legged Soay sheep, more like goats, are relics of an ancient breed; this is their last habitat in Britain. When St Kilda was evacuated the stock was transferred to Hirta, where the sheep have continued to breed successfully: quite a number are seen now on farms and in wild-life parks on mainland Britain.

The Soay sheep are only one unique species: the St Kilda field mouse, reddish and weighing twice as much as the mainland species, and the St Kilda wren are others.

BORERAY is the 'gannets' isle'; this, above all, is one of the great fascinations of St Kilda. It is Britain's most important sea-bird breeding place: here is the largest gannetry in the world, with, probably, more than 40,000 pairs of these birds; here is the oldest colony of fulmars in the UK – there are said to be 6,000 breeding sites on Conachair alone. Puffins, razorbills, kittiwakes, manx shearwaters, and petrels are others that breed in great numbers. These birds were vital to the existence of the St Kildans, who otherwise lived mainly on sheep (the wool was also important); there was little fishing, and not much agriculture. Trade was by barter, and rents were paid in feathers. Fulmars not only provided food, but oil for lamps; along with gannets, the fulmars were caught in vast quantities by men descending the cliffs on ropes, while puffins were caught from their burrows by the women and children. The birds were stored in 'cleits', small drystone chambers, which are dotted over Hirta.

Conditions were hard indeed on these bare islands, where winds over 200km./h. have been recorded near sea-level: the force of the gusts above sea-level – around the islands' fantastic rock formations – can hardly be imagined. It was a primitive society that lived here, an extremely religious society where, every visitor noticed, the work was done mainly by the women; but it became less and less tolerable, and the dwindling community asked to be evacuated in 1930, and was taken to the mainland.

Scourie   Highland   18B3

The world's most northerly palm trees in the open air grow in the sheltered gardens of Scourie House: not many of them, but indubitably there – a witness to the benevolent effects of the Gulf Stream on the west coast of Scotland.

That apart, Scourie, set back from a long, sandy bay, is a typical and charming example of a crofting township. In summer it is happily visited by anglers, after the brown trout in the scores of lochans found in the rough moors and hills to the east; by holidaymakers who may have a boat or a tent with them (though a good hotel and a few bed-and-breakfast places also provide accommodation); and by bird watchers. Round the corner of the north side of Scourie Bay is HANDA ISLAND, once inhabited by perhaps a dozen families, who eked out their diet with sea birds and their eggs. There are no people now on Handa; but there are vast colonies, with populations running to many thousands, of guillemots, razorbills, and kittiwakes, along with lesser numbers – but still running to many hundreds – of puffins and fulmars.

Since 1962 Handa has been a bird sanctuary under the care of the Royal Society for the Protection of Birds, which has a bothy on the island where its members may stay. There are day trips to the island from Scourie, and also from Tarbet, a small harbour across the Sound of Handa, reached by a very minor road off the A894 east of Scourie. On Handa there are fine cliffs riven by chasms and geos (clefts), natural rock arches and stacks, and on the moorland are dark lochans; the only interruption to admiring the birds and the view is in dodging the dive-bombing attacks of the bonxies (great skuas), which also, with many other birds – including, on occasions, the golden eagle – are to be seen here.

South from Scourie, the crofting clachan of BADCALL looks across a score or more of islets in Eddrachilis Bay, where, as around Scourie, there is lobster fishing. Crimson sunsets seen across the Minch can be memorable indeed – as can the all-night harsh calling of the corncrake, a bird heard, but seldom seen, on the crofters' fields around Scourie Bay.

Seil Strathclyde 4A3
The long, narrow islands of Seil and Luing, with their attendant scatter of other islands and islets, lie just off the coast in the Firth of Lorn, south from Oban.

The distance from the mainland to Seil is short: the link, by the road from Kilninver at the south end of Loch Feochan, is the Clachan Bridge, often called the 'only bridge across the Atlantic'. It is a harmless enough conceit: this single-arched bridge, designed by Telford in 1792, actually spans Seil Sound, which could be said to be part of the Firth of Lorn, which in its turn might be said to be part of the Atlantic: but there are other bridges with as good a claim!

Cross the bridge and rejoice that the caravan site that was partly built on the other side was eventually banned by the Secretary of State for Scotland, and demolished. The road runs to Balvicar Bay, then branches across the island for the ferry (not a car ferry) to Easdale. Here, and at Balvicar just south of the bay, were the two main places for what was the main industry of Seil for centuries: the islands' slate quarries; there are many signs of this industry, but it has now lapsed completely. At Easdale, where quarrying started about 1631, work had to be largely abandoned when the sea flooded in; the last quarry, at Balvicar, closed a few years ago, killed by high freight charges and by the demise of slate as a popular roofing material.

Despite the remains of an industry, and the battered remains of piers, Easdale is an attractive place, with the peak of Dun Mor towering over it. At Ellenbeith, on the Seil side of the strait, are craft and souvenir shops: this is a destination for coach tours from Oban. The gardens at An Cala, with rose and water gardens, are open one or two afternoons a week from April to September.

From Balvicar, the road south to Luing passes Kilbrandon church, with interesting modern stained glass windows, to Cuan Sound and the car ferry to Luing. There were slate quarries at Cullipool; but they closed down in 1965. There were good dairy farms, also: but in recent years Luing has achieved something of a reputation in agricultural circles for the beef cattle reared there.

West of Luing, beyond clusters of small islands, are the GARVELLACHS, the Isles of the Sea, named after the largest one, Garbh Eilach. On one of these islands, Eilach an Naoimh, are some of the earliest Celtic monastic remains in Scotland. Traditionally associated with St Columba, the ruins are more probably of ninth-century date; they include 'beehive' cells (one rebuilt 3m. high to show its construction), a chapel, and a graveyard, from which, unfortunately, most of the stones of interest have been removed. Local lobster fishermen may take you out to these islands, and to Scarba, from which the famous Corryvreckan whirlpool (*see* Ardfern) may be seen. Special interests apart, though, these are beautiful islands, with a wealth of bird life and with seals basking on offshore rocks.

Shetland Highland 23   (*pop.* 18,445)
It is often said of Shetland that it is nearer to Bergen in Norway than it is to Aberdeen in Scotland. In fact, it is not: Lerwick, the Shetland capital, is 340km. north of Aberdeen, 400km. west of Bergen. But the story does have a grain of poetic truth: these 100-odd islands, less than twenty of which are inhabited, are nearer in spirit and atmosphere to the Norse than to the Scots.

Because there is so much sea between the northern Scottish mainland and the southern tip of Shetland, with only Orkney and Fair Isle in between, map-makers must usually perforce put Shetland on an inset somewhere, often on a reduced scale. As a result it is not always realized that from Dunnet Head, the northernmost point of the Scottish mainland, to Sumburgh Head, the southernmost tip of Shetland, is some 180km. And the road that runs the length of narrow Mainland, the main Shetland island, from Sumburgh in the south to Isbister in the north, is over 130km. long.

Sumburgh Head (the islands' airport is at Sumburgh) is on the same latitude – 60° north – as Cape Farewell in Greenland and as Leningrad, which gives rise to another misconception about Shetland. Its climate is not Arctic at all, thanks to the Gulf Stream; neither, obviously, is it Mediterranean; and neither is it predictable: brilliant sunshine, grey skies, or scudding clouds in fierce gales can alternate with remarkable rapidity.

Neither, despite all the seas between, is Shetland remote: it is an hour's flight from Aberdeen, from which ships and the newly-introduced car ferries do the journey overnight. But, sadly, for the past few years Shetland has been rather inaccessible as far as the traveller is concerned; nearly all the visitor accommodation, except in places some considerable distance from Lerwick, the island capital, is permanently taken by those concerned with the development of Shetland as a service base for North Sea oil (some of the most important fields lie east of the islands).

The birdwatcher – assuming he finds somewhere to stay! – knows that he will see huge colonies of seabirds, including the great skuas (the name 'bonxie' by which they are often known is a Shetland word), which breed

Jarlshof, Shetland

on Herma Ness (at the north end of Unst, the most northerly Shetland isle) and Noss (off Bressay, east of Lerwick). He knows that he will see gannets, puffins, guillemots, razorbills, and kittiwakes as well as gulls, and that red-throated divers breed on many lochs; but perhaps the most exciting sighting will be the snowy owl – a pair arrived on Fetlar in 1967 and came annually thereafter until 1976. And there may be other varieties

that the birdwatcher does not really expect, or even hope, to see in Britain. Shetland is on the main migration route for many birds, and even such exotics as bee-eater and crane have been recorded there.

For the angler it used to be Orkney for brown trout, Shetland for sea trout; and to a certain extent this is still true – certainly for Orkney. But in recent years the sea trout in Shetland have declined in number, though there are still good runs, in August and September especially. But with something like 100 lochs on Mainland alone, most of which have brown trout, the angler is still likely to look on Shetland as a good spot to visit, particularly as there is virtually no difficulty in getting angling permits, and very cheap ones at that.

While there are birds to watch and trout to catch in most of the Highlands, only one other area of Britain (Orkney) equals Shetland for its archaeological remains. Here, it is claimed, are more prehistoric sites than in any place in the UK; and Shetland certainly has the finest remains of those unique structures, the brochs. The best example is Mousa Broch (on Mousa Island off the east coast of Mainland, some 22km. south of Lerwick). It still stands over 13m. high, with drystone walls 6m. thick round the circular courtyard. Clickhimin Broch, near Lerwick, is another impressive example: extensive excavations in the 1950s showed it to be a complex of buildings and one of the most important prehistoric sites in Britain. Here the broch is comparatively recent; like Mousa, it seems to have been built during the first two centuries AD, but there were dwellings here in the early Iron Age, perhaps 800 years earlier, and occupation continued for some hundreds of years after the broch was built. The site at Jarlshof, Sumburgh Head, was probably occupied for even longer than Clickhimin: Bronze Age people lived there, as did those of the Iron Age; remains of Norse dwellings range from the ninth to the thirteenth century; and a farmstead there was followed by a laird's house, which gave the place its name: Sir Walter Scott called it 'Jarlshof' in his *The Pirate* – rather a misnomer for a site where people dwelt, off and on, for over 2,000 years.

The Norsemen arrived about AD 800 and here, so far as can be determined, they came not as raiders but as settlers. What had been a few Pictish settlements became, in due course, one of the busiest crossroads of the world: Shetland became a major centre for the organization of Viking raids, not only along the Highland coast but as far as France, for exploring and establishing new territory in Iceland and Greenland, and for discovering the route to 'Vinland' – North America – to which, almost certainly, the Norsemen sailed five centuries before Columbus.

For that five centuries the Norse ruled Shetland, and the islands are still essentially Norse. In 1469, when the King of Denmark had to find 60,000 florins as the dowry for his daughter Margaret's marriage to James III, he first, in 1468, pledged Orkney for 50,000, then, the next year, had to find another 8,000 by pledging Shetland. The pledges have never been redeemed, though there are Shetlanders who have considered, from time to time, that it might not be a bad idea.

James III might have got a bargain, but the Shetlanders did not. Scottish law and usage gradually took over from the Norse system and eroded certain rights of the islanders to the land; in 1564 James V gave Shetland

to his illegitimate son Earl Robert Stewart, whose tyrannical oppression of the people was only exceeded by that of *his* son, Earl Patrick. The latter built the fine castle at Scalloway (the ruins are well worth seeing), some 8km. west of Lerwick, in 1600: the story – apocryphal, we may safely assume – that blood was mixed with the mortar reflects the extent of Earl Patrick's cruelties. He was executed in 1615; and his death gave the Shetlanders an opportunity to assert some of their rights, although later, under a succession of rapacious landowners, any rights they had vanished.

Their miserable state did not improve until the passing of the Crofting Act in 1864, which at last gave them some security of tenure.

Yet at the same time LERWICK, beside the great natural anchorage of Bressay Sound, grew and prospered through its fishing, not only by the Shetlanders but by Dutch vessels, which used it extensively in the seventeenth century. Lerwick, a fascinating town (*pop.* 6,307), looks across its harbour, beside which some of the older houses rise directly out of the water. As in Stromness (Orkney) the main street, paved with flagstones, twists between buildings, following the line of the shore. The newer houses stand further back. The fishing, which from a peak in the early nineteenth century dwindled to only a small number of boats in the 1930s, has revived considerably, in other parts of Shetland as well as Lerwick. Fish-processing factories have followed, to deal with the catches from modern vessels.

Shetland is perhaps particularly well known for its shawls and its ponies. But the famous Shetland shawls, made by women using the finest wool from the necks of Shetland sheep to weave gossamer-light shawls – so fine that they can be pulled through a wedding ring – are probably on their way out: fewer and fewer people have the time or the skill to make them. Less specialized forms of knitwear, however, continue to flourish. The delightful Shetland pony, bred mainly on Unst, is now mostly in demand as a pet – and fetches a high price.

Another aspect of Shetland to have received a fair amount of publicity in recent years is the Fire Festival 'Up Helly A' in January: a Viking longship, 9m. long with a huge dragon's head ·as its prow, and heraldic shields on its gunnels, is burnt after a torchlight procession of 'Vikings' through the streets of Lerwick; flaming torches – up to 800 of them – are hurled into the galley, and months of building goes up in flames. This Viking festival, continuing an old Norse tradition, marks the end of the winter solstice.

But neither this nor the history, nor even its archaeological interest, make for the real fascination of Shetland. From its coasts, with cliffs and long sandy beaches on the west, and Atlantic rollers breaking almost incessantly, each island is a green, treeless landscape with small crofts, whitewashed cottages, often fields with strip cultivation, a straggle of roads, and, above all, the omnipresence of the sea. Nowhere in Shetland is it possible to be more than 5km. from the sea, for long voes' – sea lochs – everywhere bite deep into the land. The quality of the light on Shetland is quite striking: the sun dips below the horizon for but a brief few hours, and the light never goes completely for weeks on either side of Midsummer Day (it is this that produces the 'simmer dim', a particularly serene and beautiful twilight).

Nowhere more than in Shetland has care been taken to keep the new industry, oil, in its proper place. Changes

there have been, and will be; but Shetland is still very much a land apart from any other.

Shiel Bridge   Highland   14A5
When only a narrow road straggled down Glen Shiel to the head of Loch Duich perhaps travellers were more inclined to stop at Invershiel, just across Shiel Bridge. Here the main road turns sharp right, with a smaller road to the left almost unnoticed.

Scalloway Castle (1600), Shetland

In the spate of road improvements that followed World War II the main road was widened and tailored; then, in 1969, a new bridge was built to save the motorist a 3km. drive round by Croe Bridge. The route to Kyle of Lochalsh for Skye was then fast indeed compared to what it had been in pre-war days, particularly with the new road along the shores of Loch Alsh cutting out a rather awkward hill-climb.

Encouraged by these road improvements, many motorists rush down Glen Shiel, ignoring the great slopes of the Five Sisters of Kintail, soaring up, at Scour Ouran, to 1,069m. Certainly these great mountains are better seen from Mam Rattachan, for which you take that unobtrusive left-hand turn before Shiel Bridge. Travelling briefly beside the loch, the road then climbs up through dark woods, with acute bends and tantalizing glimpses through the trees of Loch Duich below. Out of the trees, at the top, it is a good idea to stop, climb briefly above the road, and see one of the most superb panoramas in the western Highlands. The road continues down to Glenelg (qv).

If you do not leave the south side of Loch Duich to climb Mam Rattachan (Dr Samuel Johnson, then aged 64 and without the benefit of the internal-combustion engine, did it over a much worse surface in 1773), you can follow the shores of the loch (beside which there is a well-known youth hostel). The track – it is no more – continues to the little township of Letterfearn and

Totaig, the latter looking across to Eilean Donan Castle: there was a ferry across the strait once, but not now.

Beyond Totaig, a km. walk leads to Caisteal Grugaig, the remains of an ancient broch, with 3m.-thick walls. Traditionally, this was built or owned by the lady whose sons, Telve and Trodden, built the Glenelg brochs.

If you go through Invershiel, not taking the new bridge across the water, much can be found out about Kintail at the NTS visitor centre in Morvich: the NTS owns over 5,000ha. here, which include the Five Sisters, Ben Attow, and the Falls of Glomach (see Dornie). Campers and caravanners can stay at the NTS site at Morvich, and permission may be obtained there for salmon and sea-trout fishing at certain times.

Skipness   Strathclyde 3F2

There is no finer view of the mountains of Arran than from the road (the B8001) that goes from Kennacraig on West Loch Tarbert to Claonaig on the Kilbrennan Sound. It is a view that comes suddenly, although the pass across the peninsula is not lofty – only some 127m. above sea-level. The road drops down from the pass to Claonaig, just a few houses and a pier, from which during the summer months there is a car ferry to Lochranza on Arran.

North-east from Claonaig a minor road goes along the coast to Skipness: it makes a fine walk, 8km. in all,

Skipness Castle: view from the NW

returning, if you feel that way inclined, along the track above the coast. This is a good example, incidentally, of the raised beaches found so often along the coasts of the Highlands, including all Kintyre: when the immense burden of ice melted, perhaps 10,000 years ago, the land gradually rose above what is sea-level today: the flat beaches or machairs backed by low cliffs (often holding caves in which prehistoric man took refuge) are the result.

Skipness lies around a wide bay, and literally at the end of the road from Claonaig a path leads through parkland to Skipness House, Castle, and Chapel. The House is not open to the public. The Castle, a remarkably fine ruin, dates back to the early thirteenth century: in 1247 it was recorded as belonging to one Dufgal, son of Syfyn. To the original building, 2m.-thick curtain walls were added early in the fourteenth century. In 1499, when James IV was trying to bring the Lords of the Isles under control, the Castle came into the possession of the Campbells of Argyll: it was around this time that the keep was added. Unusual in that it never had to endure a major siege (which in part accounts for its good condition today), the Castle was deserted about 1700. The Chapel, roofless but well preserved considering that it was built in 1261, is across the fields. Over the low stone wall beyond the graveyard a great tarmac arrow set in the grass points down Kilbrennan Sound. The Ordnance Survey map marks it as an 'Automatic Radar Station': would that all such innovations were as innocuous!

Skye Highland 16,17 (*pop.* 7,340)
The Romantic Isle . . . The Misty Isle . . . The Winged Isle . . . these are only a few of the phrases used to describe the largest and most northerly island of the Inner Hebrides. The magnificent ridges of the Cuillins, the aura of 'Bonnie Prince Charlie', the long sea lochs penetrating the coast, the castle of a famous clan, and a picturesque 'capital' on an attractive bay – these features attract tourists and make Skye the most visited of the Western Isles. Skye of course attracts not only the holidaymaker, but also the archaeologist, the historian, the nature-lover, the geologist, the artist, and a host of others (including, obviously, the mountaineer and climber).

Skye is easier to get to than any other Hebridean island. The car ferry from Kyle of Lochalsh to Kyleakin runs virtually a shuttle service for seventeen hours a day during the summer months, the crossing taking about ten minutes. Until a few years ago it was a weekday service only: when Sunday services were proposed local protest extended to lying down in front of cars when the boats docked. But the protests were by no means unanimous among the people of Kyleakin; now the only concession to Sabbatarianism is that boats do not start until ten o'clock on Sundays.

The longer crossing, from Mallaig to Armadale, tak-

ing half an hour, runs five times each way daily – but not on Sundays. A further service, from Glenelg to Kylerhea, the traditional crossing (*see* Road to the Isles), ran for many years, but its future is uncertain.

Skye is a very large island, and most of it is moorland and mountain. For all the summer pressure of people, it is rare to feel a sense of crowding; there are exceptions, of course, ranging from Portree harbour and Dunvegan Castle to boat trips to Loch Coruisk, but generally it is not difficult to find seclusion.

There have been people on Skye from time immemor-

Skye: looking across Loch Cill Chriosd, SW of Broadford, with the slopes of Blaven in the background

ial: chambered cairns on the island date back to the Stone Age. The Vikings raided Skye many times, and eventually settled; and King Haakon's fleet stayed in Portree Bay on the expedition of 1263, when Haakon made a final, vain attempt to subjugate all the west coast. He sailed on to the Firth of Clyde and defeat at the Battle of Largs. In 1746 Skye's most famous visitor, Prince Charles Edward Stuart, arrived, although his stay lasted only a week. It was at what is now the Royal Hotel in Portree that the Prince said farewell to Flora MacDonald; and at Portree, twenty-seven years later,

Dr Johnson and James Boswell dined at what they believed was 'the only inn of the island'. Historically, there is little else to be said of Portree, except that it got its name, Port Righ ('King's Haven'), from another visitor, James V. Yet it is an attractive centre on the side of a very pleasant bay, and it is a pity that visits to the island cannot have it as a taking-off point, instead of Kylerhea or Armadale.

The only regular car-ferry service from Portree is to RAASAY, a 20km.-long, narrow island, the development of which was the subject of long and acrimonious legal

proceedings in the early 1970s. This, fortunately, does not prevent one visiting it, and a new, thrice-daily, ferry from Sconser to Raasay opened in 1976. There are only a few km. of road, and this makes more pleasant a walk up the length of the island, between the coast and the long volcanic spine, to Brochel Castle, the ruin of an ancient Raasay MacLeod stronghold, set above a beautiful bay.

North from Portree a road circles the long Trotternish Peninsula. It is one of those excursions that, only 75km. long, gives time to stop and look. There are buses – but only twice a day in summer and not that in winter. The road, the A855, runs beside two beautiful lochs, beyond which the castle-like Storr soars up to 720m. The incredible Old Man of Storr, nearby, is a thin isolated pinnacle rearing 45m. high. Further on, the road runs above the cliffs; ahead the Kilt Rock stands over the sea, and eastwards are fine views of the Torridon mountains. At Staffin Bay, a minor road climbs and swoops – with a notorious hairpin bend – into the fantastic scenery of the Quiraing, where a single column, the Needle, 36m. high, and the Table Rock stand among forbidding black

TOP: *Skye: looking N across Loch Fada with The Storr and The Old Man of Storr in the background*
BOTTOM: *Skye: The Old Man of Storr (centre)*

Dunvegan Castle, Skye

cliffs rent with clefts. This road goes through to Uig Bay; but the main road goes round the point of Trotternish to Duntulm, where the ruins of an ancient fortress of the MacDonalds of Sleat perch on a cliff.

Flora MacDonald is buried in the churchyard at Kilmuir; and from here, given no mist, are fine views across the Vaternish Peninsula to Harris and the Uists (for which there is a car ferry from Uig Bay). At Kilmuir, also, is the Kilmuir Croft Museum, a 'black house', with reminders of crofting life.

At Kingsburgh Johnson and Boswell were guests of 'Mr MacDonald and his lady Flora MacDonald', the latter 'a name that will be mentioned in history, and if courage and fidelity be virtues, mentioned with honour', wrote Dr Johnson. On Skye it is difficult to escape from the image of Flora MacDonald. It was she who brought Prince Charles Edward from South Uist, disguised as her maid 'Betty Burke', when he was on the run from Culloden (the reward for his capture was £30,000). For her part in his escape Flora MacDonald was sent to the Tower of London, but was later released and married Allan MacDonald of Kingsburgh.

After the circle of Trotternish, the road to Dunvegan is somewhat of a scenic anti-climax, as is the Vaternish Peninsula, though given the weather – always an important qualification on Hebridean islands – it is worth going along the B886 (a dead-end road to Trumpan from Fairy Bridge) for views to Harris and North Uist, with the high sheer cliffs of Dunvegan Head in the foreground.

En route to Dunvegan are reminders of the past: the Clach Ard stone, carved with typical Pictish symbols, stands on the east side of Loch Snizort Beag; and about $1\frac{1}{2}$km. north of Fairy Bridge, at Annait, the site of an early-Christian settlement stands on a green promontory, with the remains of walls and the foundations of a chapel and some cells still to be seen.

At the entrance to Dunvegan Castle is another Pictish stone, much worn by time and weather. But it is of scant interest compared to the Castle. This has been the home of the chiefs of Clan MacLeod for 700 years, and has a splendid setting on an almost sheer rock, 7–8km. high, by the side of Loch Dunvegan. The oldest part, the keep, dates back to the fourteenth century; the great keep, with its deep dungeon, was built rather later; the Fairy

SKYE

Tower dates from the sixteenth century; and there were extensive changes in the nineteenth century. Despite all these changes over the centuries, Dunvegan seems the epitome of a Highland stronghold. Inside, it has the charm of being very much a lived-in castle, and among the treasures to be seen are the 'Fairy Flag', a flag – now a tattered piece of silk – of oriental design, thought to have been captured from the Saracens during a Crusade; it is said to have twice saved the clan from disaster, and allegedly has the power – as yet untested – for one more such rescue. Relics of a famous MacLeod chief, the seventeenth-century Rory Mor, include his drinking horn, which subsequent chiefs were expected to drain of claret at one go: it holds about two litres! The family portraits include two by Allan Ramsay and two by Raeburn.

No chiefs in recent times have been more concerned for the welfare of their clan than the MacLeods: the twenty-eighth chief, Dame Flora MacLeod of MacLeod, who died in 1976, for many years travelled extensively, to America and the Commonwealth, to keep the family ties together: she was still doing this well past her nine-tieth birthday.

From about 1540 the most famous of all piping families, the MacCrimmons, were hereditary pipers to the MacLeods, and across Loch Dunvegan at Borreraig a cairn marks the site of the piping school run by this family for nearly 250 years. In 1976 a Canadian professor, Hugh MacCrimmon, opened a piping centre here.

A minor road from south of Dunvegan goes up the east side of the loch to Borreraig, with views of the high, flat-topped hills Healaval More (469m.) and Healaval Beg (488m.), which are known as Macleod's Tables (in this case, 'More', meaning big, does not mean it is higher than 'Beg', meaning little!). At Colbost is another crofter's house that has been turned into a museum: it includes a replica of a whisky still; 3km. down the road is an old water-mill for grinding corn.

The seas around the Duirinish Peninsula abound in fish, and sea-angling is based on Glendale, west of Colbost; north from Colbost, by the west shore of Loch Harport, are the ruins of Dun Ardtreck broch, built around 100 BC, in a striking setting above a low, sheer cliff.

Around Dunvegan – the village is about 1½km. south of the Castle – is more colour than anywhere in northern Skye. The green fields contrast sharply with the moorland in the centre of the island; there are woods around the Castle, and along the east side of Loch Dunvegan, towards Claigan, are beautiful stretches of white coral sand (and for archaeological interest, a ruined broch on the Fiadhairt Peninsula). In the spring seals and barnacle geese may be seen on the offshore islets, and in summer there are masses of wild flowers.

The Cuillin Hills are a different story indeed. (It is odd that these, the most challenging peaks in Britain – there are upwards of a score of them – should be 'hills'

Skye: the Cuillin Hills, with the Sligachan burn in the foreground

and not 'mountains'.) For over 20km. this huge horseshoe of hard, bare pinnacles and ridges stands over 900m. above sea-level; and its climbing is not for the inexpert.

En route for the Cuillins from Dunvegan, the ruins of the Dun Beag broch, built about 2,000 years ago, stand on a knoll near Bracadale. From the head of Loch Harport, one road runs west to Carbost and Talisker, home of a famous distillery; another goes south, climbs to nearly 100m. – a good viewpoint – then goes down Glen Brittle, west of the Cuillin ridge. If the full scale of the mountains cannot be seen from here, at least their roughness can be appreciated.

Glenbrittle, which has a youth hostel, is popular with climbers. If an excuse is needed for making the 11km. return walk along the east coast of Loch Brittle, there are other prehistoric remains to be seen: a neolithic horned cairn, still standing some 3½m. high, and an Iron Age broch – now only about 2½m. high – on Rudh an Dunain Point.

The major centre for the Cuillins, though, is Sligachan, where the roads from Dunvegan and Portree

Skye- Loch Coruisk seen from Sgurr a Ghreadaidh; Loch Scavaig is to the right

join. But the ordinary non-mountaineering mortal sees the stark magnificence of the Cuillins by taking a boat from Elgol (the road to it goes south-west from Broadford, round the head of Loch Slapin, to the shores of Loch Scavaig). The boats from here go 'subject to demand'; and demand is high indeed, when the weather is good, in July and August. The boats land at the northern end of the loch; then it is but a short walk to the shores of dark Loch Coruisk, a lake, formed by Ice Age glaciers, whose bottom is 30m. *below* sea-level; around it is a vast amphitheatre of dark, dramatic peaks.

From Elgol a side road goes to the east shores of the peninsula and to Dun Grugaig, another of the many prehistoric brochs on Skye; 6km. further up the coast, at Dun Ringill, there is yet another broch.

The Cuillin Hills – the Black Cuillin – are magnificent, if rather awe-inspiring. The Red Hills, the Red Cuillin, are more friendly, and there is a wonderful view of them across Loch Slapin on the way back to Broadford, a view across blue water to white crofts and flower-filled fields lying under the 700m.-high red ramparts.

Colour reaches its peak, though, in the southern peninsula of the island, Sleat. While the road from Broadford to Armadale, where the car ferry from Mallaig docks, is much used, Sleat itself is not as well known as the more impressive area further north. Sleat has a lushness unknown elsewhere on the island, with trim crofts and farms, and, from the road, fine views across the Sound of Sleat. North from Armadale Bay is Armadale Castle, built 1815–19. Beyond it a very minor road strikes across the Peninsula to the township of Achnacloich on Tarskavaig Bay. It turns north to Tokavaig, near which, on a high headland above Loch Eishort, are the ruins of Dunscaith (Dunsgiath) Castle. The ruins are not extensive; but the views of the Cuillins across Loch Eishort are perhaps the best of all on this most scenic island. From this road, too – from Tarskavaig Bay in particular – the mountains of Rum (*see* Small Isles) dominate the Cuillin Sound, as they do from the Point of Sleat, the southernmost end of the island, which can be reached by a minor road, and then a track, from Armadale.

The Small Isles: Rum seen from Traigh on the mainland

The Cuillins make for superb views; but they are also notorious rain-gatherers, and heavy, sometimes prolonged, downpours are not unknown on the island. Then placid burns become raging rivers, waterfalls plunge over mountain cliffs, and the views are blotted out by cloud. It is unwise to go to Skye, at any time, without rainwear; and, after midsummer, unwise to travel without midge repellent. But rain and midges are minor irritants to set beside the beauty and charm of Skye.

The Small Isles Highland 6, 17

Eigg, Muck, Rum, and Canna: these are the Small Isles, listed in the order that the boat from Mallaig calls at them on Mondays, Wednesdays, and Saturdays. On Thursdays the boat goes the other way round; on Tuesdays – and of course on Sundays – it does not go at all (though Highland timetables can often change!).

The Small Isles are in one parish – the Small Isles – and their combined populations do not exceed 200 people. But all the islands are different – in shape, size, and character.

Taking that boat from Mallaig – a most worthwhile journey, which takes seven to eight hours out and back – the first stop is normally EIGG, where a long ridge reaches its pinnacle at the steep cliffs of An Sgurr, a spectacular landmark 393m. high. Its cliffs and broken rock columns are formed of pitchstone lava, which erupted some 50 million years ago. Despite its rocky appearance from a distance, it is a rich land, supporting about half the parish population, who live by crofting. The next island is MUCK, though the boat does not always stop there; the smallest of the Small Isles, it is low and fertile, and only 3km. long. It is just one estate, on which the laird lives. RUM, the next stop, is the largest Small Isle, and utterly different. Much of it is a mass of wild mountains, rising at three points to over 760m. These mountains, like those of Eigg, are volcanic in origin; and as only the low island of Barra (qv) stands between them and Labrador, they tend to catch the Atlantic rain clouds. Geologically and botanically, Rum is an outstandingly interesting island; but the opportunities for following either study are restricted. Rum is owned by the Nature

Conservancy Council, and is used primarily for the study of red deer – about 1,500 of them. The whole island is closed to visitors for short periods in early April and again in early June, and the Council has powers to close it at any other time it wishes. Within these limitations, however, it can be landed on – but only by day visitors: there is no accommodation (campers who carry their tents on their backs may stay if they have prior permission and can face the voracious midges, for which the island is notorious). Again within the limitations, there are certain facilities for visitors. There are a couple of nature trails from Loch Scresort, where the boats call, and there are a post office and a shop.

Rum's history is not particularly edifying. Until 1826 it was inhabited by at least 400 crofters and their families. In that year, however, they were all, except one family, cleared off – most went to America – and the island was turned into a single sheep farm, looked after by the remaining family. In 1845 the whole island was turned into a sporting estate, red deer were brought in, and until 1939 nobody was allowed to land except the proprietor and his friends and employees. Kinloch Castle, overlooking Loch Scresort, was built early this century by George Bullough, a member of the Lancashire family that owned the island from 1888 to 1957. The Castle is now occupied by the Nature Conservancy Council, and is still not open to visitors (although sustained by the state).

CANNA is a different story indeed. Here are people rather than red deer: not a lot of them, but, with a sympathetic laird and fertile ground, they keep going. Possibly the 180m.-high cliffs on the north of the island – the whole island itself, for that matter – stem from the volcanic eruptions on Rum; at the eastern end of the island is Compass Hill, whose basalt rock is so strongly magnetized that it is said to disturb the compasses of passing vessels.

Canna has the best pier in the Small Isles, sheltered by Sanday Island just off-shore. But the main impression here is one of green pastures and rich soil, and of superb views to the Cuillins of Skye. And while the only accommodation for visitors is in cottages, there is a general feeling of welcome, and there are no objections if you have a tent on your back or a boat to sleep in.

Southend   Strathclyde   2D6

There are two roads from Campbeltown (qv) to Southend: the direct, inland route, which runs through dairy land then down Conie Glen, in all 16km.; or, much longer in time as well as distance, for it is a road better walked over than driven, the old drove road round the coast, winding steeply among the hills. This latter has good views across the Kilbrennan Sound, first to Arran and then, further on, to the Ayrshire coast.

Whichever route is taken, once at Southend there is no resemblance whatever to the better-known Southend in Essex. Here are two sandy beaches separated by

Dunaverty Head, where once a stronghold of the Lords of the Isles stood above a sheer drop to the sea: little of it now remains. Here are an old boathouse and a pier, reminders of once busy fishing days: only a few men go out now for lobsters or salmon; here is a small village, with farms round about; and from here it is possible to walk – cars cannot go all the way – to the real South End of Kintyre – the Mull – where you are nearer to Ireland than to Ayrshire. The rather spectacular lighthouse was built in 1788.

Along the shore between Dunaverty and Carskey Bay is ruined Keil Chapel, near which are 'St Columba's Footsteps', where, tradition has it, the Saint first landed on Scottish soil. Finding that he could still see Ireland – it is not much over 20km. away – and having been banished from the sight of his country, he sailed on, eventually to Iona (qv).

But he was a late-comer to these parts. Up Glen Breakerie from Carskey Bay there are duns on the hillside; there is another on the Borgadel Water, on the way to the Mull of Kintyre; and there are others on the low hills east of Southend. They are, it must be said, fragmentary. The latest of them pre-dates Columba by a thousand years.

South Uist   Highlands   22   (pop. 4,059)

Although sharing many of the Outer Hebridean characteristics of its northerly neighbours Benbecula (qv) and North Uist (qv) – a causeway links the three islands – South Uist has its differences.

It is as remote in feel as, and even more Gaelic than, the others; but though it has lochs and lochans and sea-inlets in plenty, they are not as dominant as in Benbecula or eastern North Uist; it has hills over 600m. high on its eastern side; and along nearly all its western shores are beaches and machair, almost unbroken for over 30km. *Almost* unbroken: part of the machair is now taken over by the Ministry of Defence rocket range that was established for test-firing 'Corporal' missiles: an observation post for these was set up on St Kilda (qv) also. When the missiles became obsolete in 1968 the Ministry did not abandon the range but added more rockets, two for weather research. Barracks and houses were built in 1970, and further additions have been made since.

Car ferries to South Uist from Castlebay on Barra and Oban dock at Lochboisdale, sailing for over 3km. up narrow Loch Boisdale before reaching the pier. From here it is some 5km. to Daliburgh, the main, though small, centre of population on the island: another difference in South Uist is that it is more a collection of scattered crofts than of crofting townships.

The island is almost entirely Roman Catholic, unaffected by the Presbyterian faith, which maintains further north. Just south of Loch Bee on low Rueval Hill is a statue of Our Lady of the Isles, erected in 1957 with contributions from the Catholic community in many parts of the world. Standing over 9m. high on a rocky outcrop, it was sculpted by Hew Lorimer. At the south end of the island, at Garrynamonie, even more recent is Our Lady of the Sorrows, a church built in 1964, with a mosaic on the front.

South from Rueval, the Nature Conservancy Council's Loch Druidibeg reserve is the most important breeding ground in Britain of the greylag goose. When hatched the goslings are taken by their parents to the lochs nearer the machair, where a wide variety of duck, swans, and other geese feed.

South from Garrynamonie, the road ends at Ludag, and here it is possible to take the mail ferry (or hire a boat) to Eriskay (qv).

From Ludag (or anywhere else *en route*) you can take a bus that runs the whole length of the island, passing many a trout loch on the way, with the open Atlantic to the west and the hills to the east, crossing not only Loch Bee but also the south ford to Benbecula.

Spean Bridge Highland 8D3

The bridge built by Telford in 1819 here spans the River Spean, which, fed by streams from Ben Nevis, comes fast down from Loch Moy, 25km. east. This was not the first bridge. The river was originally spanned by a high bridge, 30m. above a gorge, built by General Wade in 1736: although repaired in 1893, part of it collapsed twenty years later, and sixty years later was still not repaired.

In 1745 there was a skirmish at Spean Bridge; it was the first action in the Jacobite rising of that year, but took place three days before Prince Charles Edward Stuart raised his standard at Glenfinnan.

Today's Spean Bridge is a small village, quite popular with holidaymakers, where the road from Fort William divides – left for the Great Glen and Inverness, right for the Spey Valley. West from the village, just off the A82 Inverness road, is the very impressive memorial, by Scott Sutherland, to the commandos of World War II, many of whom trained in this area. The views from here to Ben Nevis are magnificent. Near the memorial, a minor road drops down to Gairlochy, where the Caledonian Canal climbs up two locks to Loch Lochy, and from where an even more minor road leads along the attractive shores of Loch Arkaig, a well-known brown-trout loch.

Eight km. east of Spean Bridge, on the road to Laggan, with more good views of the Ben Nevis massif, is Roy Bridge, from which a minor road leads up Glen Roy. Some 6km. along this road the 'parallel roads' are easily seen across the valley: the 'roads' are in fact the beaches of lochs formed by glaciers during the Ice Age, and they are the best example of glacial action in Scotland. There

OPPOSITE TOP: *Spinningdale Mill: view from the NE*

OPPOSITE BOTTOM: *Fingal's Cave (right)*

are other 'parallel roads' on the west side of the Glen, easily reached from the road. The road follows the river to Brae Roy Lodge, and there ends. From the Lodge a long, rough track through the hills joins the Corrieyairack Pass from Fort Augustus to the Spey Valley.

Spinningdale Highland 21A7

In a land with so many ruined castles, the tall gaunt building by the shores of the Dornoch Firth at Spinningdale is often taken to be another one. In fact, it is the ruins of a cotton mill established in 1790 by George Dempster of Skibo, to give much-needed employment to the area. This it did for a brief period – over 100 people were employed at the peak – but (not for the first or last time in Highland history) costs of transport outweighed the advantage of plentiful labour. The mill burnt down in 1808, and was not rebuilt.

Three km. west, off the road to Bonar Bridge, a promontory juts into the Firth; at its point DUN CREICH, a vitrified hill-fort dating back at least to the first century BC, stands 113m. above the water: there is no approach to the summit by road.

The major castle in this area is some 15km. east, off the road to Dornoch: Skibo Castle, built in 1898 for Andrew Carnegie.

Staffa Strathclyde 7B5

This small uninhabited island, only a little over 1km. long and a third of that wide, has some of the most remarkable cliffs, and certainly the most famous cave, in Scotland.

FINGAL'S CAVE is only one of several caves in the cliffs of high hexagonal pillars, formed when the basalt from the volcanic activity on Mull cooled down. The huge 'organ pipes' inspired Mendelssohn to write his *Hebrides* overture (also known as *Fingal's Cave*); they inspired Wordsworth to three – admittedly little-known – sonnets; Queen Victoria rhapsodized about Staffa; other nineteenth-century figures, from Turner to Tennyson, were among its visitors; and it became an established 'tourist visit' in the early days of steamer trips around Mull.

Queen Victoria was able to take a boat inside Fingal's Cave, which can only be done when the sea is quiet: usually the Cave can only be seen from the outside, through a great natural arch. This cave is some 20m. high and 13m. wide; there are others – McKinnon's and the Boat caves on the south-west side of the island among them – and a causeway also.

For all its natural wonder, the island was not known to visitors until 1772. Once it was inhabited, and black cattle were pastured on it: the last family to live there all the year round begged to be taken off over a century ago because of the terrifying roaring of the sea, which, in strong winds, can force its way out through holes above some of the caves.

Steamer trips from Oban go past Staffa; but there are

boat excursions from Mull, on some of which – weather permitting – it is possible to land on the island.

Strathpeffer Highland 15E2

The immediate surroundings of this pleasant resort are most un-Highland, with fields, woods, and hedges instead of stone walls. But not far to the north rise the slopes of shapely Ben Wyvis, 1,045m. high, a major landmark in this part of the country; from the summit – not difficult to attain – both the North Sea and the Atlantic may be seen on a clear day.

Strathpeffer has been well known for over 150 years. Sulphur and chalybeate springs were discovered here towards the end of the eighteenth century; the place soon became a spa, with the first pump room built about 1820, and it retained its fame as such for nearly 100 years.

Its prosperity was prophesied by the Brahan Seer (*see* Conon Bridge), the most famous of the Highland soothsayers, who was born *c.* 1600. 'Uninviting and disagreeable as it now is, the day will come when it shall be under lock and key and crowds of pleasure and health seekers shall be seen thronging its portals', he foretold.

Three km. east is the low hill KNOCKFARRIL with its vitrified fort. Such forts, found mostly in north-east Scotland, were made of rubble walls with a timber framework, which, when burnt in a strong wind, fused

Knockfarril vitrified fort, nr Strathpeffer

the stone into a slaggy mass. Although Knockfarril is among the best known of these forts, its origins are unknown: it might date back as far as 800 BC.

Just north of Strathpeffer, CASTLE LEOD, a four-storey tower, built in 1619 by Sir Rorie Mackenzie of Coigach, and now the seat of the Earl of Cromartie, is set in fine parkground. It is not open to the public.

The A834 south-west from Strathpeffer joins the A832 for Gairloch and Ullapool at Contin, whose bridge over the River Blackwater was built by Thomas Telford: the original bridge was swept away by floods in 1811, but was speedily replaced. Across the river, at Achilty, west of Contin, there is an old coaching inn, and just beyond this, off the road, are the Falls of Rogie.

Sunart Highland 6F2

Although the smallest of the areas of mountain and loch bounded by the Sound of Mull, Loch Linnhe, and the Road to the Isles, Sunart does not lack interest.

It has but one village, Strontian (*pron.* Strontcheean), which has twice in 150 years undergone a complete renovation and which has given the root of its name to a metal discovered in 1790 (the radioactive form of which is present in nuclear fallout). Lead mines in the glen north of the village were worked from the beginning of the eighteenth century, when Strontian was a miserable clachan; and it was there that strontium – along with a variety of other rare metals – was found. The village had a complete face-lift in 1828 under the direction of the local landowner, Sir James Riddell. The lead mines ceased to be worked in 1855, but were later reopened.

In 1968 the village was the first to benefit from a scheme initiated by the Secretary of State for Scotland to bring new life to small villages: the developments since have made this a most attractive centre.

A very minor road runs north from the village and climbs to over 342m. before dropping down to the south-east shores of Loch Shiel; it passes Bellsgrove Lodge and has recently been made suitable for cars; the mines are on the hillside beyond the Lodge.

From the top of the ridge over which the road passes is the approach to Ben Resipol, a 16km. return walk, which can also be made along a track just west of Strontian village, taking about the same distance. There are superb views to reward the very necessary exertion, particularly looking seaward along Loch Moidart to the Small Isles and the Cuillins of Skye – and, in clear weather, to the Outer Hebrides.

For some 15km. west from Strontian the road runs beside Loch Sunart – a beautiful route – to Salen, a small village with a hotel, at the head of a bay; here the main road turns north to Acharacle; beyond Salen the coast road, much smaller now, enters Ardnamurchan (qv).

Tain Highland 21B7 (*pop.* 2,151)

To the people of Tain 1066 was important for reasons

quite remote from the tumult of William's Norman conquest, for 1066 was the year when Malcolm Canmore (Malcolm III of Scotland) granted Tain a charter as a Royal burgh.

About sixty-six years before that, St Duthac, also known as Duffus or Duthus, was born in Tain, on the site where a ruined chapel now stands. In due course, the Saint's remains were brought back to Tain – but that was not until 1253, 188 years after his death. At the Chapel of St Duthac the wife and daughter of Robert the Bruce sought sanctuary in 1306, after they had fled from Kildrummy Castle on Donside (Grampian region); but the sanctuary was violated, they were seized by the Earl of Ross and handed over to Edward I: Bruce did not see them again for many years. The sanctuary was again violated in 1427 when MacNeil of Creich pursued Mowat of Freswick into it and burnt it over the heads of Mowat and his followers. The ruins may still be seen.

St Duthac obviously had an appeal for Stewart kings: James IV made an almost annual pilgrimage to Tain from 1493 until a month before he was killed at Flodden Field in 1513; and James V made a pilgrimage, barefoot, also.

These are a few incidents in the long and fairly stormy history of Tain. In the town there are a chapel, with some good stained glass, and the Collegiate College of 1371; the Tolbooth was built in the seventeenth century, but was restored after gale damage in 1730: the bell cast in 1630 is still there. Balnagown Castle, an ancient seat of the Ross family, has been modernized. The Castle is not open to the public. The cheese factory, where visitors can see the processes, is more welcoming; other local industries include a distillery at which one of the great malt whiskies of Scotland is produced, and, at Aldie, nearby, a water-driven mill, which still makes oatmeal.

Tarbert Strathclyde 3E1
Whether by day or night (while the world is still awake and the street lights are reflected in the water, and the houses and hotels around the harbour are lit), Tarbert is a picturesque spot. It stands at the head of East Loch Tarbert, on the narrow neck of land that separates Knapdale from Kintyre: not much over a km. away is the head of West Loch Tarbert: Kintyre is almost an island.

The East Loch is a good natural shelter both for fishing boats – there are not as many as there used to be, though Tarbert is still a prosperous fishing port – and for yachts and other pleasure craft.

It was an obvious place in earlier centuries for a stronghold. An early one was destroyed in the eighth century, and to a later one Robert the Bruce made additions: he occupied it in the late 1320s while trying to get control of Kintyre. Here he emulated the feat of Magnus Barefoot, the Norse king who in 1093 dragged his galley across the isthmus (as did Haakon 170 years later to another Tarbet – without the 'r' – see Arrochar):

Bruce, using logs as rollers, did the same thing from East to West Loch Tarbert.

Buses link the two lochs more comfortably and quickly now, to take passengers to the Caledonian–MacBrayne car ferry, which sails down the 16km.-long loch, then crosses to Islay. Further down the loch, on the south side, is Kennacraig, where the opposition, non-subsidized Western Ferries, also sails to Islay. The road leaves the coast here and is only moderately interesting until it comes back to it after the village of Clachan, beyond which, the loch now passed, there is an intriguing sign – 'To the Seals' – at the side of the road. The sign is usually accurate: a path leads to Ronachan Point, where seals regularly bask on offshore rocks.

Tayinloan Strathclyde 2D3
From Westport, where the road west from Campbeltown reaches the sea, to the mouth of West Loch Tarbert the A83 is never out of sight of the coast, and for much of its way runs beside it. All the way there are views to Islay and Jura, magical when the sun is sinking – and after it has disappeared behind the islands.

There are few villages – but plenty of farms and crofts – along this 30km. stretch of road. Tayinloan is one: the village lies just off the road, and at its pier is the ferry to the Isle of Gigha (pron. Geea, with a hard 'g'), not 5km. away. Gigha is a rich island, sustaining, despite its small size – narrow and not 10km. long – dairy farms. Its main claim to attention is the gardens of Achamore House (now a hotel), at their best (as is usual in most west-Scotland gardens) in the late spring and early summer, when the rhododendrons and, later, azaleas are at their peak; camellias and semi-tropical shrubs also grow here. There are bays around the island, with a wealth of interest for ornithologists; the black-throated diver is among the many species to be seen.

Of the many prehistoric remains along the Kintyre coast, the three Ballochroy Standing Stones (take the track inland from Ballochroy north of Tayinloan) are an enigma, as are so many of these stones. They are believed by some to be an astronomical observatory for the summer solstice: the centre stone is oriented to a similar stone on Jura – that island's peaks rise across the water – and would have been accurate c. 1800 BC, which is probably when these stones were erected. Be that as it may, it is an excellent view.

Another impressive remain is the single standing stone near Killean, just south of Tayinloan; it stands over 5m. high. Less impressive are the caravans, by no means new, that for many years have been permanently parked between the road and the shore.

After Glenbarr, going south, the rocky coast mellows to sandy beaches at Bellochantuy and Westport.

Taynuilt Strathclyde 4B2
Just off the main road from Dalmally to Oban, Taynuilt and the nearby village of Bonawe (previously spelt

Taynuilt: the memorial to Nelson

lain nearby for centuries, and added an inscription. It was probably the first monument to Nelson, erected before he was buried in St Paul's, and was forty-four years in advance of the monument erected in Trafalgar Square.

Across Loch Etive from Bonawe are extensive granite quarries: there is a ferry across the loch.

Thurso Highland 20D1 (*pop.* 9,107)
The people of Thurso will tell you in all seriousness that Thurso Bay rivals the Bay of Naples. It is of course merely a display of local patriotism. No Vesuvius lies behind Thurso – only the flat Caithness moorland – but the headlands it looks out to are the clean cliffs of Holborn Head and Dunnet Head. No Italian water can offer the fine salmon and sea trout to be had in the Thurso River; nor are there better halibut and skate to be had than from this sea-angling centre. One sails not to Capri but to the infinitely less commercialized islands of Orkney: Hoy rears its bulk 25km. away across the Pentland Firth.

Harold's Tower, built over the grave of Earl Harold, twelfth-century ruler of much of Caithness, Orkney, and Shetland, stands near the ruins (not open to the public) of Thurso Castle, home of Sir John Sinclair (1754–1835), a well-known statistician and agricultural improver of the eighteenth and early nineteenth centuries. It was Sinclair who launched the *First Statistical Account of Scotland* in 1790, and he was the first president of the Board of Agriculture. The Sinclairs have been the leading family in this area for centuries.

Another notable native, not a Sinclair, was Sir William Alexander Smith, founder of the Boys' Brigade, who was born at Pennyland House in 1854.

There are old buildings to be seen in this grey town, from restored fishermen's cottages to eighteenth-century houses; but it is for the bay with its long sands that visitors come, in considerable numbers, in summer. Many others stay but briefly in the town: nearby Scrabster is the main embarkation point for Orkney: a roll-on, roll-off ferry went into operation in 1975.

More than visitors have come to Thurso in post-war years. During the 1950s this town doubled its population, to house workers at the nuclear power station at Dounreay (*see* Melvich); and considering the pressure under which the new houses had to be provided, the result is praiseworthy – which is perhaps why Thurso did not suffer the kind of social upheaval that has often been associated with more recent incursions of alien industry into the Highlands.

Tighnabruaich Strathclyde 3F1
It is not necessary to travel to the far north-west Highlands for superb views over lochs, mountains, and islands. One of the finest such is not 60km. from Glasgow – as that proverbial crow flies, though it is almost exactly twice that distance by road – by Arrochar to the east

Bunawe) are interesting mainly for their link with early industry in the Highlands.

In the eighteenth century the area was densely forested with oak and beech trees, and iron smelters who had moved from England (where felling such trees for fuel was stopped by Queen Elizabeth to conserve the trees for ship-building) to Scotland eventually came here.

In 1753 a Lancashire company established extensive ironworks, bringing the iron ore from Furnace on Loch Fyne (*see* Inveraray) and from England, and bringing also large numbers of Lancashire workmen. When blast furnaces were introduced this industry ended; the old furnace is preserved.

In October 1805 the workmen at the ironworks heard of the death of Nelson at Trafalgar, and to his memory they promptly erected a large standing stone that had bank of Loch Fyne, then over to Glendaruel and the head of Loch Riddon.

Until 1969 the route continued along Loch Fyne to cross the Ardlamont Peninsula before reaching Tighnabruaich; or from Glendaruel the tortuous road – known locally as the Khyber Pass – was climbed to Otter Ferry, to get round the point to the western leg of the Kyles of Bute. Now, a new road runs above the west shores of Loch Riddon, and at the top you look down the Kyles and cross the Sound of Bute to the high peaks of Arran, immensely impressive, even if a haze softens the jagged tops.

With this as a prelude, the road drops down to perhaps the most attractive village in the Firth of Clyde area. Tighnabruaich's houses – with gardens where subtropical plants flourish – line the shore irregularly. It is a sailing centre, and, when there were more cruises on the Firth of Clyde than now, was a popular target for the cruise ships: the pier is still in use.

KAMES, a village just south, has the same atmosphere, though not Tighnabruaich's charm.

South along the Kyles, there are some beaches before rounding the point, and there are minor roads to the shores of Loch Fyne, before passing through Kilfinan and reaching the loch at Otter Ferry. Returning to the head of Loch Riddon makes a good round trip for the motorist happy to leave his car for a spell now and then. GLENDARUEL, to the north, is richly wooded and a blaze of colour in late autumn, and, south again, above Loch Riddon, near Caladh Castle (now demolished), the Forestry Commission has established a wildlife centre with photo-safari hides. These look across a lochan (duck, roe deer, and blue hares may be watched), from which a 2km. nature trail leads to more splendid views.

Tiree Strathclyde 7A7
Only 3km. of water separate this island from Coll (qv) (and in between them is the tiny island of Gunna, where barnacle geese may often be seen).

Coll and Tiree have much in common. Each is about 20km. long, and fairly narrow – though Tiree's western hammerhead does widen out to about 10km. across. Each looks east to Mull, and west across the open Atlantic. Each is very low; and being so, the rain clouds from the ocean often pass over them, to precipitate on the mountains to the east. Each has a mild climate and a remarkable sunshine record: in Britain only the south coast of England has as many hours' sunshine annually as Tiree. Each has immense stretches of shell sand on its western shore.

But there are differences. Tiree supports many more people: in 1974 the total population of the two islands was 999, and of this only about 150 lived on Coll. Whereas Coll consists mainly of farms, Tiree is almost entirely devoted to crofting; and Tiree attracts more visitors. The car-ferry link with Oban is a little more frequent than it is with Coll, but it is pointless (the same

applies to Coll) to take a car unless the aim of a holiday is just to get without effort to the many bays around the island; two long, usually lonely, beaches, Hynish Bay and Gott Bay, lie on each side of Scarinish, the main township of the island, where the boats from Oban call.

Tiree has not always been a crofting island. In St Columba's time it was Tir Iodh, 'the Land of Corn', and for centuries it was the 'granary of the Hebrides', sending grain to Iona. In the 1950s another crop was added by the introduction of bulb growing.

Tiree is the lowest of all the Hebrides, though in the south there is a hill, Ben Hynish, rising to 140m.; the main effect of the hill is to emphasize the remarkable flatness of the island.

There are no castles on Tiree. But Iron Age people lived there, and in a number of places there are remains of their forts, the best being a broch, excavated in the early 1960s, at Vaul, north from Gott Bay: there was a settlement here over 2,000 years ago, a broch was built in the first century BC, and this was converted to a farm in about AD 200.

Nearly 20km. south-west from Tiree the famous Skerryvore lighthouse stands 42m. high on a low rock pounded by Atlantic waves, which exert immense pressures at times of south-westerly gales (to combat this, the lower 8m. of the lighthouse are of solid masonry). Built by Alan Stevenson (Robert Louis Stevenson's uncle) between 1838 and 1843, it was manned for over a century; the tower was damaged by fire in 1954, and after renovation it became an unmanned light.

Tomatin Highland 15G4
This village, notable only for its distillery, lies in Strath Dearn, through which flows the River Findhorn; this river, with its tributaries, rises over 30km. to the southwest among the wild Monadhliath mountains. The Findhorn is a good river for angling, and very beautiful in its lower stretches; but in this area the surrounding countryside is bleak indeed.

The main road, now bypassing Tomatin, and the railway climb to the south-east through a narrow ravine, Slochd Mor, to Slochd Summit, over 400m. above sealevel, before dropping down to Carrbridge.

Some 6km. north-west from Tomatin, Loch Moy lies beside the road, and just beyond it is the approach to Moy Hall, seat of the chiefs of Clan Mackintosh, whose country this has been for over 600 years. Originally the Mackintosh of Mackintosh dwelt on an island in the loch; the move to the mainland was made in about 1700, but today's mansion dates only from the 1950s. A major event in the clan's history was the 'Rout of Moy', in 1746. While the Mackintosh supported the King, his wife raised the clan for Prince Charles Edward Stuart; believing that the Prince was at Moy, 1,500 government troops marched there during the night, but, forewarned, the Moy blacksmith and four companions hovered in the darkness around this army, fired their guns and shouted commands to imaginary troops to such effect that the 1,500 panicked, retreating in utter disorder. Or so it is said.

Tongue Highland 18F2

Set almost beside one of the long sea lochs that bite deep into the north coast of Scotland, the Kyle of Tongue, this village might be expected to be a bleak spot. But it is nothing of the sort: although not improved by the new road that leads to the bridge over the Kyle of Tongue, in summer, at least, its houses and two hotels have a warmth about them, and the land immediately around is fertile. It contrasts oddly with the bleak moors so near, from which, a few km. south, one of the most shapely mountains of the north, Ben Loyal, rises to 763m. Its granite peaks, well seen from just outside the village, might appear to have some potential for mountaineers; but, in fact, it is of little interest to climbers, and it is rather anglers, after trout – and the possibility of a salmon – in Loch Loyal, who find Tongue to their liking.

Tongue House, north of the village, was once the home of the Lords of Reay, the chiefs of Clan MacKay, whose territory covered much of the extreme north-west corner of the Highlands, the most sparsely inhabited part of Britain. Sir Donald MacKay of Farr, who became the first Lord Reay in 1628, acquired a reputation as a wizard, and is said to have had frequent encounters with the Devil, who allegedly chased him from Padua to Sutherland. The estates were sold to the Duke of Sutherland in 1829.

High on a hilltop at the mouth of the Allt an Rian, fed by streams off Ben Loyal, are scant remains of CASTLE VARRICH, about which little is known, though it is reputed to have been the stronghold of an eleventh-century Norse king.

Until recently the road to the west went round the head of the Kyle; now there is a bridge, which saves some 13km. By the road a church of 1724 stands on the site of two earlier churches; here the Lords of Reay, chiefs of Clan MacKay, are buried. The 'laird's loft', inside the plain, white church, is hung with MacKay tartan. Across the water, a road runs north to Melness, a scattered collection of cottages and crofts, and continues for some 3km. or so around the bay, looking out to the three Rabbit Islands (their sandy soil is ideal for rabbits). Originally these islands were collectively known as Eilean na Gaeil, 'the Island of Strangers', because the Norsemen landed there. In 1745 a French sloop bringing gold for Prince Charles Edward's rising ran aground near the Rabbit Islands.

Torridon Highland 14A2

Travelling west along Glen Torridon, among wildly impressive as well as very ancient hills (see Kinlochewe), Upper Loch Torridon comes suddenly into view as the Glen widens. At the head of this beautiful sea loch, by a cluster of unexpected trees, are Torridon, a small village,

and, where the minor road forks right, the NTS visitor centre. There is a deer museum also, and guided walks through the area, for small parties, may be arranged. The NTS has in its care over 5,400ha. of the Torridon estate, north of the loch and stretching from the summit ridge of Beinn Eighe in the east to west of Beinn Alligin.

The road along the north shores of the loch used to be tortuous indeed. Even now that much of it has been reconstructed, some of it above the old road, which wandered round the shore to the tiny village of Alligin, it still does not give a driver much opportunity to look at the magnificent views across the loch to the Ben Damph Forest and the mountains of Applecross. After climbing and dropping, climbing and dropping again, the road ends at the village of Diabaig. If the road has been walked – and that is the way to do it, leaving the new road by a track to join the old road – the energetic may carry on to Craig and to Red Point, where there is a road again by Badachro to Gairloch. Comparatively few people either drive or walk to Alligin and Diabaig. Most take the road above the south shores of Upper Loch Torridon, which was built in the 1960s to link Torridon with Shieldaig; there are good views from this stretch. The road bypasses the village of Shieldaig, which lies just below it. This village, a line of small houses looking across Loch Shieldaig, unfortunately looks what it now primarily is – a summer retreat too trim to be the fishing/crofting village it was not twenty years ago. Shieldaig Island, in the loch, was acquired by the NTS in 1970; it is almost entirely covered by Scots pines.

Ullapool Highland 19B7

Seen from the road running alongside Loch Broom – it comes into view 8km. distant – Ullapool looks like a single string of low whitewashed cottages stretching halfway across the loch.

Not until reaching Ullapool is it apparent that it is a 'planned village', its few streets on a grid pattern backing from the shore road to the pier.

The herring fishing in the Minch had been a lavish source of food for a couple of hundred years before the British Fisheries Society built Ullapool in 1788; the fisher cottages along the harbour road are still there, though renovated to twentieth-century standards. The herring fishing remains important. It declined almost to the point of extinction in the mid nineteenth century; but the shoals revived during World War II when boats could not fish the Minch because of mines. In recent years the herring has been threatened again with overfishing; but landings at Ullapool continue.

Fish have also played a notable part in Ullapool's holiday trade. Fishing for a wide variety of catch from here is so good that the European Sea Angling Championships were held in Ullapool in 1965, when over 4,800kg. of fish were caught in a week.

The sheer beauty of the surroundings, the boat trips (these are even laid on to see the sunsets over the Summer Isles – which can be unforgettable), and the fact that this is the last place of any size (though its normal population is only around 1,000) on the road to the north mean that it is better to be in Ullapool before the main holiday season starts. Holidaymakers throng the place in July and August. The traffic has been added to with the introduction in 1974 of a car ferry from Ullapool to Stornoway in Lewis.

There is only a shingle beach, but there is a sandier one at Ardmair Bay, just across the point north of Ullapool, where the cliffs of Ben More Coigach (783m.) make a huge background.

North from Ullapool, a wide road, the A835, carries traffic to the far north-west. This is a new road, built in post-war years; alongside it, or climbing over hillocks or beside the river, is the old road, remarkably narrow by today's standards. The incredible hills rearing from the loch-fretted moorland – Stac Polly, Cul Mor, Suilven, and Canisp – were perhaps better appreciated at the leisurely pace enforced by the old road than at the speeds normal on the new one.

Wick Highland 20F3 (*pop.* 7,842)
Wick spreads grey and uncompromising around the

Upper Loch Torridon seen from the Shieldaig road; Beinn Alligin is in the background

head of Wick Bay. It is the most northerly town on the east coast of Britain, only 27km. south of John o' Groats, and makes few concessions to the picturesque. Yet it has a fascination not uncommon in this bleak north-east corner of Scotland: the frequent drama of high skies over flattish, largely treeless, land, and impressive cliff and rock scenery along the coast.

Wick has a long history: *vik* is Norse for bay, and it seems probable that Viking raiders – and eventually settlers – harboured in this bay, which is the mouth of the Wick River meandering down from Loch Watten.

There are many reminders of the centuries after the Vikings. Not 5km. north of the town is NOSS HEAD, with a lighthouse overlooking Sinclair's Bay, its shoreline a sweep of sandy beach over 6km. long. Just west of the lighthouse, on high rocks, are the stark ruins of castles Girnigoe and Sinclair. GIRNIGOE, of which more remains, dates from the late fifteenth century, and was probably built by a son of William Sinclair, third Earl of Orkney, who, compelled to resign this earldom, was created Earl of Caithness. The grimmest event in its history was the imprisonment, for seven years, of John, Master of Caithness, by his father, the fourth Earl, who suspected his son of plotting against him: the son eventually died after having been fed on salt beef and deprived of water. The Castle was deserted after an attack in 1679. CASTLE SINCLAIR, built around 1607 as the home of the Earls of Caithness, was deserted at about the same time; both castles, twenty years later, were reported as ruins.

Another tall cliff-top castle is at KEISS, at the north end of Sinclair's Bay; in a similar state of ruin, it was also a residence of the Earls of Caithness. Yet another is the Castle of Old Wick, just south of the town – a fourteenth-century windowless square tower, also in ruin. As impressive here is the rock scenery, which includes an arch, the Brig o' Tram, spanning from the cliffs to a high stack. The reasonably energetic should take the track above the cliffs for some 5km. to Sarclet and its harbour, called the Haven. But the most unusual harbour on this coast, which has so many, is just south of Ulbster: there, in a picturesque sea inlet, with a waterfall, 365 steps lead down to WHALIGOE BAY.

Much of Wick's industrial story is closely connected with fish. The suburb of Pultneytown, on the north side of the bay, was founded by the British Fisheries Society early in the nineteenth century. At the peak of fishing activity, in 1840, 765 boats were using the harbour; but towards the end of the century the herring gradually disappeared: today only about thirty seine-net boats, mainly catching white fish, and half a dozen small boats for lobsters, are all that remain. Though the fishermen live in Wick, the boats do not normally unload their catches there but go to ports more appropriate to the fishing grounds.

Vast sums of money were spent on the harbour, designed by Thomas Telford (but not his most successful

ABOVE: *Some of the 365 steps down to Whaligoe Bay, S of Wick*

OPPOSITE: *Castles Girnigoe and Sinclair, nr Wick*

effort). It was improved by Thomas Stevenson in 1868; Stevenson's son, Robert Louis, worked there for a time, but the life of an engineer was too much for his health. The harbour is still only usable – however small the vessel – at high tide.

Wick does not rely on tourists, though it has its quota of holidaymakers. Its biggest tourist attraction, it is said, is a factory – the Caithness Glass Works – where beautifully-designed hand-blown glassware, known far beyond Scotland, is produced. There are tours of the factory on weekdays.

Conversion Tables for Weights and Measures

The figures in bold type can be used to represent either measure for the purposes of conversion, eg 1in. = 2·540cm., 1cm. = 0·394in.

kilometres		miles
1·609	**1**	0·621
3·219	**2**	1·243
4·828	**3**	1·864
6·437	**4**	2·485
8·047	**5**	3·107
9·656	**6**	3·728
11·265	**7**	4·350
12·875	**8**	4·971
14·484	**9**	5·592
16·093	**10**	6·214
32·187	**20**	12·427
48·280	**30**	18·641
64·374	**40**	24·855
80·467	**50**	31·069
96·561	**60**	37·282
112·654	**70**	43·496
128·748	**80**	49·710
144·841	**90**	55·923
160·934	**100**	62·137

centimetres		inches
2·540	**1**	0·394
5·080	**2**	0·787
7·620	**3**	1·181
10·160	**4**	1·575
12·700	**5**	1·969
15·240	**6**	2·362
17·780	**7**	2·756
20·320	**8**	3·150
22·860	**9**	3·543
25·400	**10**	3·937
50·800	**20**	7·874
76·200	**30**	11·811
101·600	**40**	15·748
127·000	**50**	19·685
152·400	**60**	23·622
177·800	**70**	27·559
203·200	**80**	31·496
228·600	**90**	35·433
254·000	**100**	39·370

hectares		acres
0·405	**1**	2·471
0·809	**2**	4·942
1·214	**3**	7·413
1·619	**4**	9·884
2·023	**5**	12·355
2·428	**6**	14·826
2·833	**7**	17·297
3·237	**8**	19·769
3·642	**9**	22·240
4·047	**10**	24·711
8·094	**20**	49·421
12·140	**30**	74·132
16·187	**40**	98·842
20·234	**50**	123·553
24·281	**60**	148·263
28·328	**70**	172·974
32·375	**80**	197·684
36·422	**90**	222·395
40·469	**100**	247·105

metres		yards
0·914	**1**	1·094
1·829	**2**	2·187
2·743	**3**	3·281
3·658	**4**	4·374
4·572	**5**	5·468
5·486	**6**	6·562
6·401	**7**	7·655
7·315	**8**	8·749
8·230	**9**	9·843
9·144	**10**	10·936
18·288	**20**	21·872
27·432	**30**	32·808
36·576	**40**	43·745
45·720	**50**	54·681
54·864	**60**	65·617
64·008	**70**	76·553
73·152	**80**	87·489
82·296	**90**	98·425
91·440	**100**	109·361

kilograms		av. pounds
0·454	**1**	2·205
0·907	**2**	4·409
1·361	**3**	6·614
1·814	**4**	8·819
2·268	**5**	11·023
2·722	**6**	13·228
3·175	**7**	15·432
3·629	**8**	17·637
4·082	**9**	19·842
4·536	**10**	22·046
9·072	**20**	44·092
13·608	**30**	66·139
18·144	**40**	88·185
22·680	**50**	110·231
27·216	**60**	132·277
31·752	**70**	154·324
36·287	**80**	176·370
40·823	**90**	198·416
45·350	**100**	220·462

Further Reading

Geology and Natural History

Darling, F. Fraser and Boyd, J. Morton. *The Highlands and Islands* (1969).
Holiday, F. W. *The Great Orm of Loch Ness* (1968).
MacNally, L. *Highland Year* (1968).
Stephen, David. *Highland Animals* (1974).

History

Campbell, Marion. *Mid Argyll, a Handbook of History* (1970).
Daiches, David. *Charles Edward Stuart* (1973).
Linklater, Eric. *The Prince in the Heather* (1965).
Mackie, Euan W. *Scotland: An Archaeological Guide* (1975).
Piggott, Stuart and Simpson, W. Douglas. *Scotland: Illustrated Guide to Ancient Monuments* (1970).
Prebble, John. *Culloden* (1967),
       Glencoe (1968),
           The Highland Clearances (1969).
Tranter, Nigel. *The Fortified House in Scotland*, vol. V (*North & West Scotland and Miscellaneous*) (1970).

Travel and Description

Glenmore & Cairngorms Forest Park Guide (1966).
Journey to the Western Islands of Scotland (Johnson) and
   Journal of a Tour to the Hebrides (Boswell) (ed. R. W. Chapman, 1970).
Lindsay, Maurice. *The Discovery of Scotland* (1964),
       The Eye is Delighted (1971).
Linklater, Eric. *Orkney and Shetland* (1971).
Murray, W. H. *The Companion Guide to the West Highlands of Scotland* (1968),
       The Hebrides (1966).
Nicholson, James R. *Beyond the Great Glen* (1975).
Simpson, W. Douglas. *Portrait of the Highlands* (1969).
Thompson, Francis. *The Highlands and Islands* (1974).
Walton, John (ed.). *Argyll Forest Park Guide* (1967).

Highland Life and Culture

Bain, Robert. *The Clans and Tartans of Scotland* (1968).
Christison, Sir A. F. *The Clarsach* (1969).
Collinson, Francis. *The Traditional and National Music of Scotland* (1966).
Daiches, David. *Scotch Whisky* (1969).
Grant, I. F. *Highland Folk Ways* (1961).
Haldane, A. R. B. *The Drove Roads of Scotland* (1968),
       New Ways Through the Glens (1962).

Menzies, Gordon (ed.). *Who Are The Scots?* (1971).
Moncrieffe, Sir Iain of that Ilk. *The Highland Clans* (1967).
Power from the Glens (North of Scotland Hydro-Electric Board, 1973).
Taylor, Iain Cameron. *Highland Whisky* (1968),
    Highland Communications (1969).
Thomas, John. *The West Highland Railway* (1965).
Thompson, Francis. *Harris Tweed* (1969).
Vallance, H. A. *The Highland Railway* (1963).

Biography and Memoirs
Darling, F. Fraser. *Island Years* (latest edit. 1973).
Duff, David (ed.). *Victoria in the Highlands* (1968).
Mackenzie, Osgood H. *A Hundred Years in the Highlands* (1949).
Maxwell, Gavin. *Ring of Bright Water* (1960),
    The Rocks Remain (1963).

Photograph and Map Credits

PHOTOGRAPH AND MAP CREDITS

Index

Map Section

KEY TO ROAD MAPS

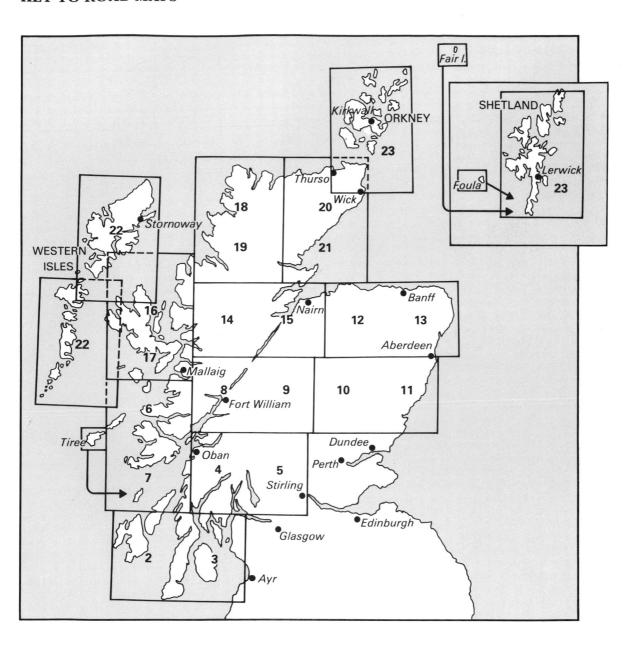

GEOLOGY OF THE SCOTTISH HIGHLANDS

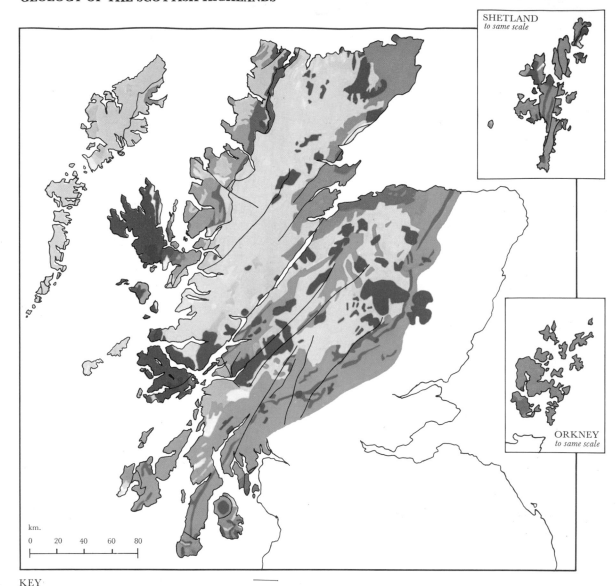

SHETLAND
to same scale

ORKNEY
to same scale

km.
0   20   40   60   80

KEY

Jurassic

MIDDLE JURASSIC: *Oolites, limestones, sandstones, and clays*

LOWER JURASSIC (LIAS): *Shales, clays, and flagstones*

Triassic and Permian

Marls, sandstones and pebble beds, some conglomerates, breccias, and volcanics

Carboniferous

LIMESTONE SERIES

Devonian (OLD RED SANDSTONE)

UPPER DEVONIAN: *Conglomerates and sandstone*

LOWER AND MIDDLE DEVONIAN: *Sandstone, flagstone, slates, shale, grits, red and green marls, and some volcanics*

Cambrian

CAMBRIAN: *Slate, shale, sandstone, quartzite, and some dolomite*

PRE-CAMBRIAN – TORRIDONIAN: *Sandstone, gritstone, flagstone, shale, conglomerates, breccia, grit, slate, and volcanics*

Metamorphic Rocks

DALRADIAN: *Limestone, mica schist, schistose grits, slates and quartzites*

MOINIAN: *Mica schist and quartzo-feldspathic schist*

LEWISIAN: *Mainly acid and basic gneisses, schists, and limestones*

CALEDONIAN AND LEWISIAN: *Hornblende-schist and amphibolites*

CALEDONIAN AND LEWISIAN: *Granite gneiss*

Igneous Rocks

Volcanics: *Basalt, Andesite, etc.*

TERTIARY

PERMO-CARBONIFEROUS

DEVONIAN

Intrusive

BASIC: *Dolerite and Gabbro*

ACID: *Granite, Diorite, and Felsite*

—— FAULTS

I

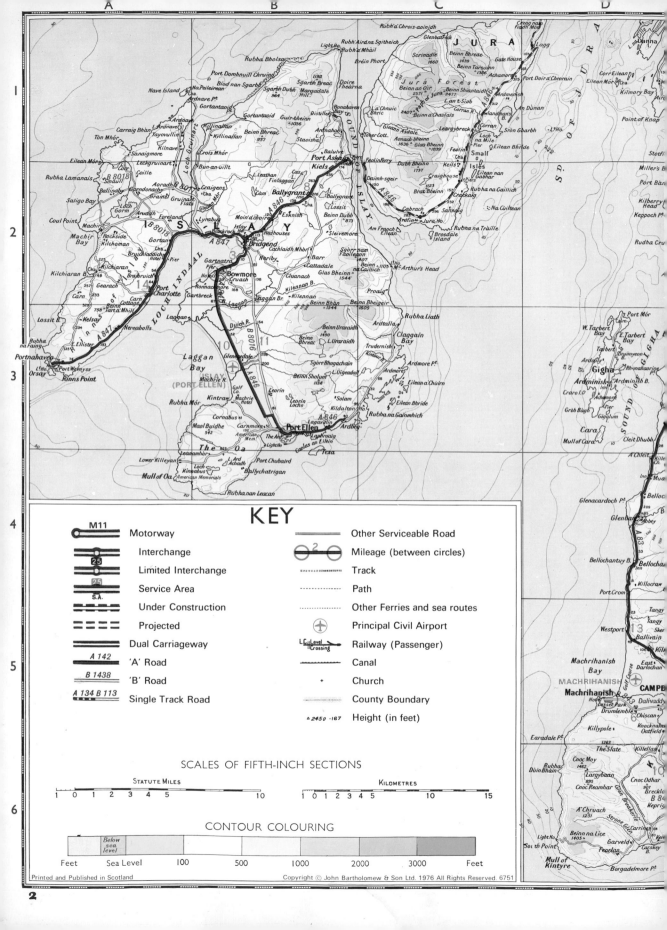

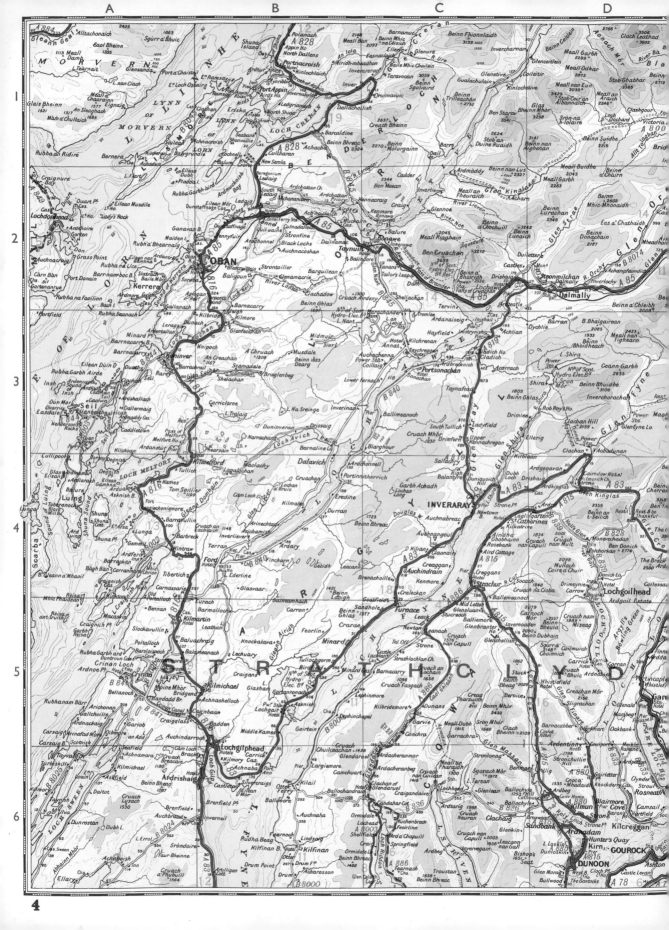

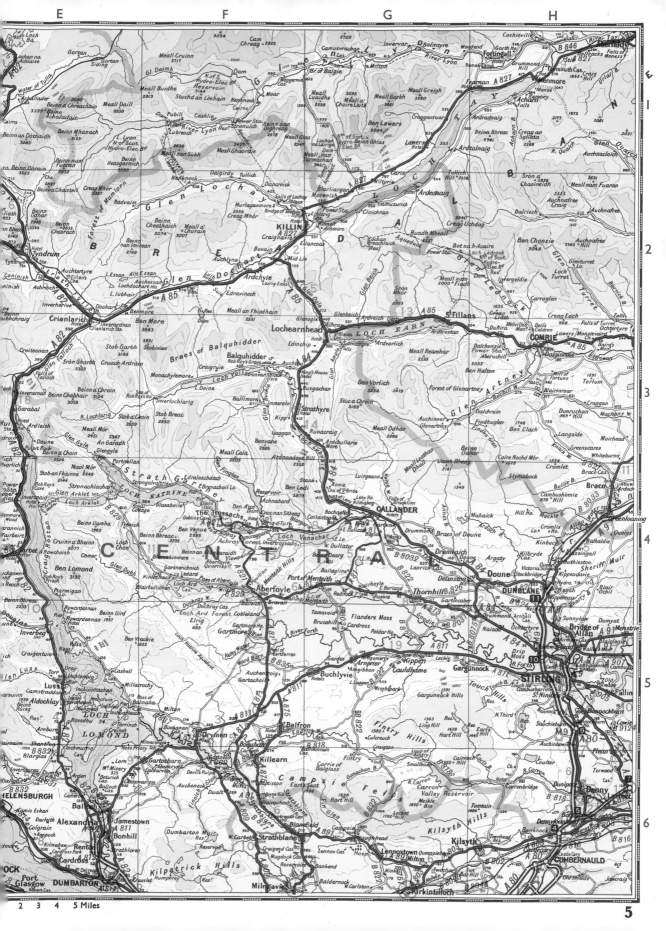

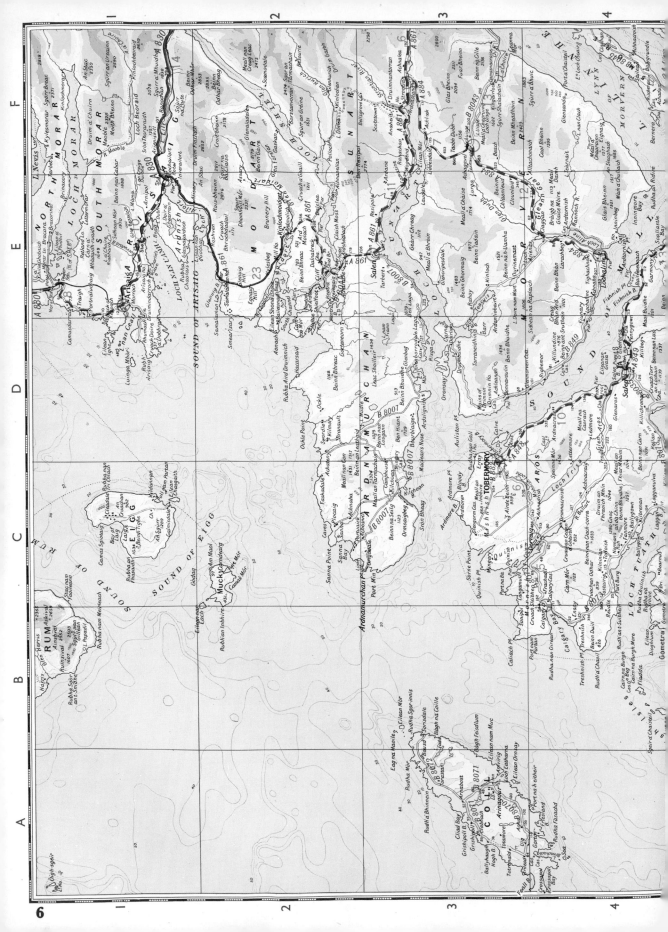

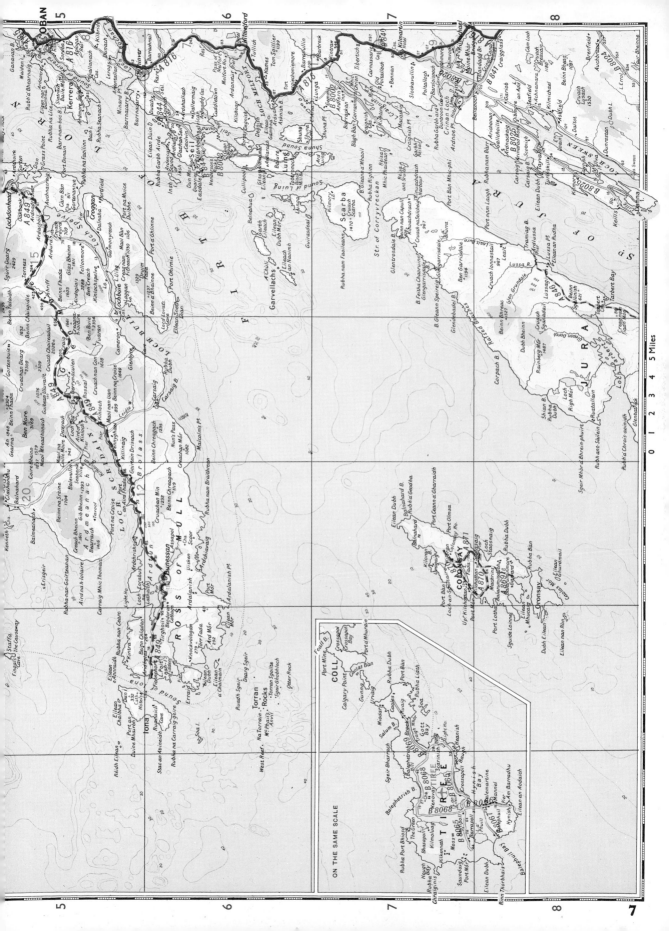

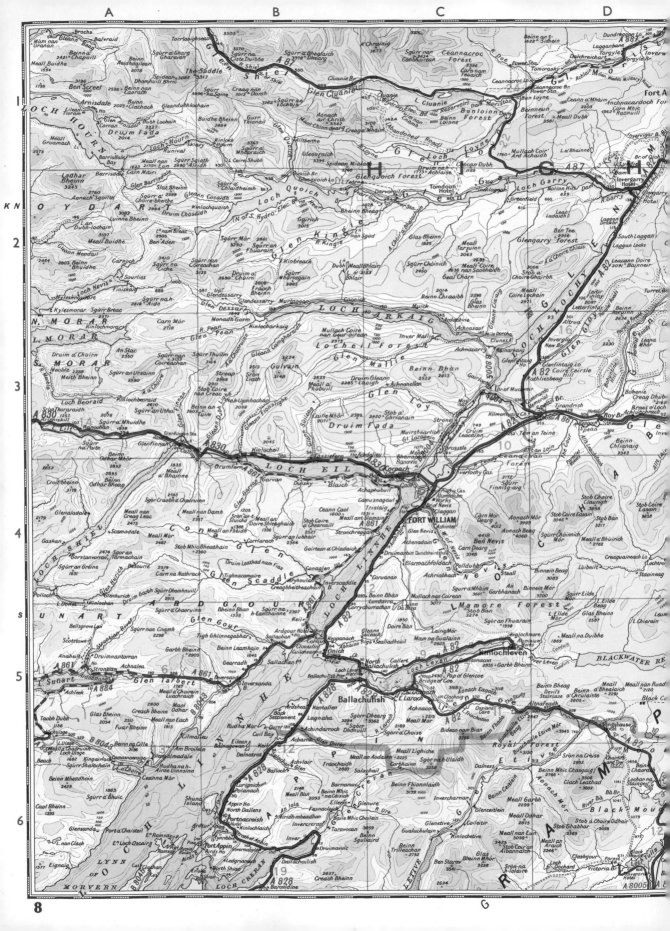

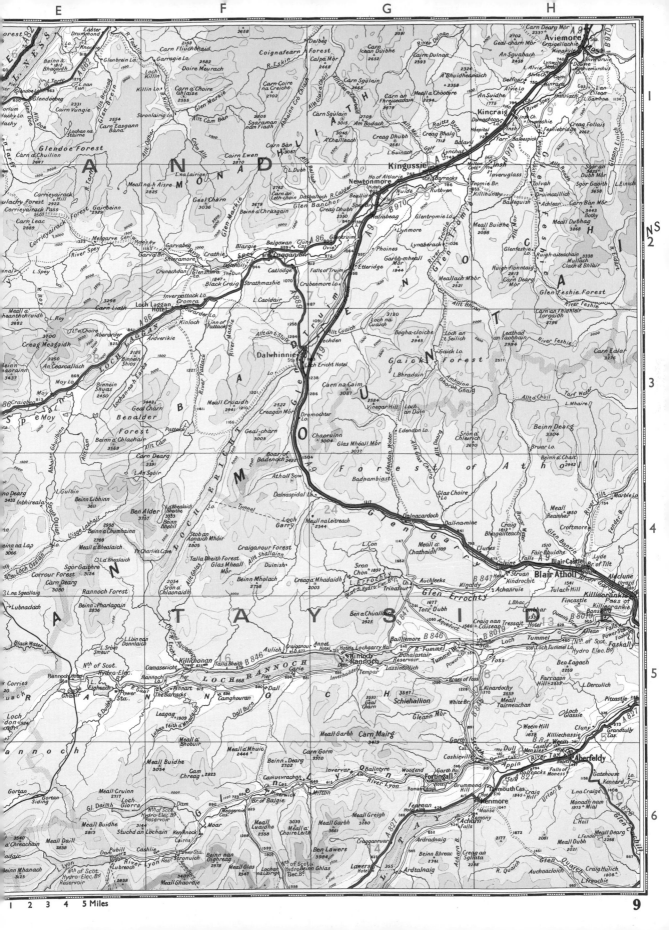

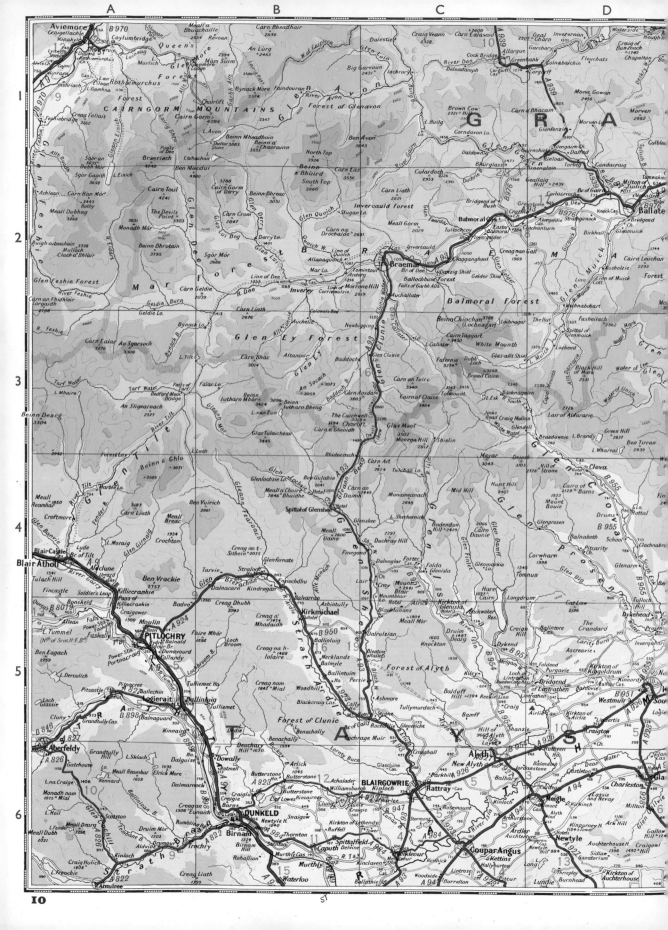

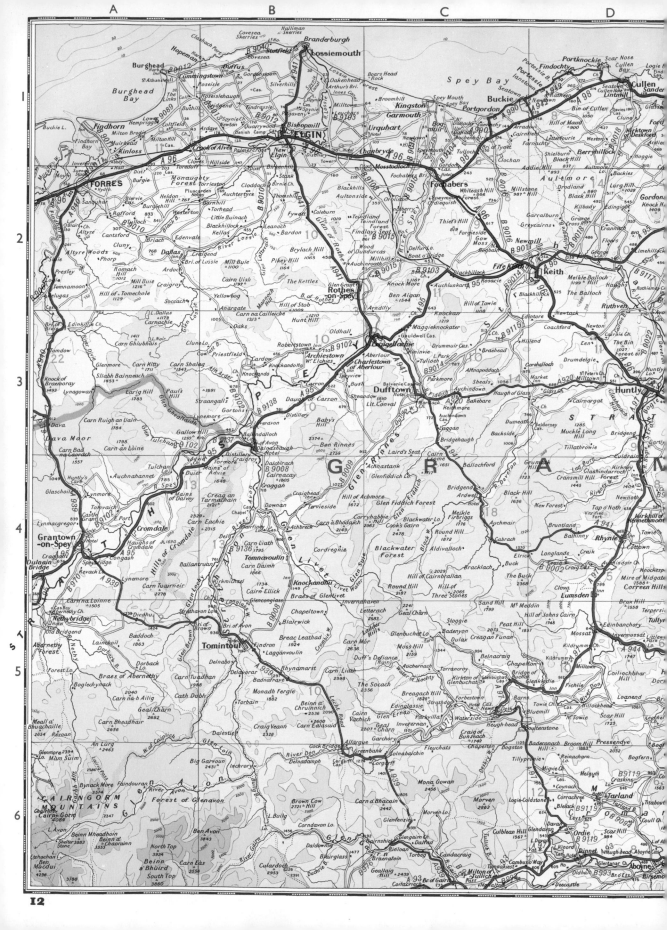

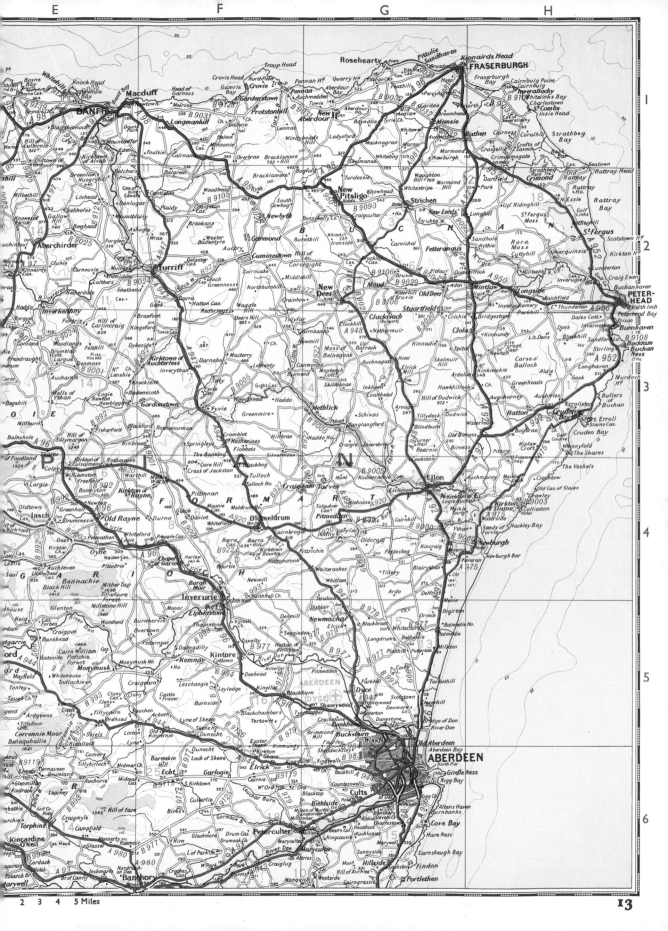

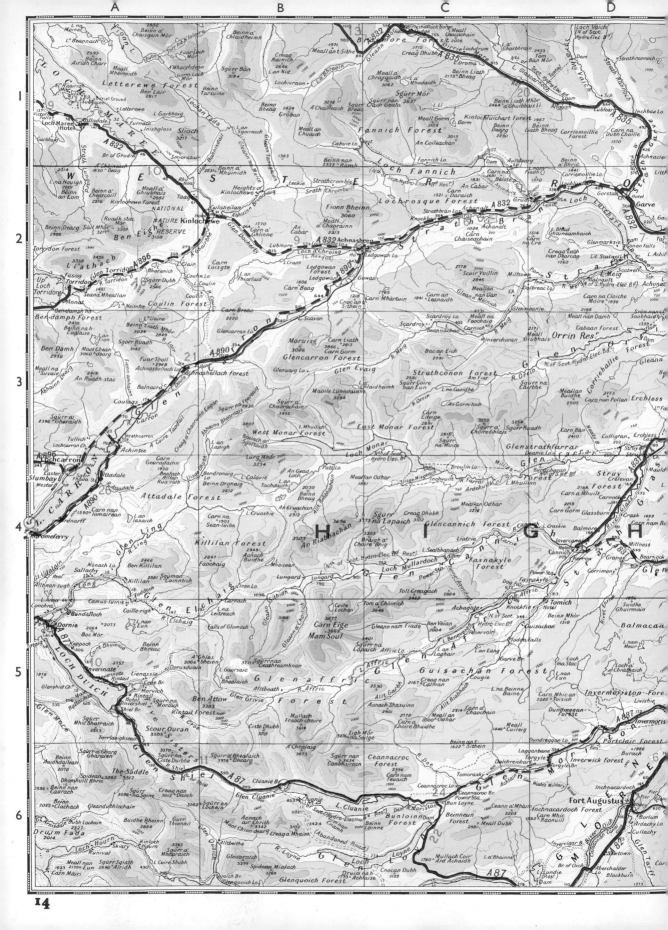

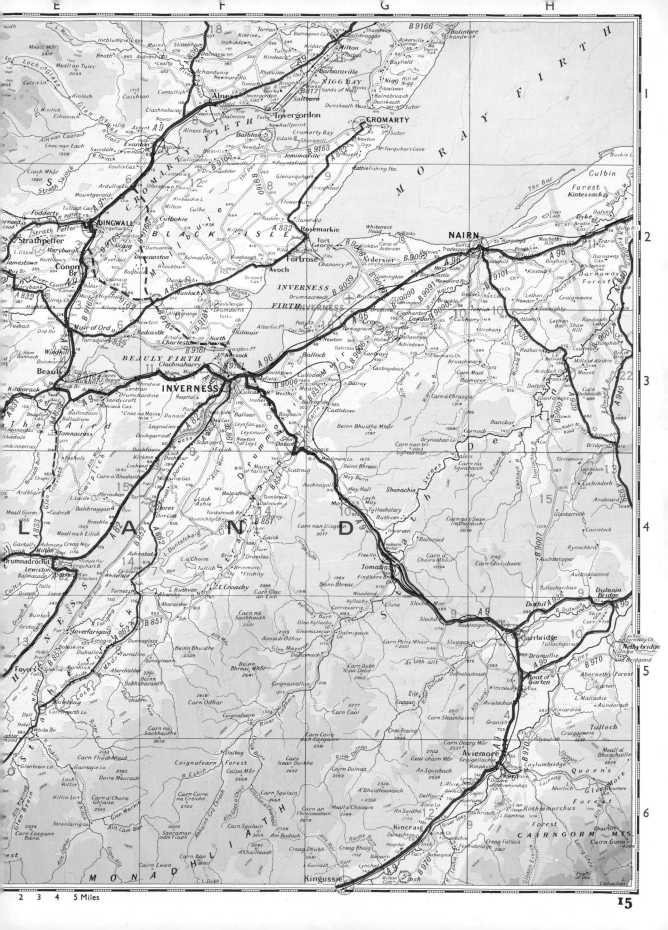

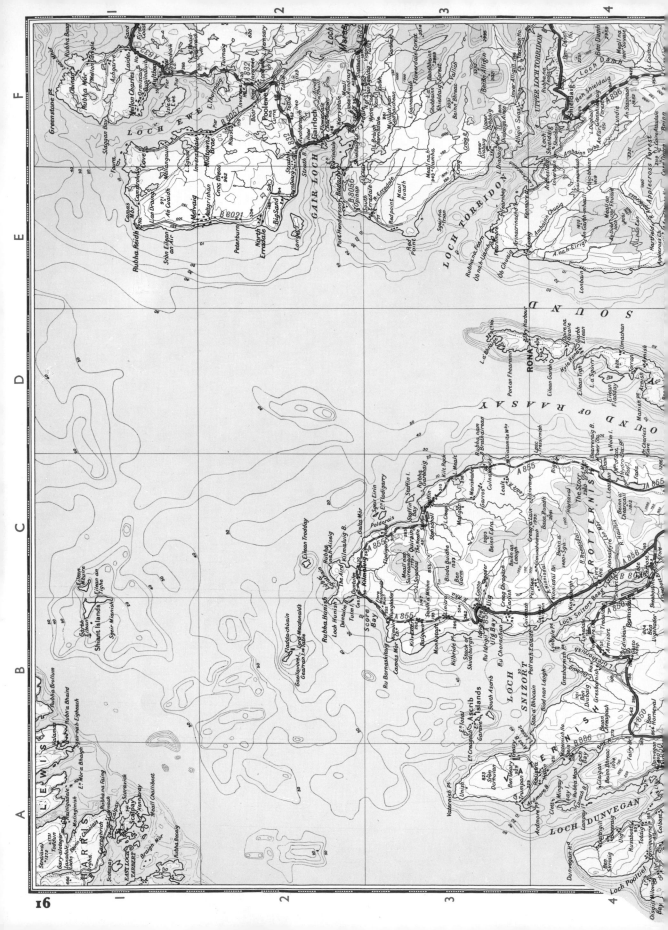

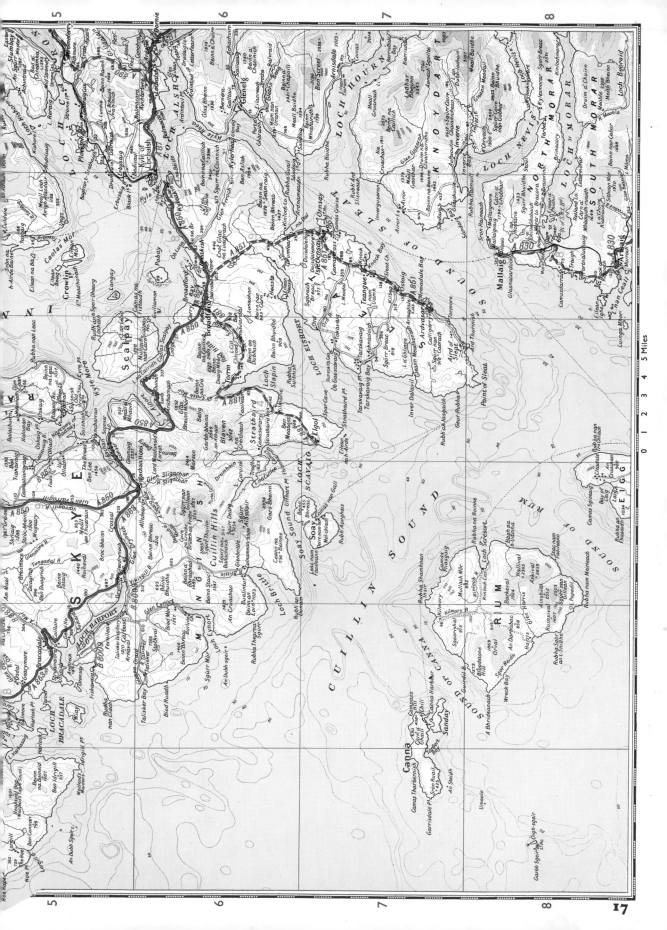

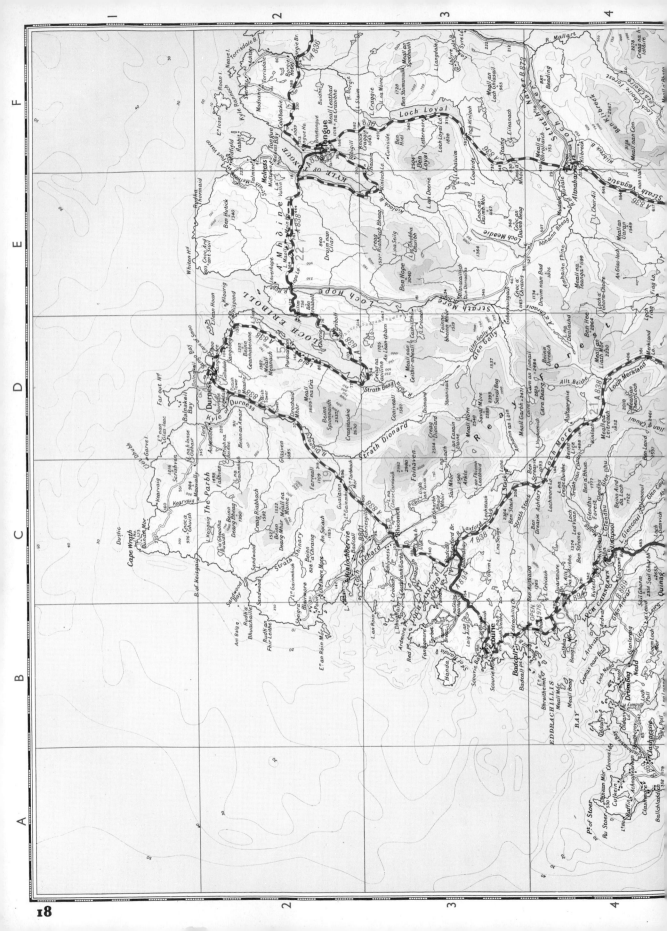

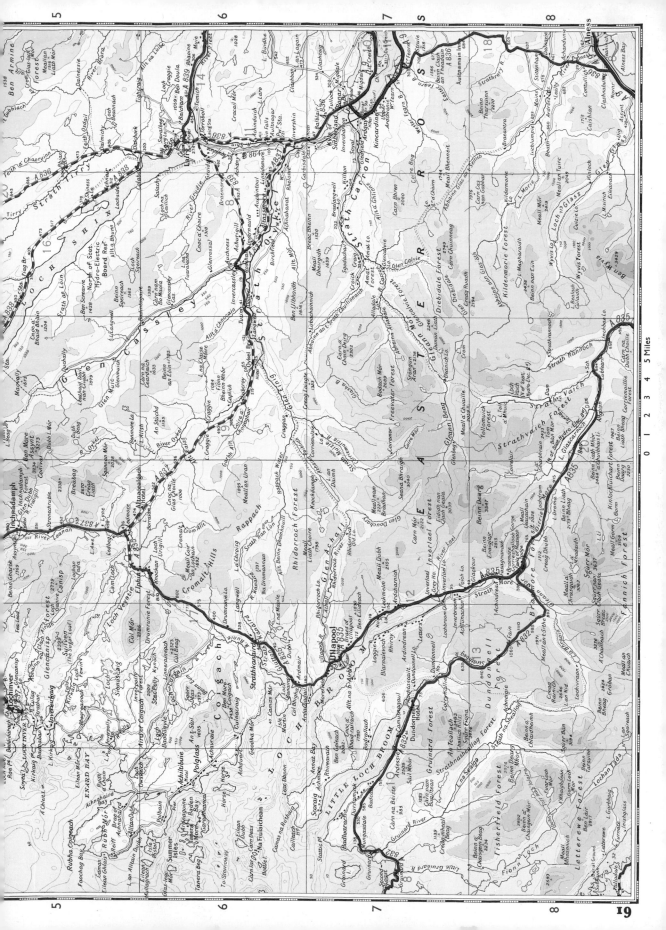

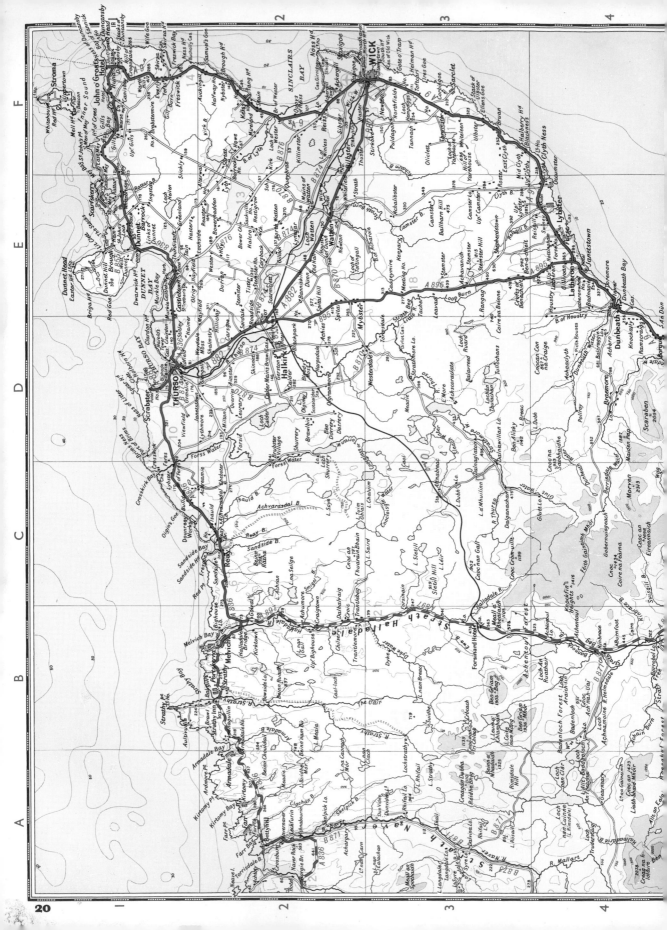

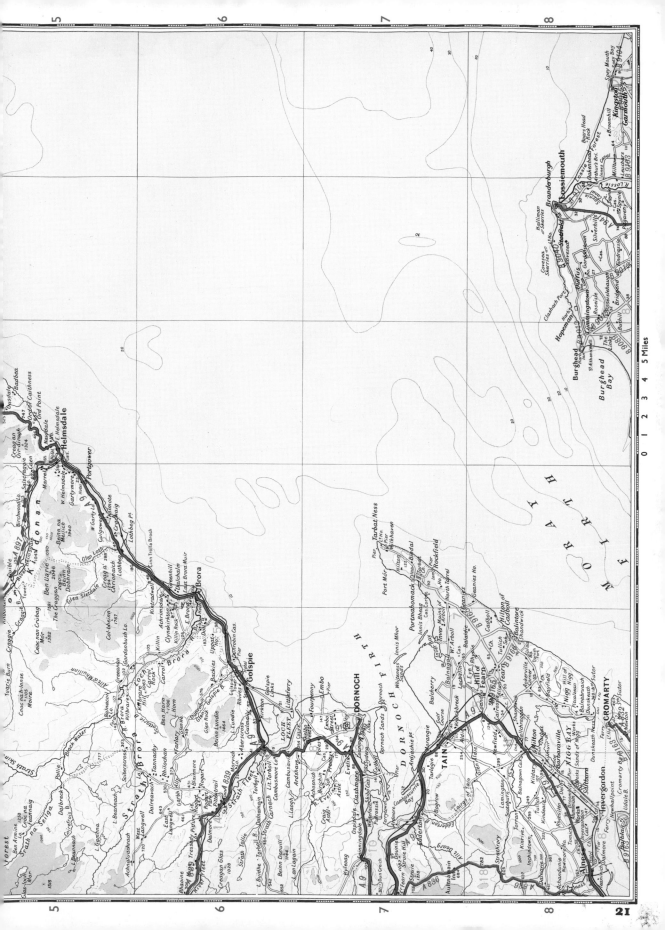

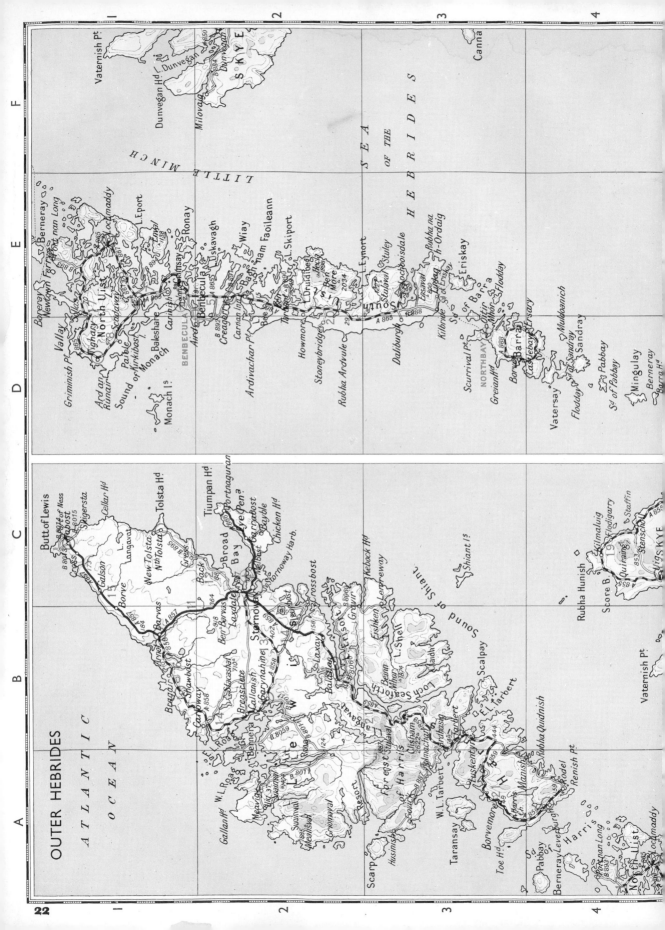

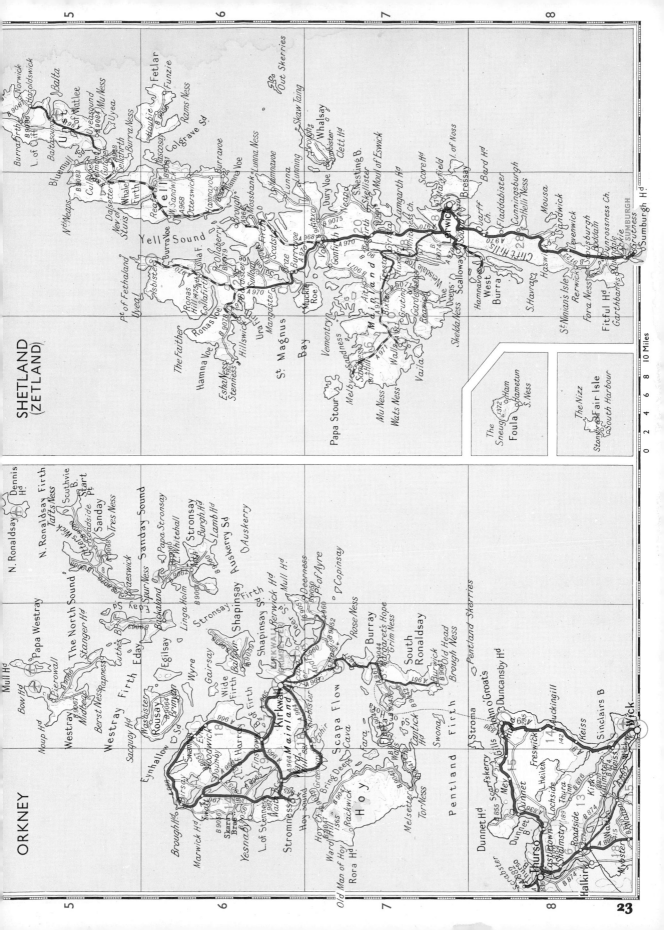